Karen Brown

IRELAND

Charming Inns & Itineraries

Written by

JUNE BROWN

Illustrations by Barbara Tapp
Cover Painting by Jann Pollard

Karen Brown's Country Inn Series

Karen Brown Titles

Austria: Charming Inns & Itineraries

California: Charming Inns & Itineraries

England: Charming Bed & Breakfasts

England, Wales & Scotland: Charming Hotels & Itineraries

France: Charming Bed & Breakfasts

France: Charming Inns & Itineraries

Germany: Charming Inns & Itineraries

Ireland: Charming Inns & Itineraries

Italy: Charming Bed & Breakfasts

Italy: Charming Inns & Itineraries

Portugal: Charming Inns & Itineraries

Spain: Charming Inns & Itineraries

Switzerland: Charming Inns & Itineraries

Dedicated with Love

to

Pam and Ann

The painting on the front cover is a farmhouse on the Ring of Kerry, Co Kerry

Editors: Karen Brown, June Brown, Clare Brown, Kim Brown Holmsen, Iris Sandilands, Gretchen DeAndre.

Illustrations: Barbara Tapp; Cover painting: Jann Pollard

Maps: Susanne Lau Alloway—Greenleaf Design & Graphics; Back cover photo: William H. Brown.

Copyright © 1992, 1994, 1996, 1997, 1998 by Karen Brown's Guides.

This book or parts thereof may not be reproduced in any form without obtaining written permission from the publisher: Karen Brown's Guides, P.O. Box 70, San Mateo, CA 94401, USA, email: karen@karenbrown.com.

Distributed by Fodor's Travel Publications, Inc., 201 East 50th Street, New York, NY 10022, USA.

Distributed in the United Kingdom by Random House UK, 20 Vauxhall Bridge Road, London, SW1V 2SA, phone: 44 171 973 9000, fax: 44 171 840 8408.

Distributed in Australia by Random House Australia, 20 Alfred Street, Milsons Point, Sydney NSW 2061, Australia, phone: 61 2 9954 9966, fax: 61 2 9954 4562.

Distributed in New Zealand by Random House New Zealand, 18 Poland Road, Glenfield, Auckland, New Zealand, phone: 64 9 444 7197, fax: 64 9 444 7524.

Distributed in South Africa by Random House South Africa, Endulani, East Wing, 5A Jubilee Road, Parktown 2193, South Africa, phone: 27 11 484 3538, fax: 27 11 484 6180.

A catalog record for this book is available from the British Library.

Library of Congress Cataloging-in-Publication Data

Brown, June, 1949-
    Karen Brown's Ireland : charming inns & itineraries / written by
June Brown ; illustrations by Barbara Tapp ; cover painting by Jann
Pollard. -- Totally rev. 6th ed.
      p. cm. -- (Karen Brown's country inn series)
    Includes index.
    ISBN 0-930328-63-9 (pb)
    1. Bed and breakfast accommodations--Ireland--Guidebooks.
2. Hotels—Ireland--Guidebooks. 3. Ireland--Guidebooks. I. Brown,
Karen, 1956- . II. Title. III. Series.
TX907.5.173B76 1997
647.944415'01--dc21   97-11554
                                                        CIP

Contents

An Irish Blessing

May the road rise to meet you,
May the wind be always at your back,
May the sun shine warm upon your face,
May the rains fall soft upon your fields,
And, until we meet again,
May God hold you in the palm of his hand.

Introduction

Writers wax lyrical about Ireland's spectacular scenery: ever-changing landscapes, splendid seascapes, purple moorlands, monastic ruins, enchanting lakes, towering fortresses, and vast patchworks of fields spread in every shade of green—believe every word they say. But realize that it's the people with their open friendliness and warmth of welcome that make a visit to Ireland special. This guide is all about Irish hospitality and staying in places where you are a house guest rather than a customer. Ireland is not conducive to rushing: the narrow country roads lend themselves to exploration at a leisurely pace where you return the smile and wave of greeting of those you pass. Take time to stop at a pub and be drawn into conversation, and when you get lost, ask directions and learn a bit of history or folklore as a bonus, along with the directions.

About This Guide

Ireland: Charming Inns & Itineraries is written specifically for independent travelers who want to experience a slice of Irish life staying as guests in country houses, farms, and family-run hotels. Our guide is not written for those who want the symmetry of worldwide hotel chains with their identical bathrooms and mini-bars. The fondest memories of a visit to the Emerald Isle are those of its warm-hearted, friendly people, and there can be no better way to meet the Irish than to stay with them in their homes.

In the title the term "inn" is generic for all types of lodgings ranging from a simple farmhouse bed and breakfast to a luxurious country estate, owned and run by a welcoming family. These are often the kinds of places where you are expected to carry your own bags; service may not be the most efficient and occasionally the owners have their eccentricities, which all adds to the allure. There are enough recommendations in every price category to enable you to tailor your trip to your budget. Rates are quoted in Irish punts in the Republic of Ireland and pounds sterling in Northern Ireland. We have recommended accommodation in the widest of price ranges, so please do not expect the same standard of luxury at, for example, Foxmount Farm, as Marlfield House—there is no comparison—yet each is outstanding in what it offers.

To keep you on the right track we have formed itineraries linking the most interesting sightseeing, enabling you to spend from a few weeks to a month exploring this fascinating island. In addition, we have designed a walking tour of Dublin's fair city that blends culture, history, shopping, and Guinness.

Introduction: About This Guide

About Ireland

The following pointers are given in alphabetical order, not in order of importance.

CLIMATE

It has been said that there is no such thing as climate in Ireland—only weather, and no such thing as bad weather—only the wrong clothes. This is because the changes in conditions from day to day and even from hour to hour seem greater than the changes from one season to the next. The Atlantic Ocean and the air masses moving east give Ireland very little seasonal variation in temperature, producing mild winters and cool summers. The ocean's influence is strongest near the coast, especially in winter when areas bordering the sea are milder than those inland. Coastal areas, particularly in the west, also have less variation in temperature between day and night. Even when it rains, and it does, it never pours—it's just soft Irish rain that keeps the isle emerald. The best thing is to be prepared for sun and sudden squalls at all times.

CLOTHING

Ireland is an easygoing place and casual clothes are acceptable everywhere, even at the fanciest restaurants. Because the weather is changeable, layers of sweaters and shirts that can be added to and removed are recommended. A lightweight, waterproof jacket with a hood is indispensable. Do not haul huge suitcases into bed and breakfasts: rather, we suggest that you have a small suitcase (of the size that fits under your airline seat) that you take into the places you stay, leaving larger luggage in the car.

CURRENCY

The unit of currency in the Republic of Ireland is punts, in Northern Ireland pounds sterling. The two currencies do not have equal value. Both are abbreviated to £.

DRIVING

It is to the countryside that you must go, for to visit Ireland without driving through the country areas is to miss the best she has to offer. Driving is on the left-hand side of the road which may take a little getting used to if you drive on the right at home, so avoid driving in cities until you feel comfortable with the system. If your arrival city is Dublin, do not pick your car up until you are ready to leave for the countryside. Car hire is expensive, so shop around before making a reservation. A valid driver's license from your home country is required. Your car will not be an automatic unless you specifically reserve one. If you intend to travel in Northern Ireland and rent your car in the Republic, make certain that the car company permits their car to be taken into Northern Ireland. Petrol (gasoline) is extremely expensive.

In the Republic, people by and large do not use road numbers when giving directions: they refer to roads as where they might lead to, e.g., the Cork road. To add to the confusion, new road signs quote distances in kilometers, while old signposts are in miles. The Irish seem to use neither, always quoting distances in the number of hours it takes them to drive.

The types of roads found in Ireland are as follows:

MOTORWAYS: The letter "M" precedes these fast roads which have two or three lanes of traffic either side of a central divider. Motorways are more prevalent in Northern Ireland though they are becoming more common between larger towns in the Republic.

NATIONAL ROADS: The letter "N" precedes the road number in the Republic, while in Northern Ireland the road number is preceded by the letter "A." They are the straightest and most direct routes you can take when motorways are not available.

REGIONAL ROADS: The letter "R" precedes the road number on maps, but their numbers rarely, if ever, appear on signposts. They are usually wide enough for two cars or one tractor.

Off the major routes, road signs are not posted as often as you might wish, so when you drive it's best to plan some extra time for asking the way. Asking the way does have its advantages—you get to experience Irish directions from natives always ready to assure you that you cannot miss your destination—which gives you the opportunity of asking another friendly local the way when you do. One of the joys of meandering along sparsely traveled country roads is rounding a bend to find that cows, sheep, and donkeys take precedence over cars as they saunter up the middle of the road. When you meet someone on a country road, do return their salute.

INFORMATION

The Irish Tourist Board and Northern Ireland Tourist Board are invaluable sources of information. They can supply you with details on all areas of Ireland and, at your request, specific information on accommodation in homes, farmhouses, and manors as well as information on festivals, fishing, and the like. In Ireland, the Tourist Offices, known as Bord Failte, have specific information on their area and will, for a small fee, make lodging reservations for you. Their major offices are located as follows:

BELFAST

Irish Tourist Board, 53 Castle Street, Belfast BT1 1GH, tel: (01232) 327888, fax: (01232) 240201

Northern Ireland Tourist Board, 59 North Street, Belfast BT1 1NB, tel: (01232) 231221, fax: (01232) 240960

DUBLIN

Irish Tourist Board, Baggot Street Bridge, Dublin 2, tel: (01) 6024000, fax: (01) 602 4100

Northern Ireland Tourist Board, 16 Nassau Street, Dublin 2, tel: (01) 6791977, fax: (01) 679 1863

FRANKFURT

Irish Tourist Board, Untermainanlage 7, D60329 Frankfurt/Main, tel: (069) 236492, fax: (069) 234626

Northern Ireland Tourist Board, Taunusstrasse 52-60, 60329 Frankfurt/Main, tel: (069) 234504, fax: (069) 233480

LONDON

All Ireland Tourism, British Travel Centre, 12 Regent Street, Picadilly Circus, London SW1Y 4PQ, tel: (0171) 839-8416

Introduction: About Ireland

NEW YORK

Irish Tourist Board, 345 Park Avenue, New York, NY 10017, tel: (800) 223-6470, fax: (212) 371-9052

Northern Ireland Tourist Board, 551 Fifth Avenue, Suite 701, New York, NY 10176, tel: (800) 326-0036 or (212) 922-0101, fax: (212) 922-0099

SYDNEY

Irish Tourist Board, 3rd Level, 36 Carrington Street, Sydney, NSW 2000, tel: (02) 9299-6177, fax: (02) 9299-6323

TORONTO

Northern Ireland Tourist Board, 111 Avenue Road, Suite 450, Toronto, Ontario M5R 3J8, tel: (416) 925-6368, fax: (416) 961-2175

MAPS

Each of our driving itineraries is preceded by a map showing the route, and each hotel listing is referenced to a map at the back of the book. These are an artist's drawings and although we have tried to include as much information as possible, you will need a more detailed map to outline your travels. Our preference is for the Michelin map of Ireland where the scale is 1 centimeter to 4 kilometers (1/400,000).

PUBS

Ireland's pubs will not disappoint—if you do not expect sophisticated establishments. Most of the 12,000 pubs where the Irish share ideas over frothing pints of porter have a contagious spirit and charm. Stop at a pub and you'll soon be drawn into conversation. At local pubs musicians and dancers perform for their own enjoyment, their audience being those who stop by for a drink. If this kind of entertainment appeals to you, ask someone wherever you are staying to recommend a local pub that will have live music that night.

ROOTS

The Potato Famine of the 1840s cut population by a fourth. Through the lean decades that followed, the Irish left by the thousands to make new lives, primarily in the United States, Canada, Australia, and New Zealand. The first step in tracing your Irish roots is to collect together as much information on your Irish antecedent as possible and to find out from relatives or documents (death or marriage certificates) just where he or she came from in Ireland. Armed with this information, your choices are several:

DO IT YOURSELF: If your ancestors hailed from Southern Ireland, visit the genealogical office on Kildare Street in Dublin. If your ancestors came from Northern Ireland, visit the Public Record Office of Northern Ireland, 66 Balmoral Avenue, Belfast BT9 6NY which is open for visitors to do their own research.

HAVE SOMEONE DO IT FOR YOU: The genealogical office charges a small fee, but due to a huge backlog often takes more than a year to do a general search. Write to Chief Herald, General Office of Ireland, 2 Kildare Street, Dublin 2, tel: (01) 603 0200, enclosing what you know about your ancestors.

A reputable genealogical service such as Hibernian Researchers, 22 Windsor Road, Dublin 6 charges higher fees, moves faster, and produces a more comprehensive report. Write to them for details.

If your ancestors came from Northern Ireland, send what you know about them, along with a letter, to one of the following: Ulster Historical Foundation, 12 College Square East, Belfast BT1 6DD; General Register Office, Oxford House, 49 Chichester Street, Belfast BT1 4HL; Presbyterian Historical Society, Church House, Fisherwick Place, Belfast BT1 6DU.

The major tourist offices have brochures on tracing your ancestors that give more detailed information and provide information on publications that may be of interest to those of Irish descent.

SHOPPING

Prices of goods are fairly standard throughout Ireland, so make your purchases as you find items you like since it is doubtful that you will find them again at a less expensive price. The most popular items to buy are hand-knitted sweaters, tweeds, crystal, china, and hand-embroidered linens.

Value Added Tax (VAT) is included in the price of your purchases. There is usually a minimum purchase requirement, but it is possible for visitors from non-EU countries to get a refund of the VAT on the goods they buy in one of two ways:

1. If the goods are shipped overseas direct from the point of purchase, the store can deduct the VAT at the time of sale.

2. Visitors taking the goods with them should ask the store to issue a VAT refund receipt. A passport is needed for identification. On departure, **before** you check in for your flight, go to the refund office at Shannon or Dublin airport. Your receipts will be stamped and they may ask to see your purchases. You will be given a cash refund in the currency of your choice.

About Itineraries

To keep you on the right track, we have formed driving itineraries covering the most interesting sightseeing. If time allows, you can link the four itineraries together and travel around Ireland. Each itinerary explores a region's scenic beauty, history, and culture, and avoids its large cities. At the beginning of each itinerary we suggest our recommended pacing to help you decide the amount of time to allocate to each region. Along the way we suggest alternative routes and side trips (indicated in italics). Each itinerary map shows all of the towns and villages in which we have a recommended place to stay. The capricious changes in the weather mean that often what appears sparkling and romantic in sunshine appears dull and depressing under gathering storm clouds. If the weather is stormy, find a nice place to stay with good company. Once the rain clears, there is much to see. Each itinerary is preceded by an artist's impression of the proposed route. We suggest that you outline this on a commercial map: our preference is the Michelin map of Ireland where the scale is 1 centimeter to 4 kilometers (1/400,000).

Overview Map: Driving Itineraries

The North

Rosgull Peninsula

Tory Island

Giant's Causeway

Glencolumbkille

Donegal

Belfast

Céide Fields

Sligo

The West

Lough Gill

Crossmolina

Achill Island

Inishbofin Island

Connemara

Clifden

Dublin

Dublin Walking Tour

Galway

Burren

Aran Islands

Kilkenny

Limerick

Dingle Peninsula

Cashel

Waterford

The Southeast

Killarney

Ring of Kerry

Kenmare

Blarney

Cork

Skellig Michael

Kinsale

Beara Peninsula

The Southwest

Itinerary Route

Alternative Routes & Sidetrips

11

About Places to Stay

This book does not cover the many modern hotels in Ireland with their look-alike bedrooms, televisions, and direct-dial phones. Rather, it offers a selection of personally recommended lodgings that cover the widest range from a very basic, clean room in a simple farmhouse to a sumptuous suite in an elegant castle hotel. In many, the decor is less than perfect, but the one thing they all have in common is that their owners offer wholehearted hospitality. We have inspected each and every one, and have stayed in a great many. The accommodations selected are the kind of places that we enjoy. We have tried to be candid and honest in our appraisals and to convey each listing's special flavor so that you know what to expect and will not be disappointed. To help you appreciate and understand what to expect when staying at listings in this guide, the following pointers are given in alphabetical order, not in order of importance.

CHILDREN

The majority of listings in this guide welcome children. A great many places offer family rooms with a double and one or two single beds in a room. If you want to tuck your children up in bed and enjoy a leisurely dinner, many of the listings will with advance notice provide an early supper for children.

CHRISTMAS

If the information section indicates that the listing is open during the Christmas holiday season, there is a very good chance that it offers a festive Christmas package.

CLASSIFICATION OF PLACES TO STAY

To help you select the type of accommodation you are looking for, the last line of each description gives one of the following classifications:

B&B: A private home, not on a farm, that offers bed and breakfast.

B&B WITH STABLES: Accommodation and the opportunity to ride.

CITY HOTEL: A hotel in Dublin.

COUNTRY HOUSE: More up-market than a farmhouse or a B&B, a home of architectural interest without all the amenities offered by a country house hotel.

COUNTRY HOUSE HOTEL: A home or establishment of architectural interest with a restaurant, bar, and staff other than the proprietors.

FAMILY HOTEL: A small, family-run hotel.

FARMHOUSE B&B: A private home on a farm that offers bed and breakfast.

GUESTHOUSE: A small, usually family-run hotel corresponding roughly to a Continental *pension*.

INN: A pub with rooms.

LUXURY RESORT: An architecturally interesting hotel that is a destination in itself. It usually offers such facilities as gymnasium, swimming pool, golf course, riding, fishing, and shooting.

RESTAURANT WITH ROOMS: A restaurant that also offers bed-and-breakfast accommodation.

CREDIT CARDS

Whether an accommodation accepts payment by credit card is indicated in the accommodation description as follows: none, AX—American Express, MC—MasterCard, VS—Visa, or simply, all major.

DIRECTIONS

We give concise driving directions to guide you to the listing which is often in a more out-of-the-way place than the town or village in the address. We would be very grateful if you would let us know of cases where our directions have proved inadequate.

ELECTRICITY

The voltage is 240. Most hotels, guesthouses, and farmhouses have American-style razor points for 110 volts. If you are coming from overseas, it is recommended that you take only dual-voltage appliances and a kit of electrical plugs. Your host can usually loan you a hairdryer or an iron.

HIDDEN IRELAND

Several of the listings are members of Hidden Ireland, a consortium of private houses that open their doors to a handful of guests at a time. All houses are of architectural merit and character with owners to match. These are the kinds of houses where you can indulge yourself by staying with people who have mile-long driveways, grand dining rooms watched over by redoubtable ancestors, four-poster beds which you have to climb into, and vast billiard rooms. The kinds of places most of us can only dream of living in, but where you are very welcome as guests because you are the ones who help the owners pay their central heating bills, school fees, and gardeners. Guests become a part of the household—you are not expected to scuttle up to your room. Family life carries on around you. Everyone usually dines together round a polished table and, unless you

make special requests, you eat what is served to you. The conversation flows and you meet people you might never have met elsewhere. Early or late in the season you may find that you are the only guests and you can enjoy a romantic candlelit dinner in a house full of character and charm. There are lakes full of salmon and stylish modern bedrooms at Delphi, gigantic old-fashioned bedrooms at Temple House, homey friendliness at Lorum Old Rectory, and a rhododendron forest at Ardnamona. We have listed members of this group at the back of the book. A brochure listing all members of Hidden Ireland is available from Irish tourist offices or from Hidden Ireland, P.O. Box 5451, Dublin 2, Ireland. Freephone from the USA: (800) 688-0299, tel: (01) 662-7166, fax: (01) 662-7144, e-mail: hidden.ireland@indigo.ie.

IRELAND'S BLUE BOOK

Several of the listings are members of the Irish Country Houses Association, usually referred to as The Blue Book because of the distinctive blue color of its brochure. This is an association of owner-managed country houses, hotels, and restaurants. The majority of the members are country house hotels offering accommodation in charming surroundings with restaurants, bars, and room service. However, there are several members who welcome guests to their ancestral homes on house-party lines (much as members of Hidden Ireland) with no bar and a set dinner menu. We have listed members of this group at the back of the book. Ireland's Blue Book, listing all members, is available from Irish tourist offices and Ardbraccan Glebe, Navan, Co Meath, Ireland, tel: (046) 23416, fax: (046) 23292, e-mail: bluebook@iol.ie.

MAPS

At the back of the book are four regional maps showing each recommended place to stay's location. The pertinent regional map number is given at the right on the top line of each accommodation's description. To make it easier for you, we have divided each location map into a grid of four parts, a, b, c, and d as indicated on each map's key.

MEALS

Owners of guesthouses, farmhouses, and bed and breakfasts are usually happy to serve an evening meal if you make arrangements before noon. Country houses offer a set menu of more elaborate fare and most offer interesting wines—arrangements to dine must be made before noon. Hotels offer menus and wine lists, giving you more dining choices. Our suggestion is that you make arrangements for dinner on the night of your arrival at the same time you make reservations for accommodation.

RATES

Rates are those quoted to us either verbally or by correspondence for the 1998 high season (June, July, and August). The rates given generally cover the least expensive to the most expensive double room (two people) inclusive of taxes and, in most cases, breakfast. **Otherwise**, we quote the cost of bed and breakfast per person per night in a room that has en-suite facilities (whenever these are available), based on two people sharing a room. When a listing does not include breakfast in its rates, we mention this in the description. We feel a great deal of resentment when an obligatory service charge of 10–15% is added to the bill and feel that establishments often use this as a way of padding their rates. Forewarned is forearmed, so we have stated if an establishment charges a service charge. Please **always check** prices and terms when making a reservation. Rates are quoted in Irish punts in the Republic of Ireland and pounds sterling in Northern Ireland. Prices vary considerably and on the whole reflect the type of house in which you will be staying. From the charm of a simple farmhouse to the special ambiance of a vast sporting estate, each listing reflects the Irish way of life.

RESERVATIONS

Reservations should always be made in advance for Dublin accommodation. In the countryside space is not so tight and a nice room can often be had simply by calling in the morning. July and August are the busiest times and if you are traveling to a popular spot such as Killarney, you should make advance reservations. Be specific as to what your needs are, such as a ground-floor room, en-suite shower, twin beds, family room. Check the prices which may well have changed from those given in the book (summer 1998). Ask what deposit to send or give your credit card number. Tell them about what time you intend to arrive and request dinner if you want it. Ask for a confirmation letter with brochure and map to be sent to you. There are several options for making reservations:

LETTER: If you write for reservations, you will usually receive your confirmation and a map. You should then send your deposit. (Always spell out the month as the Irish reverse the American month/day numbering system.)

FAX: This is our preferred way of making a reservation. It is the quickest and most efficient way to obtain confirmation of your reservation in "black and white."

TELEPHONE: By telephoning you have your answer immediately, so if space is not available, you can then decide on an alternative. If calling from the United States, allow for the time difference (Ireland is five hours ahead of New York) so that you can call during their business day. Dial 011 (the international code), 353 (Republic of Ireland's code) **or** 44 (Northern Ireland's code), then the city code (dropping the 0), and the telephone number.

SIGHTSEEING

We have tried to mention sightseeing attractions near each lodging to encourage you to spend several nights in each location.

Dublin Walking Tour

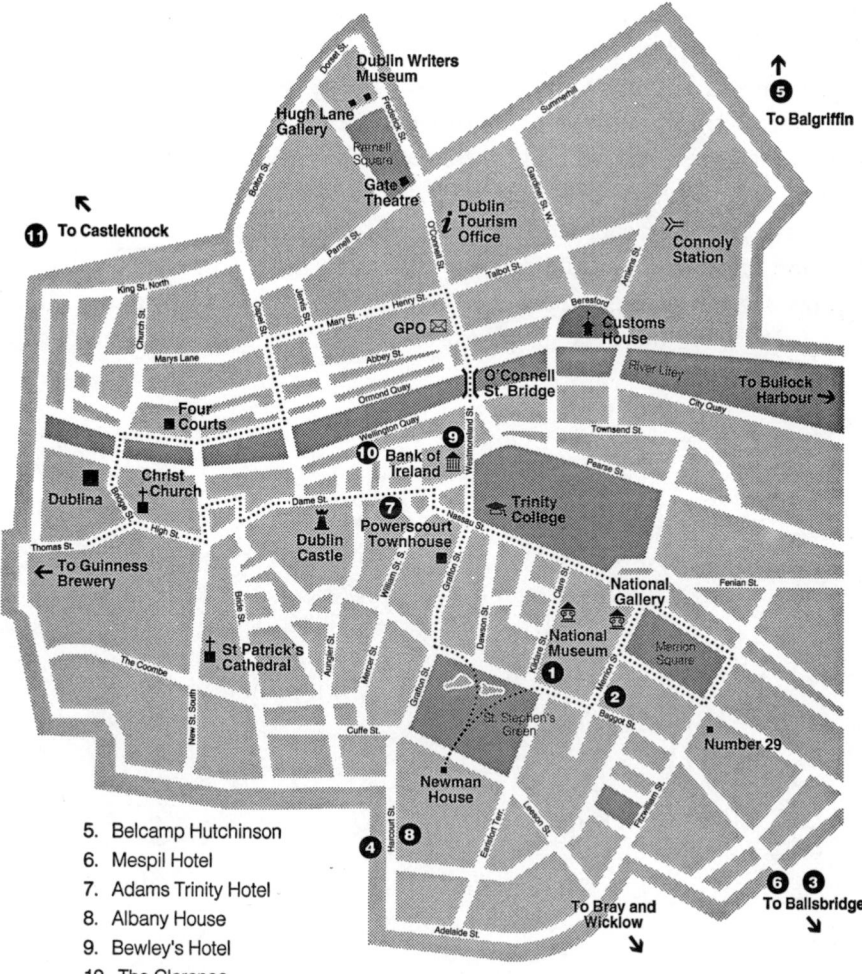

KEY

1. Shelbourne Hotel
2. The Merrion
3. Butlers
   Cedar Lodge
   Hibernian Hotel
   Raglan Lodge
4. Russell Court Hotel

5. Belcamp Hutchinson
6. Mespil Hotel
7. Adams Trinity Hotel
8. Albany House
9. Bewley's Hotel
10. The Clarence
11. Park Lodge

Dublin Walking Tour

"In Dublin's fair city where the girls are so pretty," goes the popular old ballad. The girls are certainly pretty and the city fair if you can overlook the rash of modern office developments begun in the 1960s and the areas that have been razed and seemingly abandoned. Dublin now appears to have seen the error of its ways and efforts are being made to restore what the bulldozers have spared. A car is more trouble than it is worth in Dublin. If your visit here is at the outset of your trip, we suggest that you not get your car until you are ready to leave or, if Dublin is a stop on your trip, park it for the duration of your stay. Dublin is a walking town, so don comfortable shoes and set out to explore the buildings, streets, and shops of this bustling, friendly city. If you feel weary along the way, there is no shortage of pubs where you can revive yourself with a refreshing drink.

Recommended Pacing: If you select a few museums that appeal to you and simply skirt the exterior of the others, this walking tour can be accomplished in a day, which means that you will need two nights' accommodation in Dublin.

A convenient place to begin your tour is **O'Connell Bridge** which spans the River Liffey at the southern end of O'Connell Street, dividing the north from the south of Dublin. (It is also just by the city center terminus for buses: those displaying *"An Lar,"* meaning city center, usually end up here.) Turn south into **Westmoreland Street** past the somber, windowless **Bank of Ireland** that began life in 1729 as the seat of the Irish parliament. Cross the street and enter through the front arch of **Trinity College** into the cobbled square. Founded in 1591 by Elizabeth I, it contains a fine collection of buildings from the 18th to the 20th centuries. Cross the square to the library where a display center houses the jewel of Trinity College, the ***Book of Kells,*** a Latin text of the Four Gospels. A page of this magnificent illuminated manuscript is turned every month and if you are not overly impressed by the page on display, return to the library bookshop and browse through a reproduction. (*Open daily.*) While at the college visit **The Dublin Experience**, a sophisticated audio-visual presentation that orients you to the main events of Irish history. (*Open daily Jun–Oct.*)

Retrace your steps to the front gate and turn south into pedestrians-only **Grafton Street** which teems with people and is enlivened by lots of street musicians and entertainers. Its large modern department store, **Brown Thomas**, is popular with visitors. **Bewley's Café** is a landmark, old-fashioned tea and coffee shop frequented by Dubliners. Upstairs, genteel waitress service is offered while downstairs it's self-service tea, coffee, sticky buns, sausages, chips, and the like. The food is not outstanding, but the atmosphere is very "Dublin."

If you take Johnson Court, a narrow lane off Grafton Street, you'll find yourself in **Powerscourt Townhouse**. This was a courtyard house built between 1771 and 1774 which has been converted into a shopping center by covering the courtyard with a glass roof and building balconies and stairways against the brick façades forming the quadrangle. The center space and balconies are given over to café tables and chairs— secure a balcony table and watch Dubliners at their leisure. The **Periwinkle Seafood Bar** serves delicious chowder, salads, and seafood. The surrounding maze of narrow streets are full of trendy restaurants, cafés, and interesting shops—search out **Magill's** delicatessen on Clarendon Street: it's packed with cheeses, breads, meats, and all kinds of appetizing foods.

At the end of Grafton Street dodge the hurrying buses and cross into the peaceful tranquillity of **St. Stephen's Green**, an island of flowers, trees, and grass surrounding small lakes dotted with ducks. On the far side of the square at 85 and 86 St. Stephen's Green is **Newman House**, once the home of the old Catholic University (later University College Dublin) which boasted James Joyce amongst its distinguished graduates. Number 85 is restored to its pristine, aristocratic years of the 1740s. On the ground floor are wall reliefs of the god Apollo and his nine muse daughters, done elaborately in stucco. A staircase of Cuban mahogany leads to a reception room with more riotous plasterwork figures on the ceiling. Number 86 has some rooms with interesting associations with the Whaley family and Gerard Manley Hopkins, and the Bishop's Room has been restored to its Victorian splendor. (*Open Jun, Jul, Aug, tours on the hour from noon, tel: 01 706 7422.*) **The Commons**, in the basement of Newman House, is an elegant restaurant where you can go out onto the terrace to enjoy a drink before or after your meal.

Return to the northern side of the square past the landmark **Shelbourne Hotel**, a perfect place to enjoy a sedate afternoon tea of dainty sandwiches, buttered scones with whipped cream, and homemade cakes and pastries (3 to 5:30 pm). Follow **Merrion Row** and turn left into **Merrion Street** passing the back of **Leinster House**, the Irish Parliament. It consists of two chambers—the *Dáil*, the lower house, and the *Seanad*, the upper house or senate. You can tour the building when parliament is not in session. Adjacent to the parliament building is the **National Gallery of Ireland** which is a Victorian building with about 3,000 works of art. There's a major collection of Ireland's greatest painter, Jack Yeats, and works by Canaletto, Goya, Titian, El Greco, Poussin, Manet, Picasso, and many others. (*Open daily, tel: 01 661 5133.*)

Merrion Square is one of Dublin's finest remaining Georgian squares and the onetime home of several famous personages—William Butler Yeats lived at 82 and earlier at 52, Daniel O'Connell at 51, and Oscar Wilde's parents occupied number 1. The jewel of Merrion Square is **Number 29** Lower Fitzwilliam Street (corner of Lower Fitzwilliam Street and Upper Mount Street), a magnificently restored, late-18th-century townhouse. From the basement through the living rooms to the nursery and playrooms, the house is meticulously furnished in the style of the period (1790–1820)—real *Upstairs, Downstairs* stuff. You can tour the house along with a tape telling you all about it. (*Closed Mon, tel: 01 702 6165.*)

Merrion Square

Stroll into **Clare Street**, stopping to browse in **Greene's Bookstore** with its lovely old façade and tables of books outside.

Detour into **Kildare Street** where you find the **National Museum** displaying all the finest treasures of the country. There are marvelous examples of gold, bronze, and other ornaments as well as relics of the Viking occupation of Dublin—the 8th-century Tara Brooch is perhaps the best known item here.

Follow the railings of Trinity College to the **Kilkenny Design Centre** and **Blarney Woolen Mills,** fine places to shop for Irish crafts and clothing.

With your back to the front gate of Trinity College, cross into **Dame Street** where the statue of Henry Grattan, a famous orator, stands with arms outstretched outside the parliament building. (If you want to visit the **Dublin Tourism Centre**, take the first left off Dame Street into Church Lane, a one-block street which brings you to the center located in a sturdy granite church on Suffolk Street. Here you can book sightseeing tours, purchase ferry, train, and bus tickets, arrange lodgings, find out what is on in Dublin, make accommodation reservations throughout Ireland, and enjoy a cup of coffee.) Walk along Dame Street past one of Dublin's less controversial modern buildings, the **Central Bank** which looks like egg boxes on stilts. Go under the bank and you are in **Temple Bar**, the energetic, "in place to be" for Dublin's youth. Its narrow streets are full of clubs, youth-oriented stores, and cafés that come alive at night. Returning to Dame Street and a more sedate side of Dublin, you come to **Dublin Castle,** built in the early 13th century on the site of an earlier Danish fortification. The adjoining 18th-century **State Apartments** with their ornate furnishings are more impressive inside than out. (*Open daily, tel: 01 677 7129.*)

Returning to Dame Street, you pass **City Hall** and on your right the impressive **Christ Church Cathedral** comes into view. Dedicated in 1192, it has been rebuilt and restored many times. After the Reformation when the Protestant religion was imposed on the Irish people, it became a Protestant cathedral (Church of Ireland). The large crypt remained as a gathering spot and marketplace for the locals (Catholics) who used it for many years until a rector expelled them because their rowdiness was interrupting church services. Another point of interest is **Strongbow's Tomb**: he was one of the most famous Norman lords of Ireland and by tradition debts were paid across his tomb. When a wall collapsed and crushed the tomb a replacement, unknown crusader's tomb was conscripted and named Strongbow's Tomb. (*Open daily, tel: 01 677 8099.*)

Joined to the cathedral by a covered bridge that arches across the street is **Dublinia** where you learn the history of Dublin through an audio-visual display. You conclude your tour at the large-scale model of the city and the gift shop. (*Open daily Apr–mid-Sep, tel: 01 679 4611.*)

At the junction of High Street and Bridge Street, pause to climb the restored remains of a portion of **Dublin's Walls**. When they were built in 1240, the walls fronted onto the River Liffey.

If you feel like walking the distance along **Thomas Street,** now is the time to detour about 1.5 kilometers to that thriving Dublin institution, the **Guinness Brewery,** whence flows the national drink. Be aware that this is a seedier area of town. As you near your goal the smell of roasting grains permeates the air. As you enter the Guinness hop store, your reward for watching an audio-visual show on the making of the world-famous Irish brew is a sample (pints if you wish) of the divine liquid and the chance to purchase souvenirs of all things Guinness. The 2,000,000 gallons of water a day that the brewery uses do not come from the Liffey, but from St. James's well on the Grand Canal—it is this limestone water that gives Guinness its characteristic flavor. (*Open weekdays, tel: 01 453 6700, ext. 5155, fax: 01 454 6519.*)

If you are not up to the walk to the Guinness Brewery, cross diagonally from the walls to the **Brazen Head in Bridge Street** where you can enjoy that same brew in Dublin's oldest pub. There has been a tavern on this site since Viking times, though the present, rather dilapidated premises date from 1688. It's always a crowded spot that really comes alive late in the evening when musicians gather for impromptu traditional music sessions.

Cross the River Liffey and strolling along the **Inns Quay,** you come to **The Four Courts,** the supreme and high courts of Ireland. You can look inside the fine circular waiting hall under the beautiful green dome which allows light through its apex. If it is early morning, you may see barristers in their gowns and wigs on their way to court.

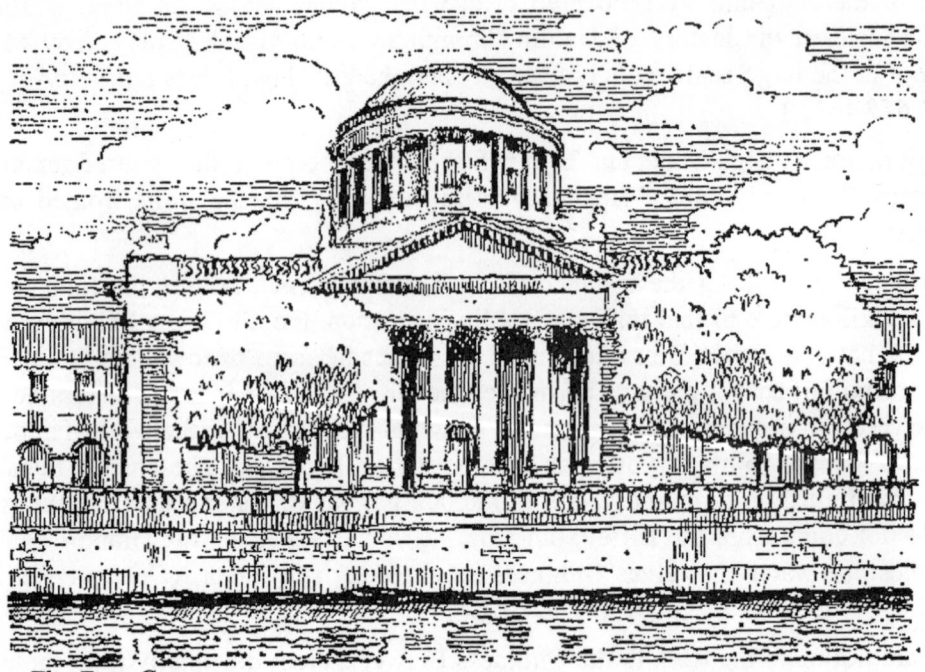

The Four Courts

Turn left up **Capel Street** and third right into **Mary Street** (a rather seedy area) where little shops sell all manner of goods and lead to the busiest pedestrian shopping street in

Dublin, **Henry Street**. Hardy ladies wrapped in warm woolen coats stand before their prams and bawl in Dublinese, "Bananas six for a pound" and "Peaches pound a basket." Policemen regularly move the ladies on but within a few minutes, they are back hawking their wares.

A short detour down **Moore Street** takes you through Dublin's colorful open-air fruit, vegetable, and flower market.

On reaching **O'Connell Street**, turn left. O'Connell Street has its share of tourist traps and hamburger stores, but it's a lively bunch of Dubliners who walk its promenades: placard-carrying nuns, nurses collecting for charity, hawkers of fruit, flowers, and plastic trinkets. All are there for you to see as you stroll along this wide boulevard and continue past the **Gate Theatre** into **Parnell Square** where at the north end of the square you find the **Dublin Writers Museum** in a restored 18th-century mansion. You go on a tour of the paintings and memorabilia with a tape telling you all about it. Among those featured are George Bernard Shaw, William Butler Yeats, Oscar Wilde, James Joyce, and Samuel Beckett. (*Open daily, tel: 01 872 2077*.) Just a few doors away is the **Hugh Lane Gallery** of modern art that ranges from works by Impressionists to contemporary Irish artists. (*Closed Mon, tel: 01 874 1903*.)

Retrace your steps down O'Connell Street to the **General Post Office**. The GPO, as it is affectionately known, is a national shrine as the headquarters of the 1916 revolution. Pass the statues of those who fought for Irish freedom and you are back at your starting point, O'Connell Bridge.

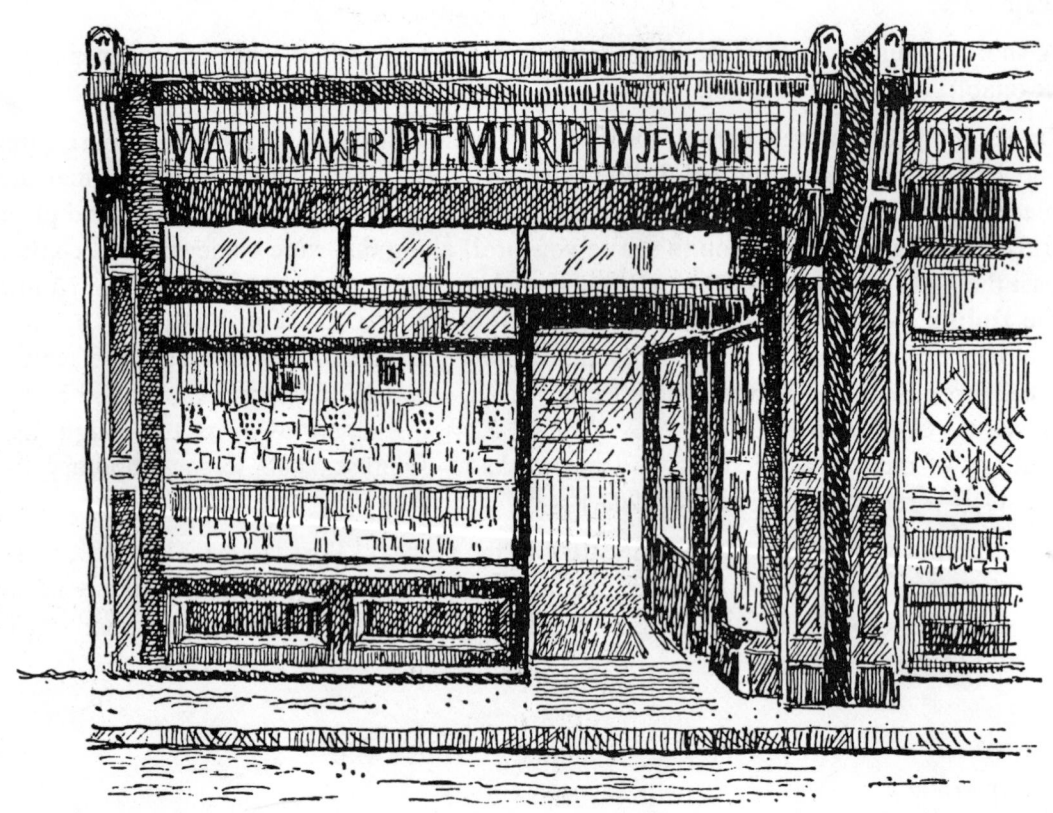

WATCHMAKER P.T. MURPHY JEWELLER OPTICIAN

28

The Southeast

- ● Places to Stay
- ○ Orientation/ Sightseeing
- ▥ Itinerary Route
- — Roads
- ▥ Alternative Route & Sidetrips
- ✈ Airport

Belfast

Dublin

Dublin
Monkstown
Enniskerry
Powerscourt
Gardens & Waterfall
Glendalough
Sally Gap
Rathnew
Laragh
Wicklow
Vale of Avoca
Ballinaclash
Avoca
Arklow
Killinierin
Gorey
N11
Castlecomer
N9
Bagenalstown
Kilkenny
Bunclody
Maddoxstown
Borris
Enniscorthy
Thomastown
Ballymurn
Cashel
Inistoge
Bansha
New Ross
Cahir
N24
Waterford
Wexford
Four Mile Water
Nire Valley
John F. Kennedy Park
Arthurstown
Cappoquin
Passage East
The Vee
Glencairn
Lismore
Tramore
Annestown
Conna
N72
Castlelyons
N25
Dungarven
Stradbally
Midleton
Killeagh
Cork
N25
Youghal
Shanagarry

The Southeast

All too often visitors rush from Dublin through Waterford and on to western Ireland, never realizing that they are missing some of the most ancient antiquities and lovely scenery along the seductive little byways that traverse the moorlands and wind through wooded glens. This itinerary travels from Dublin into the Wicklow mountains, pausing to admire the lovely Powerscourt Gardens, lingering amongst the ancient monastic ruins of Glendalough, visiting the Avoca handweavers who capture the subtle hues of heather and field in their fabric, and admiring the skill of the Waterford crystal cutters.

Glendalough

Recommended Pacing: If you are not a leisurely sightseer, and leave Dublin early, you can follow this itinerary and be in Youghal by nightfall. But resist the temptation—select a base for two nights in two places and explore at leisure. If you are not continuing westward and return to Dublin via The Vee, Cashel, and Kilkenny, select a place to stay near Cashel or Kilkenny.

Leave Dublin following the N11 in the direction of Wexford. (If you have difficulty finding the correct road, follow signs for the ferry at Dun Laoghaire and from there pick up signs for Wexford.) As soon as the city suburbs are behind you, the road becomes a dual carriageway. Watch for signs indicating an exit signposted **Enniskerry** and **Powerscourt Gardens**. Follow the winding, wooded lane to Enniskerry and bear left in the center of the village: this brings you to the main gates of Powerscourt Gardens. As you drive through the vast, parklike grounds, the mountains of Wicklow appear before you, decked in every shade of green. Powerscourt House was burnt to a ruin in 1974: a rook's nest blocked one of the chimneys, and when a fire was lit in the fireplace, the resultant blaze quickly engulfed this grand home. Restoration is now under way and while there are no grand rooms to visit, you can enjoy refreshments at the restaurant and shopping at the Avoca knitwear store. The gardens descend in grand tiers from the ruined house, rather as if descending into a bowl—a mirror-like lake sits at the bottom. Masses of roses adorn the walled garden and velvet green grassy walks lead through the woodlands. Many visitors are intrigued by the animal cemetery with its little headstones and inscriptions. Such a corner is not uncommon in Irish stately homes. (*Open mid-Mar–Oct, tel: 01 286 7676.*) Leaving the car park, turn left for the 6-kilometer drive to the foot of **Powerscourt Waterfall**, the highest waterfall in Ireland and a favorite summer picnic place for many Dubliners.

Turn to the left as you leave the waterfall grounds to meander along narrow country lanes towards **Glencree**. As you come upon open moorland, take the first turn left for the 8-kilometer uphill drive to the summit of **Sally Gap**. This road is known as the old military road because it follows the path that the British built across these wild

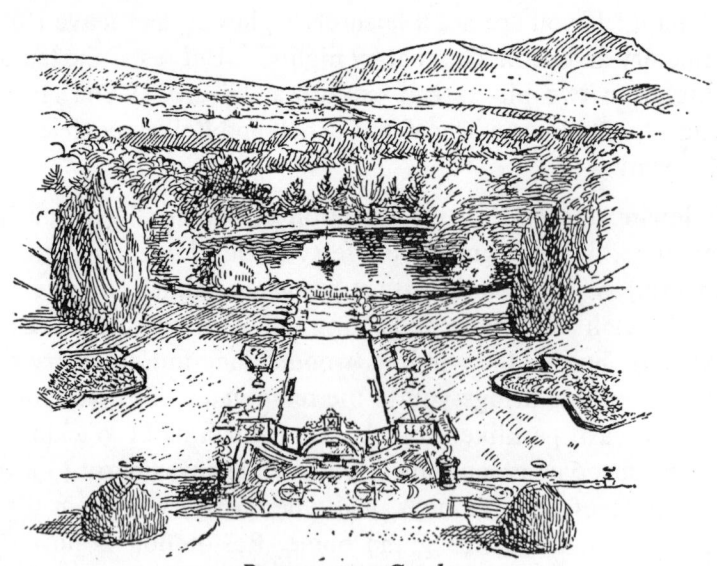

Powerscourt Gardens

mountains to aid them in their attempts to suppress the feisty men of County Wicklow. Neat stacks of turf are piled to dry in the sun and the wind. Grazing sheep seem to be the only occupants of this vast, rolling moorland. Below **Glenmacnass Waterfall** the valley opens up to a patchwork of fields beckoning you to **Laragh** and Glendalough.

Glendalough, a monastic settlement of seven churches, was founded by St. Kevin in the 6th century. After St. Patrick, St. Kevin is Ireland's most popular saint. He certainly picked a stunning site in this wooded valley between two lakes to found his monastic order. Amidst the tilting stones of the graveyard, the round tower—still perfect after more than a thousand years—punctuates the skyline. A 15-minute movie and display on the history of the area is available at the Interpretive Centre. (*Open all year, tel: 0404 45325.*) Take time to follow the track beyond Glendalough to the Upper Lake (you can also drive there). Tradition has it that St. Kevin lived a solitary life in a hut near here.

The Southeast

Farther up on a cliff face is a cave known as St. Kevin's Bed. Here, so the story goes, Kathleen, a beautiful temptress, tried to seduce the saint who, to cool her advances, threw her into the lake.

Retrace the road to Laragh, turn right, and travel south through the village of Rathdrum where sturdy stone cottages line the street and continue across the crossroad following signposts for **Avondale House**, the home of Charles Stewart Parnell. Parnell was born into the ruling Anglo-Irish gentry but, due in part to the influence of his more open-minded mother, an American, he became the leading light in Ireland's political fight for independence. His downfall was his long-term affair with a married English lady. The house is sparsely furnished and takes just a few minutes to tour. You can also wander around the estate with its wonderful trees. (*Open daily May–Sep, weekends Oct–Apr, tel: 0404 46111.*)

Leave Avondale to the left and you soon join the main road that takes you through the **Vale of Avoca** to the "Meeting of the Waters" at the confluence of the rivers Avonmore and Avonbeg. Detour into **Avoca** to visit the **Avoca Handweavers**. You are welcome to wander amongst the skeins and bobbins of brightly-hued wool to see the weavers at work and talk to them above the noise of the looms. An adjacent shop sells tweeds and woolens. (*Open daily all year, tel: 01 286 7466.*)

At **Arklow** join the N11, a broad, fast road taking you south through Gorey and Ferns to **Enniscorthy**. Amidst the gray-stone houses built on steeply sloping ground by the River Slaney lies a Norman castle. Rebuilt in 1586, the castle houses a folk museum that includes exhibits from the Stone Age to the present day, with the emphasis on the part played by local people in the 1798 rebellion against English rule. (*Open all year, tel: 054-35926.*)

On the outskirts of Wexford take the N25 in the direction of Waterford. Before reaching **New Ross** the N25 merges with the N79 where you turn left for Arthurstown and the **John F. Kennedy Park**. The great-grandfather of American President John F. Kennedy emigrated from nearby Dunganstown, driven from Ireland by the terrible potato famine of the 1840s. Row upon row of dark evergreens stand before you like an honor guard to the slain president as you climb to the panoramic viewing point atop Slieve Coillte. (*Open all year, tel: 051 388 171.*)

Return to the main road and continue south to **Arthurstown** where the **Passage East Ferry** takes you across the estuary to **Passage East,** the tiny village on the western shores of Waterford harbor. Arriving at the N25, you turn right to visit the town of **Waterford** fronting the River Suir, and left to arrive at the **Waterford Crystal Factory.** This is a very worthwhile excursion as the tours give you an appreciation for why these hand-blown and -cut items are so expensive. It takes many years to become a master craftsman and one little mistake in the intricate cutting means the painstaking hours of work are wasted and the item is simply smashed and recycled—there are no seconds (Waterford crystal items are uniformly priced throughout the country). While appointments are not necessary, if you are visiting in the busy summer months, either arrive at 9 am or make a tour reservation in advance and avoid waiting while seemingly endless coachloads of tourists go ahead of you. I thoroughly enjoyed touring with a guide (weekends) but the weekday tours have the advantage of enabling you to go at your own pace and linger beside skilled workmen. The showroom displays the full line of Waterford's production from shimmering chandeliers to glassware. The visitors' center also has a gift shop, tourist information center, and café. (*Open daily, tel: 051 73311, fax: 051 78539.*)

If the weather is inclement, stay on the N25 in the direction of Cork but otherwise meander along the coast road by doubling back in the direction of Waterford for a **very short** distance, turning to the right to **Tramore,** a family holiday town, long a favorite of the "ice-cream-and-bucket-and-spade" brigade. Skirting the town, follow the beautiful coastal road through **Annestown** to **Dungarven.**

Where the coastal road meets the N25, make a detour from your route, turning sharp left to **Shell House**. Like it or hate it, there is nothing quite like it on any suburban street in the world—a cottage where all available wall surfaces are decorated with colored shells in various patterns.

Returning to the main road after crossing Dungarven harbor, the N25 winds up and away from the coast, presenting lovely views of the town and the coast. If you haven't eaten, try **Seanachie** (a restored thatched farmhouse, now a traditional restaurant and bar) which sits atop the hill and serves good Irish and Continental food.

Youghal

After passing through several kilometers of forests, turn left on the R673 to **Ardmore**, following the coastline to the village. Beyond the neatly painted houses which cluster together lies the **Ardmore Monastic Site**. The well-preserved round tower used to have six internal timber landings which were joined by ladders, and at the top was a bell to call the monks to prayer or warn of a hostile raid. The round tower is unique to Ireland, its entrance door placed well above the ground: entry was gained by means of a ladder which could be drawn up whenever necessary. Early Christian monks built round towers as protection against Vikings and other raiders. Leaving the ruins, turn left in the village for **Youghal** where this itinerary ends. Sightseeing in Youghal is outlined in the following itinerary. From Youghal you can continue west to follow *The Southwest* itinerary, or take the following alternative route back to Dublin via the Vee, Cashel, and Kilkenny.

ROUTE FROM YOUGHAL TO DUBLIN VIA THE VEE, CASHEL, AND KILKENNY

From Youghal retrace your steps towards Waterford to the bridge that crosses the River Blackwater and turn sharp left (before you cross the river) on **Blackwater Valley Drive,** a narrow road which follows the broad, muddy waters of the Blackwater through scenic wooded countryside. The "drive" is well signposted as "Scenic Route." Quiet country roads bring you into **Lismore.** Turn left into town and right at the town square. Cross the river and take the second road to the left, following signs for **Clogheen** and **The Vee.** As the road climbs, woods give way to heathery moorlands climbing to the summit where the valley opens before you—a broad "V" shape framing an endless patchwork of fields in every shade of green.

Continue on to **Cahir Castle** which has stood on guard to defend the surrounding town of **Cahir** since 1375. A guided tour explains the elaborate defensive system, making a visit here both interesting and informative. A separate audio-visual presentation provides information about the castle and other monuments in the area. (*Open Oct–May, closed Mon, tel: 052 41011.*)

Leaving the castle, continue through the town square for the 16-kilometer drive to **Cashel.** The **Rock of Cashel** seems to grow out of the landscape as you near the town and you can see why this easily defensible site was the capital for the kings of Munster as long ago as 370 A.D. In the course of converting Ireland to Christianity, St. Patrick reached the castle and, according to legend, jabbed his staff into the king's foot during the conversion ceremony. The king apparently took it all very stoically, thinking it was part of the ritual. Upon reaching the summit of the rock, you find a 10th-century round tower, a 13th-century cathedral, and a 15th-century entrance building or Hall of Vicars Choral, a building which was sensitively restored in the 1970s and now houses some exhibits including St. Patrick's Cross, an ancient Irish high cross of unusual design. (*Open all year, tel: 062 61437.*)

Rock of Cashel

Leave Cashel on the N8 for the 40-kilometer drive northeast to **Urlingford** where you bear right for the 27-kilometer drive to **Kilkenny**. Kilkenny is quite the loveliest of Irish towns and it is easy to spend a day here sightseeing and shopping. Entering the town, turn left at the first traffic lights along the main street and park your car outside the castle.

Kilkenny Castle was originally built between 1195 and 1207. The imposing building as it now stands is a mixture of Tudor and Gothic design and is definitely worth a visit. The east wing picture gallery is flooded by natural light from the skylights in the roof and displays a collection of portraits of the Ormonde family, the owners of Kilkenny Castle from 1391 until 1967. (*Open all year, tel: 056 21450.*)

Opposite the castle entrance, the stables now house the **Kilkenny Design Centre**, a retail outlet for goods of Irish design and production: silver jewelry, knits, textiles, furniture, and crafts.

Undoubtedly the best way to see the medieval buildings of Kilkenny is on foot. A walking tour starts from the Tourist Office in the **Shee Alms House** just a short distance from the castle. Stroll up High Street into Parliament Street to **Rothe House**. The house, built in 1594 as the home of Elizabethan merchant John Rothe, is now a museum depicting how such a merchant lived. You should also see **St. Canice's Cathedral** at the top of Parliament Street. The round tower dates from the 6th century when St. Canice founded a monastic order here. Building began on the cathedral in 1251, though most of the lovely church you see today is an 1864 restoration.

Alleyways with fanciful names such as The Butter Slip lead you from the High Street to St. Kieran Street where you find **Kylters Inn**, the oldest building in town. This historic inn has a lurid history—supposedly a hostess of many centuries ago murdered four successive husbands, was then accused of witchcraft, and narrowly escaped being burnt at the stake by fleeing to the Continent.

A 100-kilometer drive along the N10 and N9 returns you to Dublin.

The Southwest

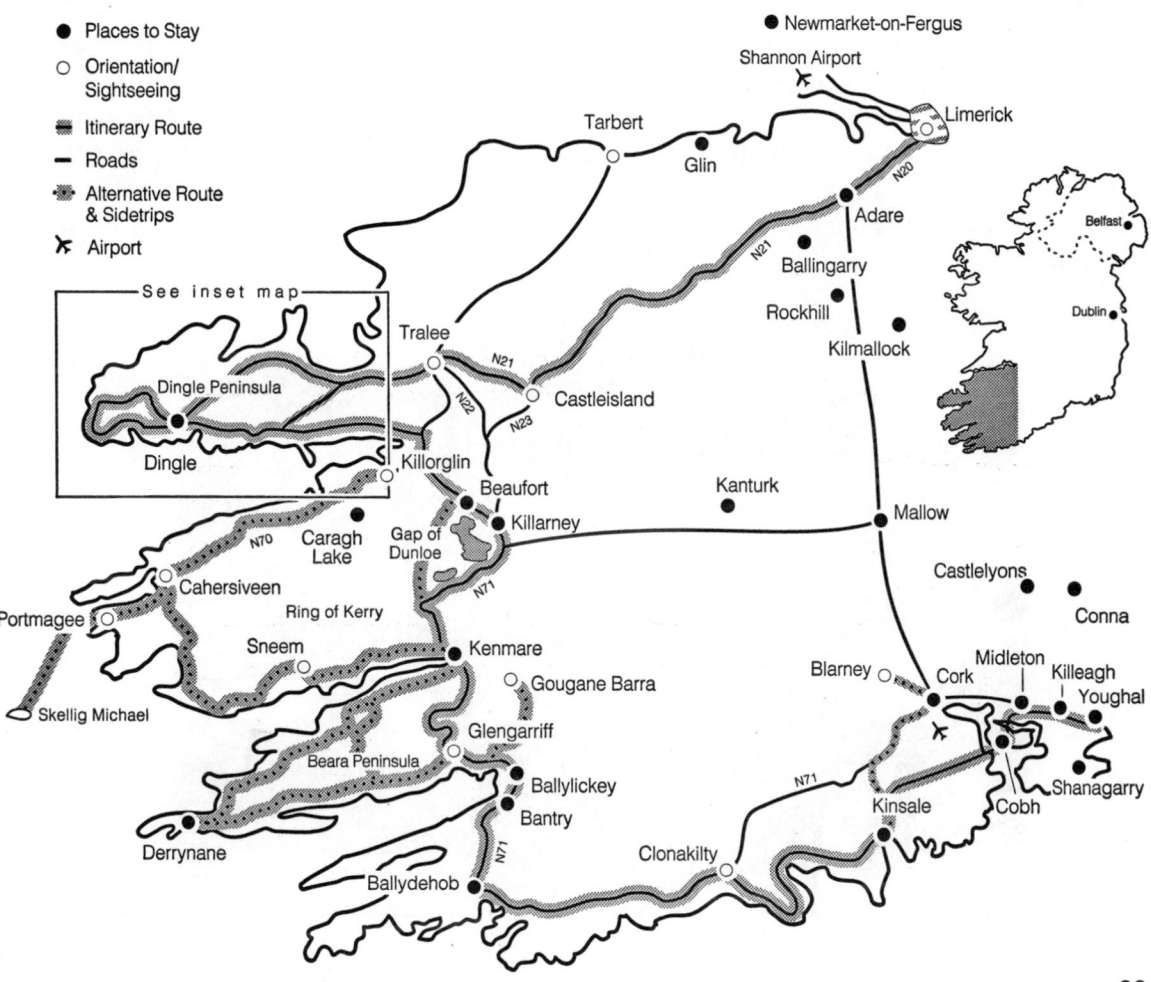

Places to Stay

○ Orientation/
   Sightseeing

▦ Itinerary Route

— Roads

▦ Alternative Route
   & Sidetrips

✈ Airport

Newmarket-on-Fergus

Shannon Airport ✈

Limerick

Tarbert

Glin

N20

Adare

Ballingarry

Rockhill

Kilmallock

— See inset map —

Tralee

N21

N21

N22   N23   Castleisland

Dingle Peninsula

Kanturk

Belfast

Dublin

Dingle

Killorglin

Beaufort

Killarney

Mallow

Caragh
Lake

N70

Gap of
Dunloe

N71

Castlelyons

Conna

Cahersiveen

Ring of Kerry

Portmagee

Sneem

Kenmare

Gougane Barra

Blarney   Cork

Midleton   Killeagh

Youghal

Skellig Michael

Glengarriff

Beara Peninsula

Ballylickey

Bantry

N71

Shanagarry

Derrynane

Ballydehob

N71

Clonakilty

Kinsale   Cobh

39

The Southwest

y of the southwest is absolutely magnificent: the mellow charm of Kinsale
e rugged scenery that winds you towards Glengarriff and its island filled with
subtropical vegetation, the pretty 19th-century town of Kenmare, the translucent lakes of
Killarney, and the ever-changing light on spectacular seascapes on the Dingle Peninsula.
Relish the fabled beauties of this lovely part of Ireland. Take time to detour to Blarney to
take part in the tradition of climbing atop Blarney Castle to kiss the stone that is said to
confer "the gift of the gab." Do not hurry: allow time to linger over breakfast, enjoy a
chat over a glass of Guinness, sample freshly caught salmon and scallops, and join in an
evening singsong in a local pub.

Kinsale

Recommended Pacing: For this portion of the itinerary select two places to stay near the coast, one in either Kenmare or Killarney, and one in Dingle. Allow one or two nights in each spot.

Your journey to the southwest begins in **Youghal** (pronounced yawl). Sir Walter Raleigh, who introduced the potato and tobacco from the New World, was once its mayor. It's a pleasant old town, dominated by the clock tower which was built in 1776 and served as the town's jail. The one-way traffic system makes it impossible to explore without parking the car and walking. Several of the Main Street shops have been refurbished, but the town still has an "ungussied-up" look to it. Make your first stop the **Heritage Centre** with its displays on the town, where you can pick up a brochure that outlines a walking tour of the old buildings.

Traveling the A25, a 30-kilometer drive brings you to the heart of **Midleton** where you find the **Jameson Heritage Centre** in the old whiskey distillery. Marvel at the world's largest pot distillery in the courtyard (capacity 143,872 liters), learn about whiskey production, visit the huge waterwheel, and be rewarded by a sample of the golden liquor. There's also a shop and café. (*Open Mar–Oct, tel: 021 631 821.*)

Just before you reach Cork, turn left for Cobh. **Fota House**, situated on a small island in Cork harbor, is popular with locals who come to picnic in its grounds and enjoy its wildlife park. The house has been restored by the University of Cork. Its interior is decorated in bright tones with daylight streaming through the skylights and tall windows. There's a repeated motif of a Greek vase and regency-style plaster panels that give the house great style. A collection of Irish landscape paintings hang on the walls. (*Open all year, tel: 021 812 555.*)

Nearby **Cobh** (pronounced cove) was renamed Queenstown to mark the visit of Queen Victoria in 1849 and reverted back to Cobh in 1922. There's a long tradition of naval operations here, as its large harbor is a safe anchorage. The **Cobh Experience**, an audio-visual display housed in the restored Victorian railway station, tells the story of this port.

Cobh was the point of departure for many emigrants off to seek a better life in America and Australia. For many it was the last piece of Irish soil they stood on before taking a boat to a new life. The ill-fated *Lusitania* was torpedoed not far from Cobh and survivors were brought here. It was also the last port of call of the *Titanic*. There's an excellent shop and café—an enjoyable place to spend a couple of hours on a rainy day. (*Closed Jan, tel: 021 813591, fax: 021 813 595*.)

Retrace your steps a short distance to the **Carriagaloe-Glenbrook ferry** which transports you across Cork harbor and eliminates the hassle of driving through Cork city. A short countryside drive brings you to **Kinsale**, its harbor full of tall-masted boats. Narrow, winding streets lined both with quaint and several sadly derelict houses lead up from the harbor. Flowers abound, with small posies tucked into little baskets and overflowing windowboxes planted artistically at every turn. As well as for its floral extravaganza, Kinsale is noted as being the gourmet capital of Ireland. A group of 12 restaurants have come together to form a good food circle. It's a pleasant pastime to check some of the menus on display as you inhale mouth-watering aromas and peek at happy people enjoying their food.

There has been a fortress in Kinsale since Norman times. A great battle nearby in 1601 precipitated the flight of the earls and sounded the death knell of the ancient Gaelic civilization. It was from Kinsale that James II left for exile after his defeat at Boyne Water. Bypassed by 20th-century events, Kinsale has emerged as a village full of character, attracting visitors who find themselves seduced by its charms.

About 3 kilometers east of Kinsale, the impressive, 17th-century **Charles Fort** stands guard over the entrance to its harbor. It takes several hours to tour the five bastions that make up the complex. The ordnance sheds are restored and hold a photographic and historical exhibition about the fort. (*Open Apr–Sep, tel: 021 772 263*.)

Across the estuary you see the 1603 **James Fort** where William Penn's father was governor of Kinsale, while William worked as a clerk of the Admiralty Court. Later

William was given a land grant in America on which he founded the state of Pennsylvania.

Blarney

SIDE TRIP TO BLARNEY

About a half-hour drive north of Kinsale lie **Blarney Castle** *and its famous tourist attraction, the* **Blarney Stone.** *Kissing the Blarney Stone, by climbing atop the keep and hanging upside-down, is said to confer the "gift of the gab." Even if you are not inclined to join in this back-breaking, unhygienic pursuit, the castle is worth a visit. (Open all year, tel: 021 385 252.)* **Blarney Castle House** *next door has been home to the Colhurst family for over a hundred years and they open up their doors in the afternoon to visitors. The light, airy rooms are furnished in exquisite taste. (Open Jun–Sep, closed Sun, tel: 021 385 252.) Just up the street,* **Blarney Woolen Mills** *is an excellent place to shop for all things Irish, particularly knitwear.*

Leave Kinsale along the harbor, cross the River Bandon, and follow country lanes to the sleepy little village of **Ballinspittle.** As you drive through the village, it is hard to imagine that in 1985 it was overwhelmed by pilgrims. They came to the village shrine after a local girl reported seeing the statue of the Virgin Mary rocking back and forth. You pass the shrine on your right just before you come to the village. Follow country lanes to **Timoleague,** a very small coastal village watched over by the ruins of a Franciscan abbey and on to the N71 and **Clonakilty** and **Skibbereen.** As you travel westwards, rolling fields in every shade of green present themselves.

Arriving at the waterfront in **Bantry** you come to **Bantry House**. Like so many other Irish country houses, it has seen better days, but the present owner, Egerton Shelswell-White, makes visitors welcome and gives a typed information sheet, in the language of your choice, that guides you room-by-room through the house. The house has a wonderful collection of pictures, furniture, and works of art, brought together by the second Earl of Bantry during his European travels in the first half of the 19th century. In contrast to his ancestors' staid portraits, Egerton is shown playing his trombone. (*Open all year, tel: 027 50047.*)

Apart from furnishing the house, the second Earl, inspired by the gardens of Europe, laid out a formal Italian garden and a "staircase to the sky" rising up the steep terraces to the crest of the hill behind the house. If you are not up to the climb, you can still enjoy a magnificent, though less lofty view across the boat-filled bay from the terrace in front of the house. A very pleasant tea and gift shop occupies the old kitchen. One wing of the house has been renovated and modernized to provide up-market bed-and-breakfast accommodation—see listing.

In the stable block next to the house the **1796 Bantry French Armada Centre** relates the story of the French Armada's attempt to invade Ireland in 1796. It failed and a model of one of the armada's ships that sank in Bantry Bay is on display—a very interesting look at a little-known piece of Irish history. (*Open Apr–Oct, tel: 027 51796.*)

Eight kilometers north lies **Ballylickey**.

SIDE TRIP TO GOUGANE BARRA LAKE

From Ballylickey an inland excursion takes you to **Gougane Barra Lake**, *a beautiful lake locked into a ring of mountains. Here you find a small hotel where you can stop for a snack or a warming drink, and a little church on an island in the lake, the oratory where St. Finbarr went to contemplate and pray. The road to and from the lake takes you over a high pass and through mountain tunnels.*

Just before you enter **Glengarriff** turn left for the harbor to take a ferryboat for the minute ride to Garinish Island, a most worthwhile trip. (*Harbour Queen Ferryboats 027 63116, fax: 027 63298.*) **Garinish Island**, once a barren rock where only gorse and heather grew, was transformed into a miniature botanical paradise at the beginning of this century by a Scottish politician, Arran Bryce. The sheltered site of the island provides perfect growing conditions for trees, shrubs, and flowers from all over the world. It took a hundred men over three years to sculpt this lovely spot with its formal Italian garden, caseta, and temple. (*Open Mar–Oct, closed Sat, tel: 027 63081.*)

From Glengarriff the road winds upwards and, glancing behind, you have a spectacular view of **Bantry Bay** lying beyond a patchwork of green fields. Rounding the summit, the road tunnels through a large buttress of rock and you emerge to stunning views of sparse rocky hillsides.

Cross the River Kenmare into **Kenmare**. This delightful town of gray-stone houses, with gaily painted shop fronts lining two broad main streets, is a favorite with tourists who prefer its peace and charm to the hectic pace of Killarney. Kenmare is full of excellent shops: **Cleo's** has outstanding knitwear, **Quills** has vast quantities of woolens, **Brenmar Jon** sells top-of-the-line fine knitwear, and **Nostalgia** offers antique and new linen and lace. The town also has some delightful restaurants: **The Purple Heather**, a daytime bistro, **Packies**, a lively restaurant, the charming **Lime Tree** restaurant in the Old Schoolhouse, and **The Park Hotel** with its opulent afternoon silver-service teas and superb restaurant. Visit the **Heritage Centre** with its displays of locally made lace (*064 41233*). Just a short walk from the Heritage Centre, the **Kenmare Stone Circle** is the largest in the southwest of Ireland. Walks abound, from strolling along the broad river estuary to strenuous hill hikes. Kenmare is a perfect base for exploring both the Iveragh (Ring of Kerry) and Beara peninsulas and for visiting Killarney. It also serves as a stepping-off point for a side trip to Skellig Michael.

SIDE TRIP TO THE BEARA PENINSULA

*If you do not stop along the way, it will take you between two and three hours to drive the **Beara Peninsula** where the scenery is wild, but gorgeous. From Kenmare a minor road (R571) takes you along the north shore of the peninsula to **Ardgroom**, a picturesque village nestling beside a little harbor at the foot of the mountains. Farther west, **Eyeries** village looks out over the Skellig Rocks and several rocky inlets. Behind the village, the mountain road rises up through the Pass of Boffickle for a fantastic view back over the bay. In the 19th century **Allihies** was a center of the copper-mining industry, but now it is a resort with a magnificent beach curving along the bay. At the most westerly point of the peninsula lies **Garinish** where a cable car takes visitors over to **Dursey Island**.*

Dursey is a long, mountain island encircled by high cliffs. Offshore are a number of other islands, the most interesting of which is Bull Rock, a roosting place for gannets. A cave passes right through it, creating a massive rock arch.

*Skirting the southern shore of the peninsula, the narrow road hugs the ocean through **Castletownbere** and **Adrigole** from where you can follow the coastal road into **Glengarriff** or take the opportunity for a spectacular view by turning left and ascending the **Healy Pass**. It's hard to turn and admire the vista of **Bantry Bay** as the road gently zigzags up the pass, so stop at the top to relish the view before continuing down to **Lauragh,** where you turn right for Kenmare.*

The Southwest

SIDE TRIP TO IVERAGH PENINSULA—RING OF KERRY

Rather than follow the itinerary, you can use the Ring of Kerry as a route to Dingle or Killarney.

*The drive round the **Iveragh Peninsula** is, in my opinion, somewhat overrated, but if you want to see the much-publicized **Ring of Kerry**, hope that the fickle Irish weather is at its best, for when mists wreathe the Ring, it takes a lot of imagination to conjure up seascapes as you drive down fog-shrouded lanes. Even if the weather is dull, do not lose heart because at any moment the sun could break through. Driving the ring can be a trial during the busy summer months when the roads are choked with tourist coaches.*

*Beginning the Ring, a pleasant drive takes you along the Kenmare river estuary and you get tempting glimpses of water and the Beara Peninsula. Arriving at **Sneem**, enjoy the most picturesque village on the Ring, with its tiny, gaily painted houses bordering two village greens. (The most beautiful coastal scenery lies between Sneem and Waterville.)*

*Continuing your journey westward you come to **Caherdaniel** village where you turn left for **Derrynane House**, the home of Daniel O'Connell "The Liberator," a title he earned for winning Catholic emancipation. If the weather is inclement, concentrate on the house with its furnished rooms, audio-visual presentation, museum, and tea rooms. But, if the weather is fine, spend your time outdoors walking along the sandy beach of Derrynane Bay and crossing the narrow strip of sand that separates the mainland from **Abbey Island** where St. Fionan founded a monastic order over 1,000 years ago. Just round the point lies **Iskeroon** (see listing) and **Bunavalla** pier where boats leave for the Skellig Islands (see "Side Trip to Skellig Michael"). A panoramic view of Derrynane Bay can be enjoyed form the **Scariff Inn**—you cannot miss the landmark bright yellow pub sitting beside the road three kilometers above the seashore.*

*Cresting the Coomakesta pass you turn north for **Waterville**, an aptly named town surrounded by water. Its main street with several colorfully painted houses is built along the shore. From here a pleasant drive takes you to **Cahersiveen,** a classic Irish town* with a long main street made up of shops and pubs. *Concluding the ring, you follow the seashore to* **Killorglin**. *However, our suggested route for your return to Kenmare is to take a right-hand turn to* **Caragh Lake** *(5 kilometers before your reach Killorglin) and follow the narrow lanes around this beautiful lake and across the rugged* **Macgillycuddy's Reeks** *(Ireland's highest mountains) to Blackwater Bridge (on the Ring) and Kenmare—a trip to be undertaken only on a clear day.*

View to Little Skellig from Skellig Michael

The Southwest

SIDE TRIP TO SKELLIG MICHAEL

*The trip to **Skellig Michael** cannot be counted upon until the actual day because it depends on calm seas. Book two days in advance. Boat service operates from several harbors on the Ring of Kerry—Bunavalla: Seamus Shea, tel: 066 75129; Portmagee: Des Lavelle, tel: 066 76124, fax: 066 76309; or Brendan O'Keefe, Fisherman's Bar, tel: 066 77103. Remember to wear flat-heeled shoes and take a waterproof jacket, an extra sweater, and lunch. The morning departure for the island and the late afternoon return necessitate your spending two nights on the Ring of Kerry (see listings Caragh Lake, Derrynane, and Kenmare). The boats run daily between Easter and October. Call in advance to make a reservation.*

Skellig Michael is a very special place, a rocky island topped by the ruins of an ancient monastery lying 12 kilometers off the coast of the Ring of Kerry. After you arrive at the cove beneath the looming rock, the first part of your ascent follows the path to the abandoned lighthouse, past seabirds' nests clinging to tiny crevasses in the steep rock slopes. As you round a corner, the monks' stairway appears and you climb up hundreds and hundreds of hand-hewn stone steps to the monastery perched on a ledge high above the pounding ocean. Pausing to catch your breath, you wonder at the monks who set out in fragile little boats to establish this monastery and toiled with crude implements to build these steps up the sheer rock face.

At the summit six little beehive huts, a slightly larger stone oratory, and the roofless walls of a small church nestle against the hillside, some poised at the edge—only a low stone wall between them and the churning ocean far below. The windowless interiors of the huts hardly seem large enough for a person to lie down. Remarkably, the monks' only water source was rainwater runoff stored in rock fissures.

It is reputed that the monks arrived in 600 A.D. According to annals, the Vikings raided in 812 and 823 and found an established community. It is documented that the last monks departed in the 13th century. When it is time to leave this spot, you feel a sense of wonder at the men who toiled in this rocky place, enduring deprivation, hardship, and solitude to achieve a state of grace. The Office of Public Works is maintaining and restoring the site and there may be someone to impart information.

As a complement (or an alternative) to visiting Skellig Michael, visit the **Skellig Heritage Centre** on Valencia Island. The center is found where the road bridge meets the island, directly opposite Portmagee. An audio-visual presentation, "The Call of the Skelligs," takes you to the Skellig Michael monastery while displays show the bird and

Ladies' View, Killarney

The Southwest

sea life of the islands. (Open Apr–Sep, tel: 0667 76306.)

From Kenmare travel over one of Ireland's most beautiful roads (N71) for the twisty 34-kilometer drive over mountains to Killarney, stopping at **Ladies' View** to admire a spectacular panorama with the lakes of Killarney spread at your feet.

In amongst the woodlands you find the car park for **Torc Waterfall**. Following the stream, a short uphill walk brings you to the celebrated 20-meter cascade of water.

Muckross House and Gardens is 5 kilometers out of Killarney on the Kenmare road. (Be sure to choose the entrance gate that enables you to take your car to the car park beside the house). Tudor-style Muckross was built in 1843 in an enviable position beside the lake. The main rooms are furnished in splendid Victorian style and the remainder of the house serves as a folk museum with various exhibits. There's also a bustling gift shop and tea room. (*Open daily, tel: 064 31440, fax: 064 33926.*) The gardens surrounding the house are lovely, containing many subtropical plants, and there is no more delightful way to tour the grounds than by horse and trap. Take a step back in time and visit **Muckross Traditional Farms** (the entrance is on the opposite side of the car park to the house). Stroll up the lane (or ride the old bus) to visit three farms that demonstrate what Kerry farming was like in the 1930s before the advent of electricity and farming machinery. Chat with the farmers and their wives as they go about their daily work. Muckross House and its vast estate were given to the Irish nation by the Bourne family of California who had a smaller lakeside estate, Filoli, just south of San Francisco.

Believe everything you ever read about the magnificent beauty of the Killarney lakes, but realize that **Killarney**, not an attractive town, is absolutely packed with tourists during the summer season. If you would like additional views of the lakes, then a tour to Aghadoe Hill or a boat trip from Ross Castle should give you what you are looking for. Leave Killarney on the road to Tralee (N22) and turn left for the 5-kilometer drive to **Aghadoe** where Killarney town, lakes, and mountains can all be seen from this vantage point. If you prefer a close look at the lake and its island, take the 90-minute boat tour of the Lower Lake which leaves from the jetty alongside the ruin of **Ross Castle**. Tickets for this trip can be purchased from the Tourist Office in town.

SIDE TRIP UP THE GAP OF DUNLOE

If you are in the mood for an evening adventure (this is not a trip that should be attempted on a wet, rainsoaked evening), you can drive through the beautiful **Gap of Dunloe** *and emerge back on the road to Killarney just west of* **Moll's Gap**. *If you decide to drive, you must wait until after seven in the evening as the daytime horse traffic on this narrow, unpaved road will not let you pass! Leave Killarney on the Killorglin road and after passing the golf course, make a left-hand turn at the signpost for the Gap of Dunloe.*

Kate Kearney's Cottage *is at the entrance to the ravine. Legend has it that Kate was a beautiful witch who drove men wild with desire. Now her home is greatly enlarged as a coffee and souvenir shop. Beyond the cottage the road continues as a single-lane dirt track up a 6-kilometer ravine carved by glaciers. The dramatic setting is enhanced by the purple mountains on your left and* **Macgillycuddy's Reeks** *on you right. As you drive up the gorge, the walls rise ever steeper and you pass deep glacial lakes—the farther you travel into the gap, the more you are moved by its haunting beauty. Cresting the ravine, the track winds down into another valley and becomes a single-lane, paved road with passing places that joins the N71 to the west of the narrow passage through the rocks known as Moll's Gap. Following the road back into town, you come to* **Ladies' View**, *which on a clear evening offers unparalleled views of the lakes of Killarney. From here you return to Killarney.*

The Southwest

The Dingle Peninsula

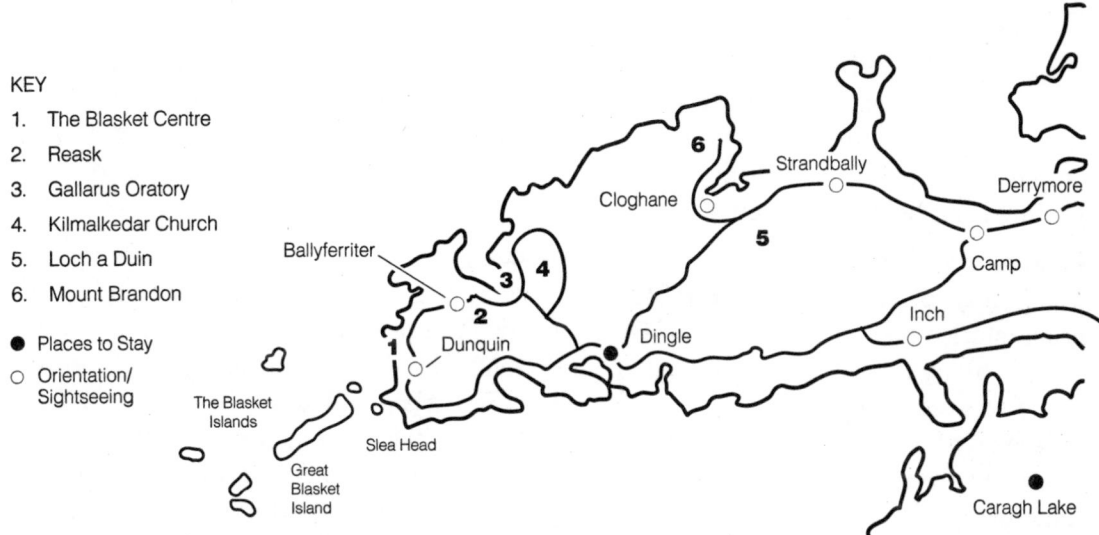

KEY

1. The Blasket Centre
2. Reask
3. Gallarus Oratory
4. Kilmalkedar Church
5. Loch a Duin
6. Mount Brandon

● Places to Stay
○ Orientation/Sightseeing

Leaving Killarney, a two-hour drive will bring you to Limerick, but rather than taking a direct route, take the time to explore the lovely **Dingle Peninsula**. It's a very special place, a narrow promontory of harshly beautiful land and seascapes where the people are especially friendly and welcoming to strangers. The road from Killarney to Dingle town takes you northwest to **Castlemaine** where you follow the coast road west through **Inch** to Dingle town, the largest settlement on the peninsula (it's only an hour-and-a-half drive from Killarney to Dingle).

Colorfully painted pubs, shops, and houses welcome you to **Dingle** (*An Daingean*) where fishing boats bob in the harbor unloading bountiful catches of fish and shellfish. It is not surprising that you find a great many excellent seafood restaurants here: **The Half Door** and adjacent **Doyle's** (see listing) are two up-market favorites. After dinner ask where you can go to hear traditional Irish music. Dingle's population is under 2,000 yet it has over 50 pubs, some of which double as shops—for example, **Dick Mack's** in Green Lane where you can buy a pair of shoes while enjoying a drink and **James Flahive's** cluttered, old-fashioned pub by the harbor. There are several interesting shops—**Brian de Staic's** jewelry store contains exquisite gold and silver jewelry inspired by Dingle's flora and ancient Celtic motifs. The town's most famous resident is **Fungi**, a playful bottle-nosed dolphin who took up residence in the harbor in 1985 and who loves to perform for visitors (tour boats leave from the harbor).

Plan to spend at least two nights on the peninsula to experience the beauty and tranquillity offered by the unspoiled scenery of the spectacular beaches and rocky promontories that lie to the west of Dingle town. Take time to wander along the beaches or walk along the lanes where fuchsia hedges divide the fields and friendly locals wave a salute of welcome and to take the trip to the Blasket Islands. Because Irish is the official language of the peninsula, signposts are in Irish (though commercial maps are in English) so we give the Irish in parentheses to aid you in finding your way. We outline a route that will take you on a half-day drive around Slea Head but for a real appreciation of the 2,000 archaeological sites of the Dingle Peninsula (peppered with lots of interesting stories) we recommend forsaking your car and taking one of **Sciuird's** mini-van or walking tours. Michael and his dad Timothy offer tours that range from an hour's walk round Dingle town to visiting ancient Ogham stones, wedge tombs, standing stones, and ring forts. (*Sciuird, Holyground, Dingle, Co Kerry, tel: 066 51606, fax: 066 51937.*)

The road to Slea Head signposted as **Slea Head Drive** (*Ceann Sléibhe*) twists and turns, following the contours of the increasingly rocky coast. Stunning seascapes present themselves, demanding that you pause just to admire the view. Several of the farms along the way have beehive stone huts and for a small fee the farmers will let you climb up to visit them. Conjecture has it that these small huts were used by early pilgrims traveling the St. Brendan's pilgrimage route. A large white crucifix marks **Slea Head** which affords the first view of the **Blasket Islands** (*Na Blascaodaí*), alternately sparkling like jewels in the blue ocean and disappearing under dark clouds a moment later.

Around the point the scattered village of **Dunquin** (*Dún Chaoin*) and the **Blasket Island Centre** come into view. The building is impressive, with exhibits lining a long corridor that leads to an observatory overlooking the island's abandoned village. Remarkably, this tiny, isolated island abode produced an outpouring of music and writing. Three classics of Irish literature emerged with Peig Sayers' *Peig,* Thomas Crohan's *The Islandman*, and Maurice O'Sullivan's *Twenty Years a'Growing*. The islands have been uninhabited since 1953 when the last islanders evacuated their windswept homes. The large airy dining room serves tempting food (excellent lemon cake) and provides enticing island views. (*Open all year, tel: 066 56444.*)

Before you visit the center, park on the cliff-top (opposite the two yellow bungalows) and walk down to **Dunquin's pier** which sits away from the scattered village and is reached by a steep path which zigzags down the cliff. As you round the last twist, you see curraghs turned upside down looking like giant black beetles stranded high above the water line. Curraghs are fragile boats made of tarred canvas stretched over a wooden skeleton. St. Brendan is reputed to have discovered America in such a boat. In clear weather a ferry takes day-trip visitors to and from **Great Blasket Island**. The little village on the island is mostly in ruins and paths wander amongst the fields where the hardy islanders struggled to earn a living—a café offers the only shelter. (*Ferry sails every hour 10 am–6 pm in summer, tel: 066 56455.*)

On the road to **Ballyferriter** (*Balle an Fheirtearaigh*), an attractive little village with a couple of pubs and a little museum, the pottery of **Louis Mulcahy** makes an interesting stop. Shortly after the pottery (just beyond Bracks pub) watch for a small signpost indicating a right-hand turn to **Reask** (*Riasc*), an ancient monastic settlement with its large slab cross, foundations of beehive huts, and slab stone with a contract ring, a small hole—people sealed agreements by touching fingers through.

Returning to the main road, a short drive brings you to the **Gallarus Oratory** (*Séipéilín Ghallarais*). Over 1,000 years ago many of St. Brendan's contemporaries lived on the Dingle Peninsula in unmortared, beehive-shaped stone huts called clochans. The most famous example is the Gallarus Oratory, a tiny church built not as a circle, but in the shape of an upturned boat. It has a small window at one end, a small door at the other, and is as watertight today as when it was built over 900 years ago. The little visitors' center shows a video and has a café.

Arriving in the nearby village of **Múirioch,** turn right at the Y for **Kilmalkedar Church** (*Séipéal Chill Mhaolcéadair*). This now roofless place of worship was built in the 12th century on the site of a 7th-century church. However, it dates back even farther, for within the graveyard is a magnificent early-Christian cross, an ancient Ogham stone, and an intricately decorated sundial. Within the church stands a rare alphabet stone which the monks used for teaching the alphabet. Locals refer to the little slit east window as the eye of the needle and folklore has it that if you climb through the window, you will surely marry within a year and a day.

Continuing uphill, the field to your right contains the ruins of the Chancellor's house. Park your car by the gate on the right that follows the little lane (not signposted) and walk into the farmer's field to examine the waist-high foundations of the **Caher Dorgan** (*Cathar Dairgáin*) ring fort with its beehive huts. On a clear day you get a magnificent view of the Three Sisters, a line of three mountains that tumble into the sea.

Cresting the rise, you travel 5 kilometers of the Dingle Peninsula's straightest road, known as *An Bóthar Fada*—The Long Road. It must have seemed a very long road for farmers walking to town. In the distance the entrance to Dingle's harbor is guarded by **Esk Tower,** built in 1847 by an English landlord to give paid work to the men of Dingle.

Its giant wooden hand serves as a marker for fishermen to the entrance to the protected harbor.

NOTE: If you get lost on the peninsula's little lanes, ask a friendly local or follow signposts for *An Daingean*, Dingle town.

There are lots of interesting walks on the Dingle Peninsula. Two of the more unusual ones are following the **Way of St. Brendan** and exploring the **Loch a Duin Valley**. The Way of St. Brendan is laid out on a map that you obtain at **Cloghane's** tiny tourist office. The route begins in nearby Brandon and follows a well-marked route that the saint supposedly took to the top of Mount Brandon (about five hours of walking). Cloghane's tourist office also sells a booklet that takes you on a self-guided tour through the Loch a Duin Valley (Sciuird also leads a walking tour). Beginning at the hut beside the road at the bottom of Connor Pass, this route leads you on a well-marked three-hour walk through the valley's boglands. Structures associated with prehistoric habitation (2,000 B.C.), ritual, and agriculture, along with several kilometers of prehistoric field wall, still survive. The valley is also of interest to birdwatchers, botanists, and geologists.

Leaving the Dingle Peninsula (signposted Tralee), the **Connor Pass** twists you upward to the summit where a backward glance gives you a magnificent view of Dingle and its harbor. The view is spectacular, but there is no guarantee that you will see it—all will be green fields and blue sea and sky until the mists roll in and everything vanishes. Follow the coast road through **Ballyduff, Stradbally,** and **Camp** to **Tralee**. (If you are heading for the Cliffs of Moher, take the N69 to the **Tarbert Ferry** which takes you across the River Shannon.) At Tralee you join the main road (N21) for the drive to **Castleisland** and on to **Adare** with its charming row of thatched cottages and tree-lined streets. Less than an hour's drive will find you in **Limerick** whose traffic-crowded streets can be avoided by taking the ring-road signposted Ennis and Shannon Airport.

Dingle

The West

Céide Fields

Sligo

Bangor

Collooney

N59

Riverstown

Crossmolina

Ballina

Ballymote

Lough Conn

N17

Achill Island

Mulrany

Newport

Rosturk

Castlebar

Knock

N59

Westport

Louisburgh

Ballintubber
Abbey

Inishbofin
Island

N59

Leenane

Lough Mask

Cleggan

Cong

Letterfrack

Clifden

Lough Corrib

Cashel

Ballynahinch

Oughterard

Aughnanure Castle

Roundstone

Bushypark

N59

Rossaveel

Galway

Dunguaire
Castle

Aran Islands

Kilronan

Thoor
Ballylee

Dun Aengus

Lisdoonvarna

Ballyvaughan

The
Burren

Kilfenora

N18

Corofin

Miltown Malbay

Ennis

Newmarket-on-Fergus

Clarecastle

Shannon Airport

Glin

Limerick

Belfast

Dublin

● Places to Stay

○ Orientation/
  Sightseeing

▓ Itinerary Route

— Roads

▓ Alternative Route
  & Sidetrips

✈ Airport

The West

This itinerary takes you off the beaten tourist track through the wild, hauntingly beautiful scenery of County Clare, Connemara, and County Mayo. Lying on the coast of County Clare, the Burren presents a vast landscape of smooth limestone rocks whose crevices are ablaze with rock roses, blue gentians, and all manner of Arctic and Alpine flowers in the spring and early summer. Otherwise there are no trees, shrubs, rivers, or lakes—just bare moonscapes of rocks dotted with forts and ruined castles, tombs, and rock cairns. Traveling to Connemara, your route traces the vast, island-dotted Lough Corrib and traverses boglands and moorlands. Distant mountains fill the horizon and guide you to the coast where gentle waves lap at rocky inlets sheltering scattered villages, and whitewashed cottages dot the landscape. Ireland's holy mountain, Croagh Patrick, and the windswept Achill Island leave a deep impression on the visitor.

Cliffs of Moher

Recommended Pacing: It is possible to tour the west in just a few days, but this beautiful area calls for you to linger. Our ideal would be one or two nights on or near the Burren, two or three nights in Connemara, and two or three nights near either Crossmolina or Sligo.

Leave **Limerick** in the direction of Ennis and Shannon airport and you soon arrive at **Bunratty Castle and Folk Park.** An interesting history and guide to the castle is available at the entrance. As the majority of castles in Ireland stand roofless and in ruins, it is a treat to visit a 15th-century castle that has been restored so beautifully. The authentic 14th- to 17th-century furniture in the rooms gives the castle a really lived-in feel. In the evenings firelit banquets, warmed with goblets of mead, whisk visitors back to the days when the castle was young. In the castle grounds a folk park contains several cottages, farmhouses, and a whole 19th-century village street of shops, houses, and buildings furnished appropriately for their era. The community is brought to life by costumed townspeople who bake, make butter, and tend the animals. (*Open daily, tel: 061 360 788, fax: 061 361 020.*) **Bunratty Cottage,** opposite the castle, offers a wide range of handmade Irish goods, and just at the entrance to the park is **Durty Nelly's,** one of Ireland's most popular pubs, dating from the 1600s.

Just to the northwest lies the strangest landscape in Ireland, the **Burren.** Burren means "a rocky place" and this is certainly the case for as far as the eye can see, this is a wilderness. A wilderness that is rich in archaeological sites (megalithic tombs, ring forts, and the remains of ancient huts) and strange rock formations whose tiny crevices are a mass of Arctic, Mediterranean, and Alpine flowers in springtime. Ludlow, one of Cromwell's generals, passing through the area in 1649, wrote, "There is not enough wood to hang a man, nor water to drown him, nor earth enough to bury him in."

Base yourself at either **Corofin** or **Ballyvaughan** (see *Places to Stay*) to explore this unique area. To help you appreciate this unusual landscape, first visit the **Burren Display Centre** at **Kilfenora** which offers a 15-minute lecture and 10-minute film on the and rare flora and fauna of the area. Models explain the pattern of settlement ...he geological makeup of the area and silk flowers show the non-botanist what to look for. Next to the display center an old churchyard contains some interesting high crosses with symbolic carvings. (*Open Mar–Oct, tel: 065 88030.*)

Turn right as you leave the interpretive center and left as you come to the main road to reach the **Cliffs of Moher**, the most spectacular section of the coastline, where towering cliffs rise above the pounding Atlantic Ocean. These majestic cliffs stretching along 5 kilometers of the coast are one of Ireland's most popular sights. The cliffs face due west which means that the best time to see them is on a bright summer evening. The visitors' center offers welcome shelter on cool and windy days. (*Open all year, tel: 065 81171.*) A short distance from the visitors' center, **O'Brien's Tower** (built in 1835 by Sir Cornelius O'Brien, member of parliament, for "strangers visiting the magnificent scenery of this neighborhood" marks the highest and most photographed point along the clifftops.

On leaving the cliffs, head north towards, but not into, Lisdoonvarna and follow the coastal road around Black Head where the rocky Burren spills into Galway Bay to Ballyvaughan where you turn right following signs for the **Ailwee Caves** on the bluff above you. The visitors' center is so cleverly designed that it is hard to distinguish it from the surrounding gray landscape. Beneath the eerie moonscape of the Burren lie vast caves, streams, and lakes. You can take a tour through a small section of these underground caverns. The first cave is called Bear Haven because the bones of a brown bear who died long ago were found here. In other chambers you see limestone cascades, stalactites, and stalagmites before the tour ends at the edge of an underground river. Remember to dress warmly, for it's cool in the caves. (*Open Mar–Nov, tel: 065 77036.*)

Retrace your steps a short distance down the road towards Ballyvaughan and take the first turn left, passing Gregans Castle hotel and up Corkscrew Hill, a winding road that takes you from a lush green valley to the gray, rocky landscape above. Take the first turn to the left and you come to **Cahermacnaghter**, a ring fort that was occupied until the

18th century. You enter via a medieval two-story gateway, and the foundations of similar-date buildings can be seen inside the stone wall.

Some 7 kilometers farther south, you come to another ring fort, **Ballykinvarga**. You have to walk several hundred meters before you see the Iron-Age fort surrounded by its defensive pointed stones known as *chevaux de frise*, a term derived from a military expression describing how Dutch Frisians used spikes to impede attackers. Ireland has three other such forts, of which the two most impressive are found on the Aran Islands.

When you leave the Burren head directly for the coast and follow it east (N67) to **Kinvara**, a pretty village with boats bobbing in the harbor and small rocky islands separating it from the expanse of Galway Bay. On the outskirts of the village, the restored **Dunguaire Castle** has a craft shop and on summer evenings hosts medieval banquets. (*Open Easter–Sep, tel: 091 37108.*)

From the castle car park, turn towards the village and immediately take a left-hand turn (opposite the castle entrance) for the 5-kilometer drive to **Ardrahan** where you turn right on the N18, and after 6 kilometers left for the 2-kilometer drive to **Thoor Ballylee**. William Butler Yeats bought this 13th-century tower house and cottage in 1917, and it was his summer home for 11 years. The cozy thatched cottage is now a bookshop and the adjacent tea room with its three-legged bog chairs and welcoming fire provides an excellent excuse to linger over tea and scones or enjoy lunch. An audio-visual presentation tells of Yeats's artistic and political achievements. Two floors of the tower are sparsely furnished as they were in his occupancy. By pressing a green button on each room's wall you receive information and hear excerpts of his poetry. (*Open May–Sep, tel: 091 31436.*) Leaving Thoor Ballylee, retrace your steps to the N18 for a 24-kilometer drive to **Galway**.

SIDE TRIP TO THE ARAN ISLANDS

*If you are planning to visit the **Aran Islands**, take the coastal route through Spiddal to **Rossaveel** where two ferry companies operate a shuttle service to **Kilronan on Inishmore**, the largest of the three Aran Islands. (Aran Ferries, tel: 091 68903, Island Ferries tel: 091 561 767.) Until a decade or so ago, time had stood still here and the way of life and the culture of the islanders had changed little. Now their traditional dress comes out only for TV cameras and special occasions, and their traditional way of life has been replaced by a more profitable one—tourism. In the summertime more than double the population of the islands arrives on Inishmore as day-trippers. On arrival, visit the Tourist Information Centre by the harbor to discuss the cost of horse and trap, bicycle (there are plenty of shops where you can rent bikes), and mini-bus transportation. The barren landscape is closely related to that of the Burren: sheer cliffs plunge into the pounding Atlantic Ocean along the southern coast while the north coast flattens out with shallow, rock-ringed sandy beaches. You will have no difficulty obtaining transportation to **Dún Aengus** (about 8 kilometers from the harbor), the best known of the island's stone forts, believed to date from the early Celtic period some two- to three-thousand years ago. It has sheer cliffs at its back and is surrounded by pointed boulders designed to twist ankles and skin shins. Despite the hordes of visitors scrambling over its walls and stones, Dún Aengus is remarkably well preserved. With four stone forts, stone-hut remains, high crosses, and ruined churches to examine, the archaeologically minded could spend many days with detailed map in hand exploring the islands.*

Those who are not island-bound should follow signs for Clifden (N59) around Galway. Leaving the town behind, the road is straight and well paved, but a tad bouncy if you try to go too fast. Accommodation signs for nearby Oughterard alert you to watch for a right-hand turn to **Aughnanure Castle**. Approaching the castle, you may be greeted, as we were, by a friendly family of goats snoozing on the wooden footbridge before the castle gates. Aughnanure Castle was the stronghold of the ferocious O'Flahertys who

Clifden

launched attacks on Galway town until their castle was destroyed by English forces in 1572. The clan regained their castle for a period of time until wars with Cromwell and William of Orange saw them expelled again. (*Open Jun–Sep, tel: 091 82214.*) Nearby **Oughterard** is a pleasant, bustling town ("the gateway to Connemara") whose main street has several attractive shops. A stay here affords the opportunity for fishing and exploring the island-dotted Lough Corrib by boat.

Beyond Oughterard you plunge into Connemara past the **Twelve Bens** mountains which dominate the wild, almost treeless landscape of bogs, lakes, and rivers, a landscape that is ever being changed by the dashing clouds that rush in from the Atlantic. Apart from the occasional craft shop, there are no houses until you reach **Clifden** on the Atlantic coast (N59, 80 kilometers). Clifden is the major market town of Connemara and the home of the annual Connemara Pony Show (third week in August). The town presents a gay face with shopfronts painted in bright hues of red, blue, yellow, and green. Craft and tourist shops alternate with the butchers, the hardware store, pubs, and restaurants. On the main street you find **Connemara Tours** where you can rent a bicycle, buy booklets on the locale, and sign up for one of the walking tours that vary from an interesting stroll through the Roundstone bogs—great walking amongst lakes full of otters and interesting plant life—to the demanding climb up one half of the great Glanhoaghan Horseshoe in the stark Twelve Bens mountains. (*Contact Michael Gibbons and Michael Nee, Connemara Tours, Island House, Market Street, Clifden, Co Galway, tel: 095 21379, fax: 095 21845.*)

SIDE TRIP TO ROUNDSTONE

*To the south of Clifden the road has more views of sea than land as little boats bob in rocky inlets and cottages gaze westward across tiny islands. The road passes the marshy area where Alcock and Brown crash-landed after the first transatlantic flight in 1919 (commemorated by a monument about 500 meters from the main road). Via **Ballinaboy**, **Ballyconneely**, and **Roundstone**, the sweeping seascapes that this route presents are so compelling that it is difficult to concentrate on the driving.*

SIDE TRIP TO INISHBOFIN ISLAND

*If the weather is fine, a delightful day trip can be taken to **Inishbofin Island**. The Inishbofin boat leaves from Cleggan pier at 11:30 am, returning at 5 pm (the crossing takes less than an hour). Be at **Cleggan** pier half an hour before sailing time and buy your ticket at the Pier Bar. Sailings depend on weather conditions so it's best to phone ahead to verify departure times (095 44261). The boat sails into the sheltered harbor presided over by the remains of a Cromwellian castle, and you wade ashore at a cluster of houses that make up the island's main settlement. Many islanders have left in search of greener pastures and their cottages have fallen into disrepair, but those who remain eke out a hard living from the land and the sea. As you walk down lanes edged with wild fuschias and brightly-colored wildflowers, whitewashed farmhouses appear and you see fields dotted with handmade haystacks. (Regrettably, the odd long-abandoned rusting car spoils the scene.) At the far side of the island a row of cottages fronts the beach, one* *of them housing a welcoming little café where you can have lunch or tea before walking back to the harbor to take the evening boat back to Cleggan.*

Clifden stands just outside the **Connemara National Park** which covers 5,000 acres of mountain, heath, and bog—there are no pretty gardens or verdant woodlands. The video in the visitors' center gives a beautiful introduction to the park which has wonderful hiking trails. If you want to tackle the smaller paths leading into the Twelve Bens mountains, consider joining one of the guided walks that begin at the visitors' center (four of the Twelve Bens, including Benbaum, the highest, are found in the park). Two signposted nature trails start at the center: one leads you through Ellis Wood while the other takes you into rougher terrain. (*Open May–Sep.*)

Leaving Clifden to the north, the N59 passes the much-photographed **Kylemore Abbey**. Originally built by a wealthy Englishman in the 19th century, this grand home, surrounded by greenery and fronting a lake, passed into the hands of Benedictine nuns who have a school here. There's ample parking and a large restaurant and gift shop. You

Delphi

can walk beside the lake to the abbey where in summer the library is open to visitors. In the grounds you can visit the restored Gothic chapel with its pretty sandstone interior and different-colored marble pillars. (*Open Apr–Dec, tel: 095 41146.*) Follow the shore of **Killary Harbor**, the longest and most picturesque fjord in Ireland, to **Leenane**, a little village nestled at the head of the inlet. Continue along the shoreline and take the first turn to the left, signposted as a scenic route to Westport via Louisburgh. This interesting side road gently winds you along the sea lough to **Delphi,** an area of pools and loughs amongst some of the highest and wildest mountains in the west. Acres of woodlands offer shelter and there is not a bungalow in sight. The Marquis of Sligo built a lodge here in 1840 and called it "Delphi" because it reminded him of Delphi in Greece. After falling into dereliction, the house and estate were bought by Jane and Peter Mantle who welcome guests to their restored home (see listing under Leenane).

Leaving Delphi, the isolated mountain road takes you along the shore of **Doo Lough** at the foot of **Mweelrea Mountain** and on through wild, remote scenery to **Louisburgh,** where, turning towards Westport, the summit of the conical-shaped **Croagh Patrick** (Ireland's most famous mountain) comes into view. Swirling mists substantiate its mystical place in Irish history. It was after St. Patrick spent the 40 days of Lent atop its rocky summit in 441 that the mountain became sacred to Christians. Every year thousands of penitential pilgrims begin their climb to the oratory at the summit at dawn on the last Sunday in July, several going barefoot up the stony track. The ritual involves stopping at three stations and reciting prayers. No climbing skills are needed as it's a well-worn path to the top and on a clear day a walk to the summit affords a panoramic view across Clew Bay to Achill Island.

Nearby **Westport** lies on the shore of Clew Bay and is unique amongst Irish towns because it was built following a pre-designed plan. The architect walled the river and lined the riverside malls with lime trees and austere Georgian homes, forming a most delightful thoroughfare. There's a buzz to the town and on a sunny day you can enjoy a drink at the tables and chairs outside **Geraghtey's Bar** and **Grand Central,** on the Octagon (the heart of the town with a granite pillar in the center of the square). At **Clew Bay Heritage Centre** on Westport Quay, postcards and old photographs show the town as it was at the turn of the century. There is also a genealogical research center and a display on the maritime traditions of Westport. (*Open all year, tel: 098 26852.*)

Croagh Patrick

From Westport the most direct route to Sligo is by way of the broad, well-paved, fast N60, N5, and N17. However, if the weather is clear and bright, it is a delightful drive from Westport to Sligo via **Newport, Achill island, Crossmolina,** and **Ballina.**

Achill Island is Ireland's largest offshore island. Traditionally the Achill islanders traveled to Scotland as migrant farmworkers during the summer, but now what population has not been enticed away by emigration remains to garner a meager living from a harsh land. This was the home of the infamous British Captain Boycott who gave his name to the English language when tenants "boycotted" him for his excessive rents during the potato famine. Today this island holds the allure that belongs to wild and lonely places: in sunshine it is glorious, but in torrential rain it is a grim and depressing place. On the island take the first turn to your left, signposted for the windswept **Atlantic**

Drive, where you drive along the tops of rugged cliffs carved by the pounding Atlantic Ocean far below. The "drive" ends at **Knockmore** where scattered houses shelter from the biting winds.

Returning to Mulrany, turn north on the N59 for the 32-kilometer drive across boglands, where vast quantities of turf are harvested by mechanical means, to **Bangor** and on to **Crossmolina, Ballina,** and **Sligo**. The many sightseeing opportunities in the Sligo area are outlined in the following itinerary.

SIDE TRIP TO CÉIDE FIELDS

From Ballina you can detour north 20 kilometers to Ballycastle and drive another 8 kilometers east to the great cliffs of **Downpatrick Head** *where the Stone-Age settlements at* **Céide Fields** *(pronounced kay-jeh) are being excavated. Under the peat has been unearthed the most extensive Stone-Age settlement in the world, with walls older than the pyramids, a vast site which once supported a community of over 10,000 people. Wander round a portion of the archaeological dig and enjoy an audio-visual presentation and a cup of tea in the pyramid-shaped visitors' center. (Open May–Oct, tel: 096 43325.) The surrounding cliffs are amongst the most magnificent you will see in Ireland. Retrace your steps to Ballycastle and take the R314 through* **Killale** *(a workaday village whose skyline is punctuated by an ancient round tower) to* **Ballina** *where you turn left for* **Sligo***.*

From the Sligo area you can go into Northern Ireland, continue north on the following itinerary, or return south. If you travel south, consider visiting either **Ballintubber Abbey,** a beautifully restored church dating back to 1216, or the village of **Knock**. A religious apparition seen on the gable of the village church in 1879 and some hearty promotion has led to the development of Knock as a religious pilgrimage site and a tourist venue. A giant basilica stands next to the little church, a large complex of religious souvenir shops is across the road, and nearby Knock airport has a runway capable of providing landing facilities for large jets. Surrounded as it is by narrow country lanes, this sophisticated complex seems very out of place in rural Ireland.

The North

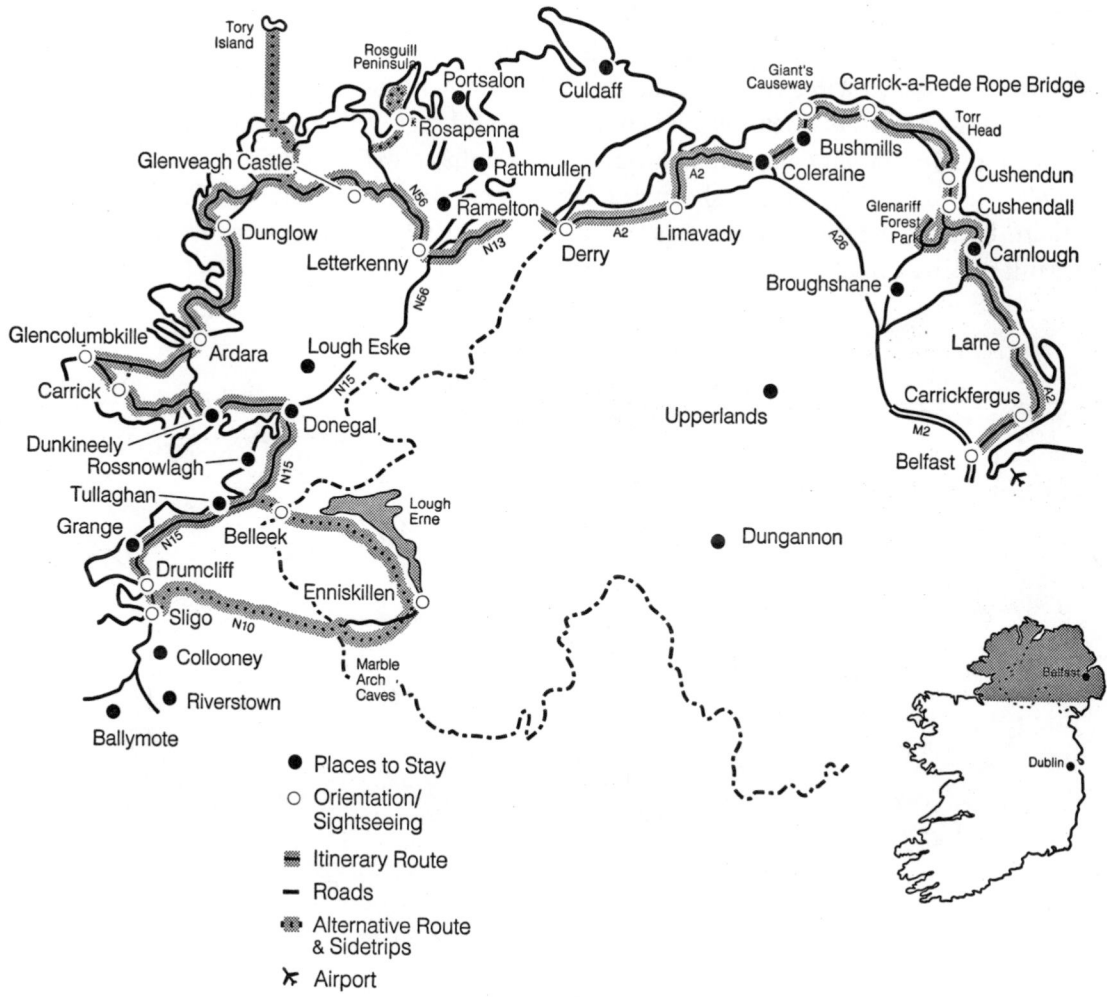

Tory Island

Rosguill Peninsula

Portsalon

Culdaff

Giant's Causeway

Carrick-a-Rede Rope Bridge

Rosapenna

Bushmills

Torr Head

Glenveagh Castle

Rathmullen

Coleraine

Cushendun

A2

Cushendall

Dunglow

Ramelton

Glenariff Forest Park

Letterkenny

N13

Limavady

Carnlough

N56

Derry

A2

Broughshane

A26

Lough Eske

Larne

Glencolumbkille

Ardara

N15

Carrick

Upperlands

Carrickfergus

Dunkineely

Donegal

M2

Rossnowlagh

N15

Belfast

Tullaghan

Lough Erne

Grange

Belleek

Drumcliff

Dungannon

Enniskillen

Sligo

N10

Collooney

Marble Arch Caves

Riverstown

Ballymote

Belfast

Dublin

● Places to Stay

○ Orientation/ Sightseeing

▩ Itinerary Route

— Roads

▩ Alternative Route & Sidetrips

✈ Airport

71

The North

The northernmost reaches of Ireland hold special appeal. Herein lies the countryside that inspired the moving poetry of William Butler Yeats. Beyond Donegal narrow roads twist and turn around the wild, rugged coastline of County Donegal where villagers weave their tweeds and Irish is often the spoken language and that written on the signposts. The Folk Village Museum at Glencolumbkille, with its authentically furnished, thatch-topped cottages, demonstrates the harsh living conditions of the far north. Crossing into Northern Ireland, the honeycomb columns of the Giant's Causeway signpost the Antrim coast full of cliffs, lush green headlands, and beautiful views.

Dunluce Castle

The North

Recommended Pacing: Two or three nights around Sligo and Donegal, a night near Glenveagh National Park (to permit a leisurely visit), and two nights along the Antrim coast will give you time to explore this lovely area.

The county and town of **Sligo** are ever mindful of William Butler Yeats, and the whole area is promoted as being Yeats country. If you are an ardent admirer of the poet, you will want to visit the **County Museum** which has a special section about his poetry and writing. Base yourself near the town for several days—Ballymote and Riverstown are our accommodation choices in the *Places to Stay* section. The countryside is very pretty and there is enough sightseeing to keep you busy for a week.

SIDE TRIP TO CARROWMORE AND CARROWKEEL

Seven kilometers to the southwest of Sligo town, sitting in fields on either side of a narrow country lane, are the megalithic tombs of **Carrowmore**. *Wander amongst the cows and explore the little stone circles and larger dolmens reputed to be the largest Bronze-Age cemetery in Europe. Farther inland take the Boyle road (N4) 30 kilometers south of Sligo to Castlebaldwin where you turn right following signposts for Carrowkeel. At the end of a mountain track you come to* **Carrowkeel**, *a 4,000-year-old passage tomb cemetery. There are 13 cairns which cover passage tombs while the 14th is a long cairn. One of the tombs can be entered (backwards) and it is claimed that, on the summer solstice, the setting sun lights up the main chamber.*

SIDE TRIP AROUND LOUGH GILL

*A half-day sightseeing trip from Sligo can be taken by driving around Lough Gill, visiting Parke's Castle and enjoying a meal at Markree Castle. Leave Sligo to the north and follow signposts for Enniskillen, Lough Derg, and Dromohair which bring you to the northerly shore of **Lough Gill**. Glimpses of the lough through the trees give way to stunning lough views as the road hugs the shore and arrives at **Parke's Castle**, a fortified manor house whose ramparts and cottages (tea rooms) have been restored. (Open Easter–Oct, tel: 071 64149.) In summer you can take a boat trip on the lake which takes you around **Inishfree Island**. Leaving the castle, follow the lough into **Dromohair** where you pick up the Sligo road. After 5 kilometers, when the road divides, take a single-track lane to the right which leads you down to the lakeside where John O'Connel's rowboat is tied to the pier. He lives by the lake and is sometimes available to row you to Inishfree Island. Returning to the main road, it's a short drive to **Collooney** where you can partake of lunch or afternoon tea at **Markree Castle** (see listing).*

Leaving Sligo, travel north along the N15 to **Drumcliff Churchyard**, which has to be the most visited graveyard in Ireland—William Butler Yeats is buried here under the epitaph he composed, "Cast a cold eye on life, on death. Horseman pass by!" In the background is the imposing **Benbulben Mountain**. Beyond the village a left turn leads to **Lissadell,** home of the Gore-Booth sisters with whom Yeats was friendly. The 1830s Greek-Revival-style house is full of curiosities and quite a sight to behold, but in need of an injection of capital to prevent its decay. The room where Yeats stayed is over the porch. While the sisters belonged to the landed gentry, Eva went on to become a poet and Constance a suffragette commander in the 1916 uprising and a minister of labor in the first Irish government. Sir Henry Gore-Booth went off with his butler to explore the Antarctic in the 1880s. (*Open intermittently, usually Jun–Sep, closed Sun, tel: 071 63150.*)

Leaving Lissadell, continue north on the N15 for the 60-kilometer drive to Donegal or follow a more circuitous route through Northern Ireland.

ALTERNATIVE ROUTE TO DONEGAL

*From Drumcliff churchyard, return towards Sligo and at **Rathcormack** turn left through the village of **Drum** to join the N16 as it travels east towards **Enniskillen**. After checking with the guard at the border post, take the first turn to your right and follow signposts to **Marble Arch Caves**. This extensive network of limestone chambers (billed as "over 300 million years of history") is most impressive. The tour includes an underground boat journey, walks through large illuminated chambers, galleries hung with remarkable stalactites, and a "Moses Walk" along a man-made passage through a lake where your feet are at the bottom of the pool and your head is at the same level as the water. Remember to dress warmly and take a sweater. It is best to telephone in advance because if there has been a lot of rain, the caves are closed. (Open Mar–Oct, tel: 01365 348 855.)*

*Leaving the hilltop cave complex, follow signposts for Enniskillen for 7 kilometers to **Florence Court**, an 18th-century mansion that was once the home of the Earls of Enniskillen. The opulent mansion is elegantly furnished and famous for the impressive Rococo plasterwork on the ceilings. (Open Apr–Oct, tel: 01365 348 249.) On leaving Florence Court, do **not** go into Enniskillen, but turn left onto the A46, following the scenic southern shore of **Lough Erne** for the 38-kilometer drive to Belleek.*

***Belleek**, on the far north shore of the lough, is famous for its ornate, creamy pottery: porcelain festooned with shamrocks or delicate, spaghetti-like strands woven into trellis-like plates. You can tour the visitors' center and then browse at the factory shop. (Open May–Sep.) Crossing back into the Republic, head for **Ballyshannon** and follow the wide N15 north for 23 kilometers to Donegal.*

Glencolumbkille

Donegal is a busy, bustling place, laid out around a diamond-shaped area surrounded by shops. Donegal is one of the best places to buy tweed goods—**Magees** sells a variety, and the **Four Masters Bookshop** is a handy place to stock up on reading material. The ruins of **Donegal Castle** (open to the public), built in the 16th century by Hugh O'Donell, stand beside the Diamond.

The N56 heads west, hugging the coast, through **Dunkineely** (see listings) and **Bruckless** to **Killybegs**, Ireland's major fishing port. Large trawlers from all over the world have replaced family fishing boats in the working harbor of this most enjoyable town. As you move west from Killybegs, the roads become more difficult, the landscape more rugged, and the signposts less frequent, and, to complicate things, they are often written in Irish (Irish names are referenced in parentheses).

If the weather is fine, you can enjoy some spectacular scenery by following the brown signs that indicate a coastal route from **Kilcar** to **Carrick** (*An Charraig*) where you turn left (in the center of the village opposite the pub) for **Telin** (*Teilean*) and follow the brown signs for **Bunglar** and The Cliffs. As the narrow road winds up, down, and around the rocky, rolling landscape you see several examples of traditional Irish cottages with small thatched pony-cart barns huddled next to them. The road narrows to a single track and takes you along the very edge of the headlands to a viewpoint that overlooks the spot where the **Slieve League Cliffs** plummet into the sea. Walkers will love the magnificent walks along the headlands. This is not a trip to be taken in inclement weather.

Retrace your steps to Carrick and turn left towards **Glencolumbkille** (*Gleann Cholaim Cille*). The road enters the Owenwee Valley where you climb before descending into the glen. Drive through the scattered village to **Glencolumbkille Folk Village Museum** at the water's edge. Glencolumbkille is a very special place which gives an appreciation of the survival of a people who endured hardship, famine, and debilitating emigration. By the 1960s, emigration was threatening to turn Glencolumbkille into a ghost town. In an effort to try to create some jobs, the parish priest, Father McDyer, formed a cooperative of the remaining local residents to develop a tourist industry by building a folk museum and holiday homes and by encouraging local crafts. Tucked against a rocky hillside, the cottages that comprise the folk museum are grouped to form a traditional tiny village, or *clachan*. Each cottage is a replica of those lived in by local people in each of three successive centuries. The thick, thatched roofs are tied down with heavy rope and anchored with stones, securing them from the harsh Atlantic winds. Inside, the little homes are furnished with period furniture and utensils. Friendly locals guide you through the houses and give you snippets of local history. A handicraft shop sells Irish cottage crafts and the adjacent tea room serves oven-fresh scones and piping hot tea on lovely Irish pottery. (*Open Apr–Oct, tel: 073 30017.*)

Leaving Glencolumbkille, the narrow road climbs and dips through seemingly uninhabited, rugged countryside where the views are often obscured by swirling mists as you climb the Glengesh Pass before dropping down into **Ardara**.

The road skirts the coast and brings you to the twin fishing villages of **Portnoo** and **Nairn,** set amongst isolated beaches that truly have an "end-of-the-earth" quality about them. A short drive brings you to **Maas** whence you travel an extremely twisty road to the Gweebarra bridge which brings you to **Lettermacaward** (*Leitir Mhic An Bhaird*) and on to **Dunglow** (*An Globhan Liath*). Nearby in **Burtonport** (*Ailt An Chorain*) more salmon and lobster are landed than at any other port. From here you drive north to **Kincasslagh** and then it's on to **Annagary,** both tiny little communities that pride themselves on speaking the Irish language. A combination of wild, untamed scenery, villages that seem untouched by the 20th century, and narrow, curving roads in general disrepair gives the feeling that the passage of time stopped many years ago in this isolated corner of Ireland.

Rejoin the N56 just south of **Gweedore** (*Gaoth Dobhair*) and follow it for a short distance as it swings inland paralleling a sea loch. As the main road swings to the right, continue straight up the mountain, following a narrow, winding road that brings you across peat bogs and purple, heather-covered moorlands inhabited only by sheep to **Glenveagh National Park,** Ireland's largest, most natural, and most beautiful park. At its center lies a sheltered glen with a lake and mighty castle. The **Glenveagh Visitors' Centre** is well signposted and well disguised, being sunk into the ground with its roof camouflaged by peat and heather. There are displays, an audio-visual program, and a café (there's another at the castle) and it is here that you leave your car to take the mini-bus around the lake to **Glenveagh Castle** and its gardens. The heather and rose gardens, the rhododendrons, the laurels and pines, busts, and statues are all lovingly maintained, but the walled kitchen garden is especially memorable, with its profusion of flowers and tidy rows of vegetables divided by narrow grass walkways. Surrounding this oasis of cultivated beauty are thousands of acres of wild countryside where the largest herd of red deer in Ireland roam. Glenveagh Castle was built in 1870 by John Adair, using his American wife's money, in a fanciful Gothic design that was popular in the later part of the century. The rooms have been beautifully restored and for a small entrance fee you can tour the house (arrive by 2 pm if you're traveling in July and August). The Glenveagh estate was sold to the nation by the castle's second owner, Henry McIlhenny, who is largely responsible for the design of the gardens. (*Open Apr–Oct, tel: 074 37072.*)

Leaving the national park, turn right across the desolate boglands and heather-clad hills—your destination is **Glebe House and Gallery** (6 kilometers away) near the village of **Churchhill**. Derek Hill gave his home, Glebe House, and his art collection to the state which remodeled the outbuildings to display his fine collection of paintings. Among the 300 paintings are works by Picasso, Bonnard, Yeats, Annigoni, and Pasmore. The decoration in the house includes William Morris papers and textiles, Victoriana, Donegal folk art, and Japanese and Islamic art. There is a tea room in the courtyard. (*Open May–Sep, closed Fri, tel: 074 37071.*)

SIDE TRIP TO THE ROSGUILL PENINSULA AND TORY ISLAND

If you would like to experience more Donegal coastal landscape, you can do no better than tour the **Rosguill Peninsula** *whose 25-kilometer Atlantic drive traces a wild coastal route from* **Rosapenna** *through* **Downies** *and* **Doagh** *to* **Tranarossan Bay** *and back to Rosapenna. The road goes up and down, most of the time high above the ocean, then sweeps down to white sandy beaches.*

If you follow the coastal road west through **Gortahawk**, *you come to* **Meenlaragh** *where you take the ferry to* **Tory Island**, *a windswept island where the inhabitants eke out a hard life farming and fishing. Sailing times of the ferry boat depend on the weather. If you want to visit the island, contact the Post Office in Meenlaragh.*

Giant's Causeway

From Glebe House it is a 16-kilometer drive to **Letterkenny**. From the town, your route into Northern Ireland is well signposted to **Derry,** with stops at customs and the army checkpoint—the only reminders that you are crossing from Eire to Ulster. The N13 becomes the A2 as you cross the border and the pound sterling becomes the currency. Skirt Derry city on the **Foyle Bridge,** then follow the A2 to **Limavady** and the A37 for 21 kilometers to **Coleraine.**

Bushmills and the Giant's Causeway are well signposted from the outskirts of Coleraine. (One of the delights of traveling in Northern Ireland is that the roads are well paved and the signposting frequent and accurate.) **Bushmills** is famous for its whiskey—a whiskey spelled with an "e"—of which Special Old Black Bush is the best. A tour of the factory demonstrates how they turn barley and water into whiskey and rewards you with a sample of the classic drink to fortify you for your visit to the nearby Giant's Causeway. (*Open weekdays, tel: 012657 31521.*)

In the last century the **Giant's Causeway** was thought to be one of the wonders of the world. Formed from basaltic rock which cooled and split into regular prismatic shapes, it stepped out to sea to build an irregular honeycomb of columns some 70,000,000 years ago. More romantic than scientific fact is the legend that claims the causeway was built by the Irish giant, Finn MacCool, to get at his rival in Scotland. Do not expect the columns to be tall, for they are not—it is their patterns that make them interesting, not their size.

The first stop on a visit to the causeway is the **Giant's Causeway Centre** where the facts and legends about the causeway are well presented in an audio-visual theater. (*Open all year, tel: 012657 31855.*) A mini-bus takes you to the head of the causeway where you follow the path past formations called "Honeycomb," "Wishing Well," "Giant's Granny," "King and his Nobles," "Port na Spaniagh" (where gold and silver treasure from the Spanish Armada ship *Girona* was found in 1967), and "Lovers' Leap" and up the wooden staircase to the headlands where you walk back to the visitors' center along the clifftops. (It's a 5-kilometer walk and you can truly say you have seen the causeway if you complete the circuit.)

Leaving the causeway, turn right along the coast to visit the ruins of the nearby **Dunluce Castle**, a romantic ruin clinging to a wave-lashed cliff with a great cave right underneath. This was the main fort of the Irish MacDonnells, chiefs of Antrim, and fell into ruin after the kitchen (and cooks!) fell into the sea during a storm. (*Open Apr–Sep, tel: 012657 31938.*)

Retrace your route down the B146 and at the causeway gates turn left along the coast road. Watch carefully for a small plaque at the side of the road pointing out the very meager ruins of **Dunseverick Castle**. Dunseverick was at the northernmost end of the Celtic road where the Celts crossed to and from Scotland.

Carrick-a-Rede Rope Bridge

Shortly after joining the A2, turn left for **Port Bradon**. The road winds down to the sea where a hamlet of gaily painted houses and a church nestles around a sheltered harbor. As you stand in front of the smallest church in Ireland, the long sandy beaches of **Whitepark Bay** stretch before you.

Farther along the coast a narrow road winds down to the very picturesque **Ballintoy Harbour,** a sheltered haven for boats surrounded by small, jagged, rocky islands. At the first road bend after leaving Ballintoy village, turn sharp left for the **Carrick-a-Rede Rope Bridge.** This is one of the famous things to do in Ireland: walk high above the sea across a narrow, swinging bridge of planks and ropes that joins a precipitous cliff to a rocky island. Hardy fishermen whose cottages and nets nestle in a sheltered cleft on the island and whose fragile wooden boats bob in the ocean below still use the bridge. (*Open May–Sep, tel: 012657 31159.*)

Life in the nearby holiday town of **Ballycastle** centers around the beach, fishing, and golf. Cross the river and turn onto the A2 to **Ballyvoy**. If the weather is clear, turn left for the scenic drive to Cushendun around **Torr Head**. The narrow road, barely wide enough for two cars to pass, switchbacks across the headlands and corkscrews down the cliffside, offering spectacular views of the rugged coastline and the distant Mull of Kintyre in Scotland.

Nestling by the seashore, the pretty village of **Cushendun** has a National Trust Shop, an excellent place to buy high-quality souvenirs. When you leave Cushendun, the landscape softens and the road, thankfully, returns to a more manageable width. You are now entering the **Glens of Antrim** where lush green fields and a succession of beautiful views present themselves. At **Cushendall** you can detour into **Glenariff Forest Park**, the queen of the glens with a series of waterfalls plunging down a gorge traversed by a scenic path crossing rustic bridges. Thackeray described this glen as "Switzerland in miniature." (*Open all year, tel: 012667 58232.*)

After your return to the coast road, **Carnlough,** a pretty seaside and fishing town, soon comes into view, its little white harbor full of bobbing boats. The **Londonderry Arms** was once a coaching inn and now is a very pleasant family hotel (see listing).

Nearby **Glenarm** is the oldest of the coastal villages, dating back to the time of King John. The pseudo-Gothic castle is the home of the Earl of Antrim, part of whose demesne, **Glenarm Forest**, climbs up from the glen and is open to the public. (*Open all year.*)

Limestone cliffs present themselves as you approach **Larne**, a sizable seaport whose Viking origins are lost amongst more modern commercial developments. Wend your way through this busy port town, following the A2 to **Whitehead**. Nearby **Carrickfergus** is the oldest town in Northern Ireland. **Carrickfergus Castle** is a sturdy Norman castle overlooking the boat-filled harbor. The castle was built as a stronghold in 1178 by John de Courcy after his invasion of Ulster, then taken by King John after a siege in 1210, fell to the Scots in 1316, and was captured by the French in 1760. Life-size models and a film recreate the castle's turbulent past. (*Open all year, tel: 01960 351 273.*)

Leaving Carrickfergus, a 12-kilometer drive along the A2 and M2/M1 whisks you through, or into, **Belfast,** where the A1 will take you south through **Newry** and into the Republic. Or, if you are staying near the Antrim coast for several days of leisurely sightseeing, take the M2 to the A26 which quickly returns you to your base.

Carrickfergus Castle

Places to Stay

Abbeyleix is a little historic gem of a town on the main Cork to Dublin road, the perfect place to break your journey for a couple of days and enjoy Ireland's lovely Midland counties. Amongst the town's treasures is Preston House, the school established in 1834 by Joshua Preston, the M.P. for Cavan, and now a welcoming guesthouse run by the energetic Alison Dowling and her husband Michael. As you enter through the hall door, saddles and riding paraphernalia lead into the inner corridor where, above the hooks that once held pupils' coats, the wall is lined with rosettes and ribbons. The small parlor, formerly the headmaster's drawing room, is country-house cozy and the delightful guests' dining room is full of lovely antiques. A door leads through to the schoolroom, now a country café serving morning coffee, lunch, and well-priced dinners. Alison is as enthusiastic about her cooking as she is about her lively town and taking care of her guests, whom she arms with information on walking in the nearby Slieve Bloom mountains. Upstairs, the four very spacious bedrooms face a tranquil garden at the back of the house. All have the modern conveniences of TV and phone, and an old-world ambiance created by antique furniture. The entire front section of the house is a huge schoolroom with a raised master dais—just the room for a hunt ball! *Directions*: Abbeyleix is on the N8, Cork to Dublin road, 16 km south of Porlaoise.

PRESTON HOUSE   New
Owners: Alison & Michael Dowling
Abbeyleix
Co Laois, Ireland
Tel & fax: (502) 31432
4 en-suite rooms
£25 per person B&B, dinner à la carte
Open all year, Credit cards: all major
Restaurant with rooms

This noble house with ornate Gothic façades stands amidst a vast estate separated from the charming village of Adare by a high stone wall and iron gates. It was rescued from decline by Tom Kane, a third-generation Galway emigrant, and his wife Judy and transformed into a luxury resort. Built as the elaborate home of the Earls of Dunraven, the house was constructed on a massive scale with a two-story-high paneled reception, over 50 hand-carved fireplaces, and an enormous, ornate gallery based on the Hall of Mirrors in Versailles. In the original manor, bedrooms and suites are baronial in size with elaborately carved marble fireplaces, king-sized beds, and seating arrangements. Bathrooms have marble floors and walls, huge tubs, and generous-sized dressing rooms. Bedrooms in the new wing are less opulent. All has been immaculately restored to reflect a luxurious, 19th-century country-house atmosphere, yet this is a mix of old and modern. In the vast grounds are the remains of a Franciscan priory built in 1464, the square keep of a feudal castle, a pets' graveyard, and a championship golf course designed by Robert Trent Jones, Sr. There are also a luxurious indoor swimming pool, gymnasium, sauna, snooker room, and tack-room bar complete with Irish music. Horse riding, fishing, golf and clay-pigeon shooting are all available on the estate. *Directions:* Adare Manor is in the village of Adare, a 30-minute drive from Shannon airport.

ADARE MANOR
Owners: Judy & Tom Kane
Adare
Co Limerick, Ireland
Tel: (061) 396566, Fax: (061) 396124
www.karenbrown.com/ireland/adaremanor.html
64 en-suite rooms
Double: £198–£320*
*breakfast not included
Open all year, Credit cards: all major
Luxury resort

The Dunraven Arms stands on the broad main street of this story-book village, its flower-filled garden adding to the picturesque scene. With its uniformed staff and formal restaurant it has more the feel of country house hotel than a hostelry. The hotel is smartly decorated and attractive antique furniture adds to the old-world feeling. The large informal bar is the gathering place for locals and residents alike, but if you want a few quiet moments, there is a snug residents' lounge with chintz-covered chairs gathered round a log fire. Request a room in the new wing that stretches down long corridors behind the inn into the peaceful garden. As well as being most attractively decorated, these new rooms enjoy immaculate modern bathrooms. The dining room has quite a reputation for its food—a laden dessert cart sits center stage and waiters hover attentively. If more informal dining is to your taste, visit the hotel's cozy restaurant, The Inn Between, in a quaint thatched cottage across the street. Enjoy the facilities of the fitness center with its swimming pool, steam room, and gymnasium. The hotel specializes in making golfing, equestrian, and fishing arrangements for guests. A 12½% service charge is added to your bill. *Directions:* Adare is on the N21, 40 km from Shannon airport, which makes it an ideal first or last stop in Ireland if you are going to or coming from the southwest.

DUNRAVEN ARMS
Managers: Louis &Bryan Murphy
Adare
Co Limerick, Ireland
Tel: (061) 396633, Fax: (061) 396541
www.karenbrown.com/ireland/dunravenarms.html
76 en-suite rooms
Double: £115–£130, Suite: £160–£170**
** breakfast not included, plus 12½% service*
Open all year, Credit cards: all major
Inn

We have a file of accolades for Margaret Liston's most valued talent—she's a caring hostess who goes the extra mile when looking after her guests. Margaret's home, Glenelg House, one of the simplest lodgings in this guide, is an attractive color-washed bungalow sitting in a pretty garden facing the vast Dunraven estate 2 kilometers from the village of Adare. All is bright and airy, as spic and span inside as out. The simply decorated bedrooms include a family room with one double and one single bed, a double room, and a twin room with its private bathroom across the hall. Guests have their own sitting and breakfast rooms and Margaret is always close at hand making guests tea and scones, answering questions, and sitting down for a chat. Many guests correspond with Margaret and a great many return. Margaret always provides a fruit dish and fresh scones for breakfast as well as traditional cooked food. Breakfast is the only meal served but there is no shortage of places to eat dinner in Adare. The very popular sightseeing venue Bunratty Folk Park is about 20 minutes' drive away, Shannon airport a 30-minute drive. *Directions:* From Adare take the N21, Limerick road for 1 km to the first crossroad. Turn left at Clounanna and Glenelg is the third bed and breakfast on the left.

GLENELG HOUSE
Owner: Margaret Liston
Mondellihy
Adare
Co Limerick, Ireland
Tel: (061) 396077, Fax: none
www.karenbrown.com/ireland/glenelg.html
3 rooms, 2 en-suite
£17.50–£19.50 per person B&B
Open Feb to Dec 21, Credit cards: MC, VS
B&B

Adare is a particularly attractive village with a wide main street and quaint, thatched cottages—a very convenient place to stay less than an hour's drive from Shannon airport. While I have two up-market listings here, I searched to find bed and breakfast accommodation and was very pleased when I arrived at Margaret and John Shovlin's home, Sandfield House. John is the food and beverage manager at the Dunraven Arms and Margaret has opened up their modern, redbrick home as a bed and breakfast. Margaret is not an effusive hostess, but she has a quiet, caring way about her and often finds herself fixing a welcoming pot of tea for exhausted guests who arrive direct from their transatlantic flights. The lounge provides a quiet place to sit and browse through the information on the village and nearby attractions. Upstairs, you find three good-sized bedrooms with snug shower rooms and a larger bedroom with a seating area and bigger bathroom. *Directions:* From Shannon airport take the N18 to Limerick and the N20 to the N21 (Killarney road) to Adare. Turn left at the beginning of the wall at the gray-stone building on the N21 and continue for 3 km—the house is on your right.

SANDFIELD HOUSE
Owners: Margaret & John Shovlin
Castleroberts
Adare
Co Limerick, Ireland
Tel & fax: (061) 396119
www.karenbrown.com/ireland/sandfield.html
4 en-suite rooms
£19–£21 per person B&B
Open Mar to Oct, Credit cards: MC, VS
B&B

Annestown House has an absolutely magnificent location high on the cliffs above a picture-perfect crescent of white-sand beach. This impressive 19th-century home, a cluster of cottages, and a little church comprise the village of Annestown—the only village in Ireland without a pub. Pippa, a former restaurateur, and John, once manager at Waterford Castle, encourage guests to make themselves at home and play the grand piano in the sitting room if they wish. Guests usually congregate in the back kitchen, now a cozy little parlor with comfy chairs drawn round the fire, or in the vast billiard room, browsing through the library of books between games. Guests really do make themselves at home—I found two guests doing press-ups beside the billiard table prior to a run. The ground-floor bedroom is handy for those who have difficulty with stairs but, to get a sweeping view of the sea, request one of the upstairs bedrooms of which the Dressing Room and Upper Room (the largest) offer outstanding views. Dinner is available, preferably with notification before noon. John is a keen walker and happy to equip you with maps, or you can content yourself with a stroll along the beach or the clifftops. Touring the Waterford crystal factory is a great attraction hereabouts. *Directions:* From the roundabout outside the Waterford factory take the coast road through Tramore and on to Annestown. Annestown House is the large white house on the cliff.

ANNESTOWN HOUSE
Owners: Pippa & John Galloway
Annestown
Co Waterford, Ireland
Tel: (051) 396160, Fax: (051) 396474
E-mail: annestown@tinet.ie
www.karenbrown.com/ireland/annestownhouse.html
5 en-suite rooms
£28.50–£30 per person B&B
Open all year, Credit cards: all major
B&B

Set about halfway between Dublin and Rosslare Harbor, Plattenstown House is an ideal base for exploring County Wicklow, "the garden of Ireland," with its heather-clad hills, pretty farmland, sandy beaches, and outstanding houses and gardens. Sitting in its own attractive gardens and surrounded by peaceful countryside, Plattenstown House was built in 1853. When their children had grown, Margaret found the house too large for herself and her husband and so decided to take guests. She is a warm, hospitable person who puts a lot of effort into pleasing her visitors. While there are several restaurants in Arklow, Margaret finds that guests often want to stay in after a day of sightseeing and she is happy to cook them dinner or a light supper (she makes the most delicious soups) with notice as late as early afternoon. Guests have a drawing room and a snug television room. Upstairs, the most spacious bedroom, Anna Livia, has an unusual set of curvaceous, light-wood furniture hand-crafted in the 1930s. Furniture by the same cabinetmaker graces the dining room while the remainder of the house is in a more traditional, old-fashioned vein. Gordon used to be a dairy farmer, but now he raises calves and is happy to take guests across the garden and introduce them to his "mums" and their gentle offspring. *Directions:* Leave the N11 at the roundabout at the top of Arklow town, take the Coolgreaney road for 4 km, and the house is on your left.

PLATTENSTOWN HOUSE
Owners: Margaret & Gordon McDowell
Coolgreaney Road
Arklow
Co Wicklow, Ireland
Tel & fax: (0402) 37822
www.karenbrown.com/ireland/plattenstown.html
4 en-suite rooms
£20–£25 per person B&B, dinner £15
Open Mar to Nov, Credit cards: MC, VS
Farmhouse B&B

Bagenalstown is sometimes signposted Muine Bheag, which can lead to a certain amount of confusion in reaching Kilgraney House, but the effort put into finding it is well worthwhile, for this is not your run-of-the-mill Irish county house—it's more like *Architectural Digest* than *Country Life*. With its crisp lines and whimsical touches, the decor is the brainchild of your hosts, designers Bryan Leech and Martin Marley. After working abroad, Bryan and Martin returned to Ireland, bringing with them unusual artwork and furniture such as tables and chairs made from coconut shells. Kilgraney House was put together with a touch of whimsy and their artistic flair, traditional Irish antiques being added to their overseas treasures, and the same attention to detail was lavished on the spotless modern bathrooms. The final ingredients are the warm welcome offered by your hosts and the lovely food they prepare for you. Because both Martin and Bryan teach design as full-time jobs their home is open for guests only during June, July, and August and on weekends in March, April, May, September, and October. Kilkenny, just a short drive away, is a particularly lovely town. A tourist map directs you to the craft shops that abound in the area. *Directions:* Take the N9 from Dublin to Royal Oak (south of Carlow), turn left into Bagenalstown (Muine Bheag), and right in the village for the 6-km drive to Kilgraney crossroads. Turn right (signposted) and Kilgraney House is the first entrance on the left (a 1½-hour drive).

KILGRANEY HOUSE
Owners: Bryan Leech & Martin Marley
Bagenalstown
Co Carlow, Ireland
Tel: (0503) 75283, Fax: (0503) 75595
www.karenbrown.com/ireland/kilgraneyhouse.html
5 rooms, 4 en suite
£27.50–£37.50 per person B&B, dinner £22
Closed Nov to Feb & see description, Credit cards: MC, VS
Country house

Ashley House is a large modern bungalow on a quiet country lane just to the north of Ballina town, built on the River Moy which is famous for salmon fishing. Carmel Murray, its owner, is a keen gardener and in summer her garden is a profusion of colorful flowers and heathers. The neat-as-a-new-pin look of the garden is extended to the home's pristine interior with its daintily papered walls and matching floral drapes. Carmel welcomes her guests with tea and cakes and has compiled a scrapbook of all the things there are to do in the area. Breakfast is served in the sunny dining room overlooking the landscaped back garden. Bedrooms, all on the ground floor, come with one, two, and three beds and while each is different in its decor, they are most attractive, with frilly muslin sheers and flowered drapes, wallpaper, and bedspreads. In summer there are often traditional Irish music and set-dancing locally on Thursdays (Carmel is an enthusiastic set-dancer). Ballina is between two very popular sightseeing venues, Céide Fields and Foxford Woolen Mills. High atop a cliff near Ballycastle, the Stone-Age settlement at Céide Fields has been excavated and a visitors' center shows you how this outpost supported people. Foxford Woolen Mills has been restored and you can see craftspeople produce tweeds, rugs, and blankets and enjoy an audio-visual presentation showing life at Foxford. *Directions:* From Ballina take the N59 in the direction of Belmullet for 1 km and turn right at the signpost.

ASHLEY HOUSE
Owners: Carmel & Michael Murray
Ardoughan, Ballina
Co Mayo, Ireland
Tel: (096) 22799, Fax: none
www.karenbrown.com/ireland/ashley.html
4 en-suite rooms
£16 per person B&B
Open Mar to Nov, Credit cards: MC, VS
B&B

Ballina and Killaloe are two villages connected by a bridge across the River Shannon as it exits Lough Derg on its way to the sea. Brid bought the large single-story Waterman's Lodge as a home and cleverly converted it into a hotel, installing a skylit roof over one of its courtyards which became her sunny restaurant at the very heart of the building. Bedrooms are off the corridor around the restaurant, making this an ideal place to stay for anyone who has difficulty with stairs. All of the spacious rooms are light and airy, with several of them enjoying views through the trees to the lake. Relax in the sitting room and plan your excursions in this very untouristy part of County Tipperary. Walk across the narrow stone bridge to quaint little Killaloe with its narrow main street lined with colorfully painted shops and its small row houses dominated by a huge cathedral where a chamber music festival is held every July. You can rent a boat on the lough, go fishing and walking, or venture farther afield to Bunratty Castle and the Cliffs of Moher. *Directions*: Ballina Killaloe is an hour's drive from Shannon. Coming from Shannon, it is best to avoid the traffic-filled streets of Limerick, so arm yourself with Brid's cross-country directions and come via Sixmilebridge. From Limerick take the N7, Dublin road, go through Birdhill, and turn left for Killaloe. Go through the village of Ballina (do not cross the bridge) and Waterman's Lodge is on your left after 200 meters.

WATERMAN'S LODGE   *New*
Owner: Brid Ryan
Ballina Killaloe
Co Tipperary, Ireland
Tel & fax: (061) 37633
10 en-suite rooms
Double: £90, dinner £26.50
Closed Jan & Feb, Credit cards: MC, VS
Country house hotel

Built in 1760, Whaley Abbey was once the shooting lodge of the playboy Buck Whiley whose outrageous exploits are celebrated in the colorful cartoons that hang on the living-room wall. For many years this was Emir's (pronounced Ema's) weekend home where she entertained friends and family: now the only difference is that the house is open year-round and friends are given a bill. While her home is beautifully decorated with great style, Emir and her assistant May Jordan takes special pride in the hot-water system that guarantees plentiful hot showers. On cool days there's always a fire ablaze in the cheery living room and guests dine together round the large refectory table where the main course is often a traditional roast. Breakfast is taken round the table in the old kitchen. Bedrooms come in all sizes, from the spaciousness of Emir's Room (all decked out in country pine with a semi-circular tub in the bathroom) to the snug attic room found up a steep flight of narrow stairs. The Conservatory Room has the advantage of opening up to a small conservatory with inviting armchairs. Riding stables are a five-minute drive away and Glendalough and the Vale of Avoca are close at hand. *Directions:* From Dublin take the N11 (Wicklow road) to Rathnew where you turn right on the R752 for Rathdrum and Avoca. About 1.5 km beyond Rathdrum turn right for Ballinaclash, and after going over the river, continue straight up the hill and take the first left, following this road until it becomes a track. Whaley Abbey is the first house on your right.

WHALEY ABBEY
Owner: Emir Shanahan
Ballinaclash
Rathdrum
Co Wicklow, Ireland
Tel: (0404) 46529, Fax: (0404) 46793
6 en-suite rooms
£30–£45 per person B&B, dinner £25
Open Mar to Nov, Credit cards: all major
Country house

Dan Mullane's famous restaurant, The Mustard Seed, has moved just a few kilometers from a thatched cottage in Adare to the spacious dining room of Dan's latest venture, a country house hotel, Echo Lodge. The move affords "foodies" the opportunity to enjoy some of Ireland's finest food and accommodation in a quiet, rural setting. Enjoy tea by the fire in the entrance-hall sitting room or curl up for a good read in the library. The emphasis is very much on a fine dining experience and guests are welcome to pop into the kitchen and chat to the chef and his brigade. The delightful bedrooms are each named after an aspect of their rather whimsical decor: Black and White, Butterfly, Nostalgia, and Lemon. As I saw each one, it became my favorite. If you are playing golf at Ballybunion, request an afternoon tee time so you do not have to rush breakfast. Adare is a 15-minute drive away and the surrounding peaceful countryside offers lots of opportunities for horse riding. *Directions:* From Adare take the N21, Killarney road for 2 km and turn left for Ballingarry. In the village take the Newcastle West road for 500 meters and Echo Lodge is on your right.

THE MUSTARD SEED AT ECHO LODGE
Owner: Dan Mullane
Ballingarry
Co Limerick, Ireland
Tel: (069) 68508, Fax: (069) 68511
www.karenbrown.com/ireland/echolodge.html
12 en-suite rooms
Double: £150, dinner £28–£30
Closed mid-Jan to early Mar
Credit cards: all major
Country house hotel

Ballydehob is a colorfully painted village set amongst ruggedly beautiful countryside. Fortunately for visitors to this most attractive spot, there is a charming bed and breakfast, Lynwood, just a short walk from town. Ann is the most welcoming of hostesses and she makes as much effort with her home as she does with her guests—her latest addition to her prettily decorated bedrooms are televisions, hairdryers, and electric blankets. All the guestrooms have tea- and coffee-makings and compact, en-suite shower rooms. A conservatory overlooks a tennis court which guests are welcome to use. For dinner most visitors go to the Ballydehob Inn or to Annie's Restaurant, because breakfast is the only meal that Ann serves. The road to Mizen Head takes travelers through Schull and past Barley Cove, a flat, sandy beach, to the southwestern tip of Ireland where vertical sandstone cliffs plunge into the sea—the last little bit of Ireland that so many emigrants saw as they sailed for America. The road back along the northern coast of the peninsula is very beautiful. *Directions:* Ballydehob is just off the N71 (Cork to Killarney road). Follow the Schull road through the village and Lynwood is on your right.

LYNWOOD
Owner: Ann Vaughan
Schull Road
Ballydehob
Co Cork, Ireland
Tel & fax: (028) 37124
www.karenbrown.com/ireland/lynwood.html
3 en-suite rooms
£16–£17 per person B&B
Open Mar to Oct, Credit cards: none
B&B

Built over 300 years ago as a hunting lodge for Lord Kenmare, Ballylickey Manor is now a deluxe country house hotel, the first Irish hotel to be accepted by the prestigious Relais & Châteaux consortium. It's a very appropriate membership, for the hotel has a definite French flavor: Christiane Graves, the owner, Gilles Eynaud, the chef, and restaurant staff are French—as is the cuisine. There's an aura of quiet luxury about the manor with its lounges, breakfast room, and five sumptuous suites. Across the gardens, just out of sight of the house, lies a lovely swimming pool surrounded by lawns and a cluster of wooden cottages. One contains the Mediterranean-style restaurant, Le Rendezvous, which serves elaborate meals (residents can choose to eat a simpler supper in the handsome green dining room at the manor). Other cottages contain delightful bedrooms (one is a suite), while two additional larger suites are found behind the manor. Ballylickey overlooks beautiful Bantry Bay and is surrounded by magnificent scenery. Drive across the mountains to the delightful town of Kenmare and farther afield to admire the magnificent lakes of Killarney (also see the following listing). *Directions:* Ballylickey Manor House is located in Ballylickey on the N71 between Bantry and Glengarriff.

BALLYLICKEY MANOR HOUSE
Owners: Christiane & Christian Graves
Ballylickey, Bantry Bay
Co Cork, Ireland
Tel: (027) 50071, Fax: (027) 50124
www.karenbrown.com/ireland/ballylickeymanor.html
12 en-suite rooms
Double: £90–£100,* Suite: £140–£180*
*plus 10% service, dinner £25
Open Apr to Nov, Credit cards: all major
Country house hotel

This tall, bright-white Victorian house is set amidst lush gardens rimming the shores of Bantry Bay. While it is worth a stay here just to soak up the spectacular scenery, the house has much to offer and Kathleen O'Sullivan is an energetic and caring hostess. The sitting room/bar, pretty in soft pinks and blues with light-wood furniture, offers plenty of places to sit, and for those in search of peace and quiet there is an old-fashioned parlor/TV room. The spacious bedrooms are individually decorated, those at the front of the house having the advantage of views of Bantry Bay through the trees. If you are looking for extra-roomy accommodation, request one of the very reasonably priced suites with two bathrooms. The Garden Room, on the ground floor, has been specially equipped for the handicapped. In addition, Kathleen has a very comfortable cottage on the grounds, just the place for families, friends traveling together, or those who prefer self catering. The atmosphere is friendly and informal, which accounts, I am sure, for the large number of guests who return here year after year. Wander off the main roads to explore the Beara Peninsula with its views of barren, rocky mountains tumbling into the sea. A "must visit" is nearby Garinish Island, a spectacular botanical garden with trees, shrubs, and plants from every part of the world. Also nearby is Bantry House, a grand mansion commanding the loveliest of views of Bantry Bay. *Directions:* Sea View House Hotel is located in Ballylickey on the N71 between Bantry and Glengarriff.

SEA VIEW HOUSE HOTEL
Owner: Kathleen O'Sullivan
Ballylickey
Co Cork, Ireland
Tel: (027) 50462/50073, Fax: (027) 51555
www.karenbrown.com/ireland/seaviewhouse.html
16 en-suite rooms
Double: £90–£110, Suite: £110–£120
Open mid-Mar to mid-Nov, Credit cards: all major
Country house hotel

Most of my family home would fit into the entrance hall of Temple House, but as a tour of the house subsequently displayed, that was just the tip of the iceberg, for beyond the enormous tiled entry hall with its array of wellington boots, fishing paraphernalia, and inclement weather gear lies a vast home with rooms of gigantic proportions. This is Deb and Sandy's family home and it's remarkable that they have made it into such a comfortable one. Those who are interested in the history of the place and wonderful stories of ancestors' exploits are directed to Sandy (he is extremely chemically sensitive so please refrain from using all scented products and aerosols). An air of warmth and faded elegance pervades this grand home which did not have electricity until 1962. All of the furniture made for the house is still here along with the original carpets and draperies, though Deb has added a lot of her own. Three of the bedrooms are gigantic. Realizing that guests enjoy the modern as well as the historic, bathrooms have been tucked into dressing rooms, good firm mattresses top historic beds, and central heating has been installed. Choose a pair of wellingtons and explore the estate from the vast parklands to the huge, walled vegetable garden. In the evening you can almost always be directed to Irish music and dancing. The Percevals can find enough to occupy your every waking moment—you will be tempted to stay for a month. *Directions:* From Sligo take the N4 to the N17 (Galway road). The house is signposted to the left. From Ballymote look for the sign beyond the Esso garage.

TEMPLE HOUSE
Owners: Deb & Sandy Perceval
Ballymote
Co Sligo, Ireland
Tel: (071) 83329, Fax: (071) 83808
www.karenbrown.com/ireland/templehouse.html
5 rooms, 4 en-suite
£38–£40 per person B&B, dinner £18
Open Apr to Nov, Credit cards: all major
Country house

Ballinkeele House was built for the Maher family in 1840, and Margaret and John are the fourth generation of Mahers to call Ballinkeele home. Set amidst 350 acres of parklike grounds, the house has all the solid quality of a grand home built in the early Victorian period: big rooms, fine ceilings, decorative doors, quality in every detail. Apart from the addition of heating and modern bathrooms, the house has not changed over the years. Soft Oriental rugs dress the flagstone entry which is warmed by a huge, old-fashioned stove, and grand oil paintings and family portraits adorn the walls. Antique furniture graces the cozy drawing room and enormous dining room where guests enjoy delicious candlelit dinners. The Master Bedroom is a particularly large room decorated in soft red and beiges with an impressive four-poster bed sitting center stage. For recreation there are walks through the estate and croquet on the lawn. Settle in for several nights and enjoy County Wexford—historic Wexford's Georgian theater is home to the October Opera Festival and on the outskirts of town is the Irish National Heritage Park with its reconstructions of old Irish buildings. The port of Rosslare is a 40-minute drive away. *Directions:* From Dublin take the N11, Wexford road, to Gorey. Turn left opposite the 64 Lounge restaurant for Wexford (R741) for 30 km and Ballinkeele House is signposted on your right.

BALLINKEELE HOUSE
Owners: Margaret & John Maher
Ballymurn
Enniscorthy
Co Wexford, Ireland
Tel: (053) 38105, Fax: (053) 38468
www.karenbrown.com/ireland/ballinkeelehouse.html
5 en-suite rooms
£30–£40 per person B&B, dinner £20
Open Mar to Nov 6, Credit cards: VS
Country house

Ballynahinch Castle, once the home of the O'Flahery chieftains, is a gray heap of a building whose architectural ugliness belies its unstuffy warmth and friendliness. The heart of the place is the bar with its old brick floor and little tables surrounded by Windsor chairs. Here a long table displays the "catch of the day" and fisherfolk hang the keys that give them access to the little huts on their fishing beats—no standing out in the rain when fishing at Ballynahinch Castle. The beats are so close to the house that folks return to the bar for lunch (packed lunches are also available). Bar food is served in the evening for those who are not inclined to partake of a more formal meal in the dining room whose windows overlook the river. Bedrooms come in two varieties: "standard" and "superior," which at Ballynahinch Castle means "large" and "larger." I particularly enjoyed my standard room Oranmore and preferred its low-ceiling coziness to the superior rooms with their higher ceilings and more spacious surroundings. Bedrooms face either the mountains or the River Ballynahinch. The natural beauty of Connemara is on your doorstep and often guests never leave the hotel's property, spending their days wandering on the well-marked footpaths through the 350 acres of grounds or just curling up with a book beside the fire. *Directions:* From Galway take the N59, Clifden road, for 68 km and turn left for Roundstone. The hotel is on your right after 4 km.

BALLYNAHINCH CASTLE
Manager: John O'Connor
Ballynahinch, Recess
Co Galway, Ireland
Tel: (095) 31006, Fax: (095) 31085
E-mail: bhinch@iol.ie
www.karenbrown.com/ireland/ballynahinch.html
28 en-suite rooms
Double: £120–£140 plus 10% service
Closed Christmas & Feb, Credit cards: all major
Country house hotel

Gregans Castle is only 57 kilometers from Shannon airport, so if you are heading north, this is the perfect spot to begin your stay in Ireland. This is not an imposing castle, but a sprawling manor house set in a lush green valley completely surrounded by the Burren, with its moonscapes of gray limestone and oasis of Alpine and Arctic plants. The entire house is delightfully decorated. Public rooms include a snug library and a cozy lounge— blazing turf fires add a cheery warmth. In the dining room, where Peter Haden supervises the production of delectable food, windows frame an outstanding view across the Burren to distant Galway Bay. My favorite room is the Corkscrew Bar with its blazing turf fire and blackened beams hung with copper and brass. Lunch is served here, and in the evening guests and locals gather for a drink and a chat. A new wing of traditional bedrooms and suites added in 1991 provides the most gracious accommodation. The older bedrooms are more modest in size, but comfortable and nicely decorated. Three large ground-floor suites overlook the garden. Local attractions include the Ailwee Caves, full of stalactites and stalagmites, and the Cliffs of Moher. *Directions:* From Shannon take the N18 to Ennis, the N85 towards Ennistymon, and the first right (R474) through Corofin. At the ruined castle turn right, and as you crest the Burren, you see the hotel in the valley below.

GREGANS CASTLE
Owners: Moira, Peter & Simon Haden
Ballyvaughan
Co Clare, Ireland
Tel: (065) 77005, Fax: (065) 77111
E-mail: gregans@iol.ie
www.karenbrown.com/ireland/gregans.html
22 en-suite rooms
Double: £120–£180, Suite: £220–£260
Open Apr 10 to mid-Oct
Credit cards: MC, VS
Country house hotel

This is just the place to stay if you want to go riding, for Bansha House has an equestrian center full of splendid horses which caters to every level of riding ability, from children (and adults) being led round the paddock to day-long treks through pretty countryside overlooking the Glen of Aherlow and the Galtee mountains. While son Con takes guests riding, Mum—Mary—stays at home, keeping everything in apple-pie-order. Mary has been offering hospitality for over 25 years, chatting with guests over a cup of tea, making them simply delicious breakfasts and evening meals and in summer sending them off to an evening of Irish dance and music in a sparkling little theater beside Cashel Rock. The foot-tapping entertainment is followed by a party of tea and cake, or a drink at the bar and a chance for the audience to dance and sing along with the professionals. The house is in tip-top shape but the premier rooms are those that have small shower rooms tucked into them. If you want to stay for a week, the Marnanes offer Primrose Cottage, a very attractive two-bedroom residence nearby. Countryside drives include the Vee and the nearby Glen of Aherlow where you can enjoy the view, and woodland walks from Christ the King Statue. The Rock of Cashel, Hoare Abbey, Holy Cross Abbey, and Cahir Castle are all within a 19-kilometer radius. *Directions:* From Tipperary take the Waterford road (N24) to Bansha, turn left in the village, and the farm is on your right after 1 km.

BANSHA HOUSE
Owners: Mary & John Marnane
Bansha
Co Tipperary, Ireland
Tel: (062) 54194, Fax: (062) 54215
www.karenbrown.com/ireland/bansha.html
8 rooms, 5 en suite
£20–£22 per person B&B, dinner £14
Closed Christmas, Credit cards: MC, VS
Farmhouse B&B

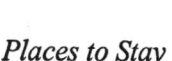

Just as you arrive in Bantry town, you see the entrance gate to Bantry House on your right. Dating from 1750, this stately home has fine views of the bay, and, like so many grand Irish homes, is struggling to keep up its elegant buildings. The current descendant of the Earls of Bantry, Egerton Shelswell-White, has tackled this problem by opening the house to the public who, with information sheets in hand, tour its lofty rooms and admire its elegant furniture, tapestries, and paintings, retiring afterwards to the tea shop in the old refectory. Yet this is a stately home with a difference, for one entire wing of the house and a couple of rooms over the tea shop have been restored in a more modern vein, offering large, bright, airy bedrooms (some with sitting rooms) on a bed-and-breakfast basis. After showing you to your room, the staff fade away until next morning when they prepare breakfast for you in the country-style dining room in what used to be the old cellars. Dinner is available on weekdays during the summer. In the evening you help yourselves to drinks from the honor bar, toast your toes by the fire, or, if you wish, play billiards in the enormous billiard room. A tour of the house is included in the tariff, so you can pop through the concealed door into the long gallery to wander at leisure through the museum-like rooms of this grand old home. *Directions:* Bantry is on the N71 between Skibbereen and Kenmare.

BANTRY HOUSE
Owner: Egerton Shelswell-White
Bantry
Co Cork, Ireland
Tel: (027) 50047, Fax: c/o (027) 50795
9 en-suite rooms
£60 per person B&B, dinner £20
Open all year, Credit cards: all major
Country house

Rosemary and Brian McAuley had Dunauley designed to take advantage of the spectacular view of the island-dotted Bantry Bay, aptly framed by a wall of windows in the living/dining room. Three most attractive double-bedded bedrooms, each with en-suite shower rooms, are found on the same level as the living room. Downstairs two additional bedrooms can be combined with a kitchen to form a self-catering unit with its own entrance. Guests enjoy both the living room and its particularly fine view as they sit round the fire in the evening and while tucking into an ample breakfast before setting out on a day's sightseeing. Breakfast is the only meal Rosemary serves, and guests usually drive into town for dinner. The drive from Bantry to Glengarriff gives a taste of the rugged landscape and exotic flora that you find in this part of Ireland. From the town you can take a boat to Garinish Island, a lush collection of interesting shrubs, trees, and flowers from all over the world. For over three years a hundred men worked to make Arran Bryce's garden, caseta, and temple, but financial hardships precluded the building of his home. *Directions:* From the center of Bantry follow white signs for the hospital through the one-way system and up the hill. Pass a church on the right and continue on this road till you see Dunauley signposted to the right—keep going uphill until you come to the house.

DUNAULEY
Owners: Rosemary & Brian McAuley
Seskin, Bantry
Co Cork, Ireland
Tel: (027) 50290, Fax: none
www.karenbrown.com/ireland/dunauley.html
5 en-suite rooms
£20–£25 per person B&B
Open May to Sep, Credit cards: none
B&B

Staying at Beaufort House in the little village of Beaufort will enable you to enjoy the outstanding beauty of Killarney National Park without having to deal with the crowds that descend on the nearby town of Killarney. Donald came to Beaufort House as a teenager and spent many years in London before he and his wife Rachel decided that they wanted to bring their two young daughters up in Ireland. Their input of capital has restored the family home to a luxurious state that it has probably never known. The decor is country-house perfection—no frayed edges here. Bedrooms come in two sizes: large with very large bathrooms or extra large with smaller bathrooms. Enjoy tea in the snug library or the sitting room, dine in the lovely dining room, and enjoy the warm hospitality offered by Donald, Rachel, and their young daughters. Enjoy a weeklong stay in one of the Cameron's lovely self catering cottages. Stroll down to the River Laune, cross the little hump-backed bridge, and enjoy views of the not-too-distant Gap of Dunloe. Look carefully amongst the bushes and you'll find the ancient Ogham stone that predates the house by several thousand years. Rachel often sends guests on a day trip that includes a jaunting car ride up the Gap of Dunloe and a boat trip across the lakes of Killarney. A drive round the Ring of Kerry is a must for many. *Directions:* Beaufort is 8 km west of Killarney on the R562 (Ring of Kerry). Turn left over the bridge and immediately left into Beaufort House.

BEAUFORT HOUSE
Owners: Rachel & Donald Cameron
Beaufort
Co Kerry, Ireland
Tel & fax: (064) 44764
www.karenbrown.com/ireland/beauforthouse.html
4 en-suite rooms, 2 cottages
£45–£55 per person B&B, dinner £25
Open Apr to Sep, Credit cards: MC, VS
Country house

Bobbie Smith is a caring hostess, carrying on the tradition of warm farmhouse hospitality started by her mother many years ago. She is also an unpretentious, fun person and her home reflects her welcoming, easygoing personality. Filled with mellow old furniture, books, pictures, and family mementos, the Old Rectory is very much a lived-in, comfortable family home for Bobbie, her husband Don, and their three daughters. Guests are welcomed with a reviving pot of tea in the drawing room, and it is here that they chat with fellow guests before dinner which is taken by candlelight round the long, gleaming dining-room table. Bedrooms have the same traditional family feel and range from a snug twin to a spacious family room with a carved four-poster and a single bed—ask for the one with the large feather bed: its comfort will surprise you. All have snug en-suite shower or bathrooms. The area is perfect for cycling, so Don organizes cycling holidays which include cycle hire, airport pickup, and baggage transportation. Those who prefer to stick to their car will find Kilkenny with its castle, fine old shops, and lovely buildings just a 20-minute drive away. Day trips can be taken to Waterford, Kildare, and Glendalough. *Directions:* Take the N9 from Dublin to Royal Oak (south of Carlow), turn left into Bagenalstown, and right in the village for the 6-km drive to Lorum Old Rectory.

LORUM OLD RECTORY
Owners: Bobbie & Don Smith
Kilgreaney, Bagenalstown
Borris
Co Carlow, Ireland
Tel: (0503) 75282, Fax: (0503) 75455
Email: 100757.16@compserv.com
www.karenbrown.com/ireland/lorumoldrectory.html
5 en-suite rooms
£30 per person B&B, dinner £20
Closed Christmas, Credit cards: MC, VS
Country house

Since moving into the spacious, rundown farmhouse that was Dunaird House, Sylvia has supervised a complete transformation, adding modern bathrooms and central heating and decorating the entire house in an elegant fashion. The graceful guest sitting room has damask sofas and elegant draperies while, by contrast, there is a country coziness to the pine breakfast room where Sylvia finds guests often sit in the evening to watch the television in spite of there being satellite TV in the bedrooms. The double-bedded pink room has a large bathroom and, like the adjacent double-bedded room, overlooks the front garden. A smaller twin-bedded room has a very fancy bathroom with shower and claw-foot tub just across the hall. Three additional cottagey bedrooms, decorated in an equally refined style, are found across the former farmyard in the old stables. Low-ceilinged beamed rooms are the order of the day here and the two ground-floor rooms have French windows opening onto a patio and the garden. Breakfast is the only meal served and guests often go the short distance into the village for dinner. Broughshane is the entrance to the Glens of Antrim which lead to the spectacular Antrim coast and the world-famous Giant's Causeway. *Directions:* Leave the M2 motorway at exit 11 for the 2-km drive to Broughshane. Turn right on the B94 (Ballyclare road) and turn first left by the church for the 1-km drive to Dunaird House on your right.

DUNAIRD HOUSE
Owners: Sylvia & John Graham
15 Buckna Road
Broughshane BT42 4NJ
Co Antrim, Northern Ireland
Tel: (01266) 862117, Fax: none
6 rooms, 5 en-suite
£20–£22.50 per person B&B
Open all year, Credit cards: MC, VS
B&B

Clohamon House has a wonderfully relaxed informality and beyond the grand old house lie some really pretty grounds full of badgers and foxes. There are also Connemara ponies, for Maria has a famous stud of ponies and is an international judge of the breed. Maria and Richard are friendly, amusing and their home has an enviable collection of antiques, for not only does it contain Richard's family furniture and portraits, but when Maria came here, she added heirlooms from her ancestral home, Waterford Castle. I particularly enjoyed Ashstand, a large twin bedroom with a panoramic view of the Slaney Valley, and Sinnotts, an elegant four-poster room. Shower rooms and bathrooms are on the smaller, more dated side. A light two-course supper is available in June, July, and August, while a county-house-style dinner is available for the rest of the year. The whole house has a comfortable, lived-in feel to it which more than overcomes the shortfalls in decorational order. If you want to stay for a week, there's a well equipped, self-catering cottage across the stable yard. You can cycle the lanes (bicycles are available), go horse riding nearby, birdwatching, and walking, visit local gardens, or take to your car and visit Kilkenny, Waterford, Wicklow, and Carlow. *Directions:* Bunclody is on the main Carlow to Enniscorthy road (N80). From Carlow turn left at the crossroads in Bunclody, cross the river and at the Y-junction go right up the hill. Halfway up the hill turn right and Clohamon House is on your right after 1 km.

CLOHAMON HOUSE
Owners: Sir Richard & Lady (Maria) Levinge
Bunclody
Co Wexford, Ireland
Tel: (054) 77253, Fax: (054) 77956
www.karenbrown.com/ireland/clohamon.html
4 en-suite rooms
£36–£48 per person B&B, dinner £23, supper £15
Open Apr to Nov, Credit cards: MC, VS
Country house

The Bushmills Inn was in a very sad and sorry state before it was rescued by Roy Bolton and Richard Wilson who transformed it in 1987 into a traditional Ulster hostelry. A rocking chair sits before an enormous fireplace and displays of old plates adorn the mantle. The ambiance of an old coaching inn continues to the restaurant with its whitewashed stone walls and tall pine settles dividing the room into intimate little areas. The inn's original kitchen, with its flagstone floor and open fire, links the hotel to the Victorian-style bar still illuminated by flickering gas light. Try a "Black Bush" from the distillery up the road—Bushmills is the home of the world's oldest licensed distillery and on weekdays you can take a tour. The bedrooms of the coaching inn are on the small side and each accompanied by a tiny shower room. More generous sized accommodation is found in the Mill House, an extension of twenty-two rooms built beside the River Bush. You may have the pleasure of seeing your nation's flag flown in your honor as the inn has the charming custom of raising the national flag of their resident who is from farthest away. Nearby are 13th-century Dunluce Castle, the Giant's Causeway and Royal Portrush golf course. *Directions:* From Coleraine take the B19 to Bushmills. As you cross the River Bush, the main entrance to the hotel is on your left.

THE BUSHMILLS INN
Owners: Roy Bolton & Richard Wilson
25 Main Street
Bushmills
Co Antrim BT57 8QA, Northern Ireland
Tel: (012657) 32339, Fax: (012657) 32048
www.karenbrown.com/ireland/bushmillsinn.html
30 en-suite rooms 1 suite
Double: £85–£98, Suite: £179–£198
Open all year, Credit cards: MC, VS
Inn

Catherine helped her mother in the antique trade for many years and as her interest in furniture grew, so did her collection—a collection large enough for her to theme her rooms depending on the period of the furniture: Art Nouveau, Victorian, Edwardian, and Regency. These bedrooms are very nice but the prize is her latest endeavor, her garden suite, a large room decorated in vivid yellow and royal blue with a bay window large enough to accommodate two armchairs overlooking a sheltered corner of her vast garden. Catherine's style is ornate—lots of different patterns with grand pieces of furniture in the dining room and six high-backed library chairs grouped around the fire in the sitting room. Breakfast is the only meal served, which is no problem as the White Gables restaurant is just down the road in Moycullan, while more adventurous food is offered farther afield at Drimcong House. Guests often go the 6½ kilometers into Galway city for city life and take day trips to the Aran Islands or to Connemara, an area of wild beauty found beyond Oughterard. *Directions*: From Galway take the N59 towards Clifden for 6½ km and Killeen House is on your right.

KILLEEN HOUSE   New
Owner: Catherine Doyle
Bushypark
Galway, Ireland
Tel: (091) 524179, Fax: (091) 528065
5 en-suite rooms
£40 per person B&B
Closed Christmas, Credit cards: all major
B&B

The Deevys have been promoting this off-the-beaten-path corner of Ireland for more than 30 years and are absolutely unflagging in their efforts. Jean and Bill bought this huge house over 30 years ago and quickly realized that it was far too large to maintain as a family home without an army of staff, so Bill pursued his career as a vet while Jean opened their home to guests. The next generation is now in place, with son Paul in the kitchen and wife Clare on duty in the evening. While Bill has retired to take care of the extensive grounds, Jean enthusiastically advises guests on where to go and what to see between breakfast and dinner. Improvements move at a slow and steady pace, with bedrooms and bathrooms that have been remodeled most recently being the most desirable. This steady pace and Paul's flair for cooking are responsible for the hotel's success and the delightful Irish idiosyncrasy of the place that new and old guests revel in. Dinner is from a set four-course menu with the flexibility of guests being able to order from it à la carte. While Jean has enough sightseeing venues to occupy a fortnight, do not miss the opportunity to visit Lismore Castle, Swiss Cottage, and Waterford Crystal and to take a drive over the Vee. *Directions*: From Waterford take the N72 (Killarney road) for about a one-hour drive to Cappoquin. Richmond House is on the left just before you enter Cappoquin.

RICHMOND HOUSE   New
Owners: Jean, Clare, Paul, & Bill Deevy
Cappoquin
Co Waterford, Ireland
Tel: (058) 54278, Fax: (058) 54988
E-mail: richmond@amireland.com
9 en-suite rooms
£30–£50 per person B&B, dinner £27
Open Mar to Dec 21, Credit cards: MC, VS
Country house hotel

The famous Ring of Kerry driving route runs quite close to Caragh Lake whose quiet shores are far enough away from the tourist path for guests to enjoy the tranquil beauty of this one-time Victorian fishing lodge with its acres of manicured gardens spilling down to the lake and its backdrop of rugged hills. Mary Gaunt was looking for an excuse to return to her native Ireland from England, so when Caragh Lodge, just across the lake from her holiday home, came up for sale, she saw its tremendous potential and made the decision to become a hotelier. Mary is a natural for the job—a caring hostess who has surrounded herself with a staff very much like herself. Nine lovely bedrooms with splendid lake views are found in the main house and an additional courtyard wing. Six less luxurious but very attractively decorated rooms are in two garden wings. Relax by the fire in one of the little lounges and enjoy an excellent meal in the dining room (Mary is the chef). More rigorous pursuits include a spin round the lake in the little boat (Mary encourages guests to fish for brown trout), a game of tennis (there's a court), or golf at one of the many local courses. Guests often make a day trip to Dingle, and Killarney is conveniently close at hand. *Directions:* From Killorglin take the N70 towards Cahersiveen for 5 km. Turn left at the sign for Caragh Lodge and Caragh Lake. Caragh Lodge is on the right after 1 km.

CARAGH LODGE
Owner: Mary Gaunt
Caragh Lake
Co Kerry, Ireland
Tel: (066) 69115, Fax: (066) 69316
www.karenbrown.com/ireland/caraghlodge.html
15 en-suite rooms
Double: £90–£132, Suite: £198, dinner £30
Open Easter to mid-Oct, Credit cards: all major
Country house hotel

Flower-filled woodlands line the driveway leading to Glendalough House, a charming Victorian hunting lodge overlooking beautiful Caragh Lake. Josephine Roder is your hostess assisted during school holidays by her son Alex. The family is completed by Fionn, the friendly Dalmatian; Jasper, the darting Jack Russell; and Pushkin, the affectionate cat. Staying here gives you the opportunity to relax and unwind, partake of candlelit dinners, and explore the area. While all the bedrooms are most attractively furnished with antiques, three are particularly appealing because of their delightful views through the treetops to the distant lake and mountains. A ground-floor bedroom (with zip-and-link beds) is perfect for those who have difficulty with stairs (its private bathroom is across the hall). Behind the house, two little bedrooms are found on either side of a comfortable sitting room in what was formerly the stables—there are no views from these rooms. Josephine feels that the house is unsuitable for children. This is an attractive spot perfectly located for trips to the Ring of Kerry, the Dingle Peninsula, and Killarney. There are also a great many golf courses in the area. Our favorite (clear-day) drive takes you through narrow lanes across the rugged Macgillycuddy's Reeks (Ireland's highest mountains) to Blackwater Bridge and Kenmare. *Directions:* From Killorglin take the N70 towards Cahersiveen for 5 km. Turn left at the sign for Glendalough House and Caragh Lake. Glendalough House is on the left after 1 km.

GLENDALOUGH HOUSE
Owner: Josephine Roder-Bradshaw
Caragh Lake
Co Kerry, Ireland
Tel & fax: (066) 69156
www.karenbrown.com/ireland/glendalough.html
7 rooms, 6 en suite
£38–£40 per person B&B, dinner £24
Open Mar to Nov, Credit cards: MC, VS
Country house

The Londonderry Arms was built in 1848 as a coaching inn by the Marchioness of Londonderry. Her great-grandson, Sir Winston Churchill, inherited it in 1921. Moira and Frank O'Neill bought the hotel in 1947, and now it is in the capable hands of their son, Frank, who has taken care to retain the old-world charm of the ivy-covered building. The old bull's-eye panes of glass and dark carved furniture in the dining room and library reflect this. Guests gather in the back lounge for tea and scones or retire to the front sitting room to read. The Old Coach House Bar is popular with the locals who enjoy a game of bar billiards as well as convivial conversation. Upstairs, the bedrooms and bathrooms have been refurbished—the nicest are the superior rooms with a view of the harbor. A lift is available for those who have difficulty with stairs. Running northward from Larne to the world-famous Giant's Causeway is the Antrim coast where the road hugs the sea and nine glens (valleys which run inland from the sea) offer diverse scenery. The coast road's sheer cliffs, rocky headlands, and succession of stunning views are breathtaking. The hotel has bicycles for guests and maps that outline scenic walks. The hotel has a car park. *Directions:* Carnlough is 56 km north of Belfast. If you are arriving from County Donegal, take the A2 to Coleraine, the A26 to Ballymena, and the A42 to Carnlough.

LONDONDERRY ARMS
Owner: Frank O'Neill
Manager: Mary O'Neill
Carnlough
Co Antrim BT44 0EU, Northern Ireland
Tel: (01574) 885255, Fax: (01574) 885263
www.karenbrown.com/ireland/londonderryarms.html
35 en-suite rooms
Double: £75–£85, dinner £17
Open all year, Credit cards: all major
Inn

Glencarne House is one of those welcoming places that guests love to return to, for Agnes Harrington is the most hospitable of hostesses. Agnes is particularly proud that her bed and breakfast has won three national awards. The perfume of flowers blends with that of the polish used to keep the lovely old furniture gleaming bright. All of the bedrooms have en-suite bathrooms—one, a family room, has two lovely old brass-and-iron beds and the large front bedroom has a beautiful brass-and-iron bed and a child's bed in the bathroom/dressing room. A hearty farmhouse dinner is served round the large dining-room table—the vegetables, fruits, lamb, and beef are fresh from the farm and carefully cooked by Agnes. The first thing you see as you cross the bridge into Carrick-on-Shannon is the flotilla of cabin cruisers for this is the premier cruising base on the River Shannon. You can hire a boat for a day or a week and meander along the River Shannon and her lakes, stopping off to visit the villages and their pubs along the way. The nearby Forest Park is found on the grounds of the former Rockingham House. The park's amenities include nature trails, a bog garden, and the relics of the former mansion. *Directions:* Glencarne House is on the N4, Dublin to Sligo road, between Carrick-on-Shannon and Boyle.

GLENCARNE HOUSE
Owners: Agnes & Pat Harrington
Carrick-on-Shannon
Co Leitrim, Ireland
Tel: (079) 67013, Fax: none
www.karenbrown.com/ireland/glencarne.html
6 en-suite rooms
£20–£22 per person B&B, dinner £16
Open Mar to mid-Oct, Credit cards: none
Farmhouse B&B

Hollywell is a lovely old house set in a large garden overlooking the River Shannon. It has a secluded riverside location, just a couple of minutes' walk to the heart of Carrick-on-Shannon, a lively riverside town which is a major terminus for weekly boat hire on the Shannon. For six generations, Tom Maher's family were the proprietors of the Bush Hotel and now Tom and Rosaleen keep up the family's tradition for outstanding hospitality as they welcome guests into their lovely home. Guests have a large sitting room with comfy sofas, books, games, and TV where they gather round the fire in the evening. Breakfast is the only meal served at the little tables arranged round the grand piano in the dining room, but there is no shortage of places to eat dinner in town. Three grandfather clocks grace the hallways and a sofa and books are grouped at the head of the stairs to take advantage of the view over a broad stretch of the river. The two very large front bedrooms share the same lovely view, while the back bedrooms are small only in comparison to those at the front. The addition of a delightfully spacious ground-floor bedroom is especially appreciated by guests who have trouble with stairs. You can fish without ever leaving Hollywell's grounds. A few of the stately houses within reach are Strokestown, Carriglass, Clonalis, and Tullynally. *Directions*: From Dublin take the N4 (Sligo road) to Carrick. Cross the river, turn up the hill by Gings Pub, and Hollywell is on the left.

HOLLYWELL
Owners: Rosaleen & Tom Maher
Liberty Hill, Carrick-on-Shannon
Co Leitrim, Ireland
Tel & fax: (078) 21124
www.karenbrown.com/ireland/hollywell.html
5 en-suite rooms
£27–£35 per person B&B
Closed Christmas, Credit cards: MC, VS
B&B

Ardmayle is a very old country farmhouse that has been owned by the De Vere Hunt family since 1840. The great attractions of staying here are that you can participate in life on a working farm with cows, sheep, and horses and enjoy trout fishing on a 2-kilometer stretch of the River Suir (no extra cost). Annette offers a warm welcome with tea and scones, and youngest son Evan will take you on a tour of the farm. The good-value-for-money dinners are delicious and include a starter, homemade soup, main course with fresh vegetables, dessert, and coffee. Four bedrooms have en-suite bathrooms, while the fifth has a large bathroom with an old-fashioned claw-foot tub down the hall. For an evening out, Annette can often direct you to local pubs that offer traditional Irish music (be warned: it begins late). If you want to venture beyond the farm, Cashel with its famous rock is just 7 kilometers of narrow country lanes away. An hour's drive brings you to Kilkenny, Cahir Castle, and the scenic drive across the Vee. *Directions:* Leave Cashel towards Dublin (N8). When you get to the Dublin road do not take it, but keep left down the hill. At the bottom of the hill (a confusing three-lane junction) keep left for 7 km through the village of Ardmayle. Outside the village, turn right at a T-junction. The first entrance on the right is to Ardmayle House.

ARDMAYLE HOUSE
Owners: Annette Hunt & family
Ardmayle
Cashel
Co Tipperary, Ireland
Tel: (0504) 42399, Fax: (0504) 42420
www.karenbrown.com/ireland/ardmayle.html
5 rooms, 4 en suite
£18.50 per person B&B, dinner £13.50
Open Apr to Oct, Credit cards: none
Farmhouse B&B

The setting for Cashel House is spectacularly impressive: at the head of Cashel Bay with Cashel Hill standing guard behind, a solid white house nestles amongst acres and acres of woodland and gardens of exotic flowering shrubs. Kilometers of garden footpaths are yours to wander along, and the beautiful seashore is yours to explore. This is not the kind of hotel to spend just a night in—once you have settled into your lovely room and sampled the exquisite food in the splendid conservatory dining room, you will be glad that you have made Cashel House the base for your Connemara explorations. Graceful antiques, turf fires, and lovely arrangements of freshly picked flowers create a warm, country-house welcome. It feels particularly decadent to have breakfast served to you in bed on a prettily decorated tray. All the bedrooms are beautifully furnished and decorated, each accompanied by a sparkling bathroom. Thirteen exquisite suites occupy a more modern wing and enjoy comfortable sitting areas overlooking the garden. Tennis rackets are available so that keen tennis players can enjoy the court bordering the bay. Riding lessons and treks are a big feature for many guests. Beyond this sheltered spot Connemara is yours to explore. *Directions:* Take the N59 from Galway (towards Clifden) through Oughterard and turn left to the village of Cashel 2 km after Recess.

CASHEL HOUSE
Owners: Kay & Dermot McEvilly
Cashel, Connemara
Co Galway, Ireland
Tel & fax: (095) 31001
E-mail:cashelhh@iol.ie
www.karenbrown.com/ireland/cashelhouse.html
32 en-suite rooms
Double: £142–£162, Suite: £182**
**plus 12½% service*
Closed mid-Jan to mid-Feb, Credit cards: all major
Country house hotel

While it looks like a modern house of rather dubious architectural merit from outside, when you enter Wandesforde House, you realize that you are in an old building. I was surprised to learn that it was built as a school by the Countess of Ormonde in 1824 for the children of the Castlecomer estate. It continued as a school until the 1970s, then lay empty for some years until it was bought by Phil and David Fleming and converted into a bed and breakfast and their family home. One of the two large classrooms is now a cheerful sitting and dining room with groupings of small chairs and tables. Phil always asks her guests what they would like for dinner and there is always a choice of meat and fish for a main course. If you arrive without having made a dinner reservation, it is usually not a problem for her to provide soup and a sandwich. The six small bedrooms are found either on the ground floor or up a narrow flight of stairs, and each has a compact shower room. Rooms come in a combination of twins and doubles and are unsuitable for large suitcases. Within a 20-minute drive are Kilkenny city, Carlow, the Barrow and Nore valleys, and the Slieve Bloom mountains. Kilkenny is renowned for its crafts, particularly in pottery, glass, and leather. *Directions:* From Kilkenny take the N78 through Castlecomer towards Naas and Wandesforde House is on your right after 6 km.

WANDESFORDE HOUSE
Owners: Phil & David Fleming
Moneenroe
Castlecomer
Co Kilkenny, Ireland
Tel: (056) 42441, Fax: none
6 en-suite rooms
£18–£20 per person B&B, dinner £15
Open all year, Credit cards: VS
Guesthouse

Ballyvolane House sits comfortably in a magnificent setting of gardens and wooded grounds—a grand old mansion, home to Merrie and Jeremy Green. Merrie is an ardent fisherwoman and takes every opportunity to go fishing, though Jeremy says that she usually just points guests in the right direction (she has 16 rods of salmon fishing). Jeremy also claims that their croquet lawn is the most challenging in Ireland—cheating to win is encouraged. Guests soon realize that Jeremy's unselfconscious humor and Merrie's straightforward sense of fun are applied to everything, which certainly means that guests to this gracious mansion do not walk around talking in hushed whispers: a cheerful camaraderie pervades the place. This is a friendly, happy house where guests wander in and out of the kitchen, which is in a vast, tall-ceilinged, drawing-type of room. After drinks in the drawing room guests gather for dinner round the long polished table watched over by a parade of benevolent ancestors. One of the lovely bedrooms has a bath so deep that you have to step up to get into it. Within a radius of a few kilometers there are no fewer than 16 golf courses and within an hour's drive are Blarney, with its famous castle, Cork city, Fota House with its paintings, and the bustling fishing and boating town of Kinsale. *Directions:* From Fermoy take the N8 towards Cork to Rathcormac where the 6-km drive to Ballyvolane House is signposted to your left

BALLYVOLANE HOUSE
Owners: Merrie & Jeremy Green
Castlelyons
Co Cork, Ireland
Tel: (025) 36349, Fax: (025) 36781
E-mail: ballyvol@iol.ie
www.karenbrown.com/ireland/ballyvolanehouse.html
7 rooms, 5 en suite
£35–£45 per person B&B, dinner £22.50
Open all year, Credit cards: all major
Country house

With its close proximity to Shannon airport, Carnelly House makes an ideal first or last night's stay in Ireland. Dramatically set at the end of a long driveway, this grand Queen-Anne-style Georgian residence offers the most spacious, luxury accommodation at grand hotel prices. On arrival, guests are offered tea or coffee in the large drawing room where softly painted paneled walls and slipcovered chairs present an inviting picture. Guests sip pre-dinner drinks here under the ornate La Francini plasterwork ceiling. Apparently the Francini brothers labored for over a year on the delicate tracery and were paid for their efforts in Irish whiskey. Dinner is wonderful and the service personnel are charming and competent. Up the grand staircase are the very large bedrooms, with old paneled walls painted in soft pastels that coordinate with elegant drapes and fitted bedspreads. Each bedroom has a very large bathroom which is nothing short of splendid. Bunratty Folk Park is just down the road. The Burren, Ailwee caves, Cliffs of Moher, and Yeats's home, Thoor Ballylee, are also worth a visit. *Directions:* From Shannon airport take the N18 towards Ennis and Galway. Watch for Dromoland Castle on your right: Carnelly House is 4 km from Dromoland's gates on your left (after you go under the pylons watch for the entrance at the end of an old estate wall).

CARNELLY HOUSE
Owners: Rosemarie & Dermott Gleeson
Clarecastle
Co Clare, Ireland
Tel: (065) 28442, Fax: (065) 29222
www.karenbrown.com/ireland/carnelly.html
5 en-suite rooms
Double: £168, dinner £30
Open mid-Feb to mid-Dec, Credit cards: all major
Country house

Mal Dua is not included because of its architectural merits (it's a stark modern building with flower-filled swans on the gateposts and concrete gnomes on the patio), but because it has most attractive, tastefully decorated bedrooms and welcoming owners in Kathleen and Ivor Duane. The house's unusual name is a combination of its owners' surnames, Maloney and Duane. The sunny lobby doubles as a sitting room with sofas and chairs in deep-pink velour which match the carpet and the balloon shades. An additional larger sitting room is decorated in shades of pink like the adjacent spacious dining room. A hearty breakfast is the only meal served. All bedrooms except the tiny single are spacious and come with different combinations of double and single beds. All have a bath or shower, hairdryer, TV, phone, trouser press, excellent reading lights, and tea- and coffee-makings. The decor is very attractive, with pastel-painted walls and coordinating drapes and bedspreads. The bedrooms are no-smoking. There are restaurants aplenty just up road in the lively little town of Clifden. During the third week in August, Clifden hosts the Connemara Pony Show and rooms are at a premium. *Directions:* Take the N59 from Galway to the outskirts of Clifden. Mal Dua is on your right as you enter the town.

MAL DUA
Owners: Kathleen & Ivor Duane
Galway Road
Clifden
Co Galway, Ireland
Tel: (095) 21171, Fax: (095) 21739
E-mail: maldua@iol.ie
www.karenbrown.com/ireland/maldua.html
14 en-suite rooms
£22–£30 per person B&B
Open Mar to Nov, Credit cards: all major
B&B

The harbormaster certainly picked a pretty site for his home on the quay, with its wide vista of the inlet of Ardbear Bay and the town of Clifden winding up the hillside. Since 1820, Quay House has served variously as the harbormaster's home, a convent, a monastery, and a hotel. Julia and Paddy bought the house and the adjacent cottages in almost derelict condition, giving them a new lease of life as a stylish hotel. They decorated the whole in a refreshingly eclectic style, blending old, modern, and unconventional in an idiosyncratic way with little jokes and quirks such as vegetarian alley, a corridor of hunting trophies, and the wall of prints with one hung upside down. The intimate dining room with its little tables and chairs extends into the adjacent conservatory. If you prefer an even more casual atmosphere, a five-minute walk brings you into town to Paddy and Julia's lively restaurant, Destry Rides Again. Upstairs, the bedrooms vary in size from spacious, high-ceilinged rooms to under-the-eaves cozy. Several are very "traditional country house" in their decor, others light, fresh, and more bohemian. Some have showers and others claw-foot tubs and showers. Three larger suites with balconies occupy an adjacent cottage. *Directions:* Take the N59 from Galway to Clifden and follow the one-way system to the top of the town where you take the lower fork at the first Y-junction down onto the quay.

THE QUAY HOUSE
Owners: Julia & Paddy Foyle
Beach Road
Clifden
Co Galway, Ireland
Tel: (095) 21369, Fax: (095) 21608
www.karenbrown.com/ireland/quayhouse.html
12 en-suite rooms
£35–£45 per person B&B, dinner from £20
Open Easter to Oct, Credit cards: MC, VS
Country house

Rock Glen is a cozy hotel converted from an 18th-century hunting lodge with all the outdoor beauties of Connemara at its doorstep. Enjoy the delights of the area, safe in the certainty that a warm welcome, superlative food, and a snug retreat await you on your return to Rock Glen. John and Evangeline Roche and their daughter Siobhan are your personable hosts. An inviting grouping of plump chairs around a turf fire, the chatter of locals and guests, and the warmth of the adjacent sun lounge invite you to linger in the bar. The dining room, decked out in shades of gold and pink, its tables laid with silver, complements the fine country-house-style cuisine that is served here. The comfortable bedrooms are uniform in size and decorated in pastel shades, all well kitted out with trouser press, hairdryer, and TV. If you book early, you may secure a room with a distant sea view. A larger room, number 35, a two-bedroom suite, has a bedroom, sitting room, and private balcony looking out to the sea. The hotel also has a full-sized snooker table and an all-weather tennis court. A 12½% service charge is added to your bill. Connemara's stunning scenery is on your doorstep. *Directions:* Take the N59 from Galway to Clifden, then just after passing the church turn left towards Ballyconeely. Rock Glen is to your right about 1 km from town.

ROCK GLEN HOTEL
Owners: Evangeline, Siobhan, & John Roche
Clifden, Connemara
Co Galway, Ireland
Tel: (095) 21035, Fax: (095) 21737
www.karenbrown.com/ireland/rockglenhotel.html
29 en-suite rooms
Double: £100–£110*
*plus 12½% service
Open mid-Mar to Oct, Credit cards: all major
Country house hotel

The Border counties between the Republic and Northern Ireland have their own distinct personality—very different from the west or the hubbub of more oft-visited tourist destinations. Hilton Park is a very grand home built by Johnny's forbears in 1734 and modified by subsequent generations. It's a grand formal house of lovely rooms where guests' bedrooms range from vast, with grand floor-to-ceiling beds which you climb into (accompanied by huge bathrooms with claw-foot tubs), to more modest in size, with regular-sized bathrooms containing lovely old soaking tubs. Guests relax in the beautiful drawing room, enjoying pre-dinner drinks, conversation, and views across the terrace of formal gardens to the lake. The same enchanting view is enjoyed in the elegant dining room where guests dine at separate tables by the gentle flicker of candlelight. Breakfast is taken "below stairs" in the former servants' hall. Guests often explore the early Christian sites found around Lough Erne and travel to Enniskillen to visit the stately homes of Castle Coole, a restored Palladian mansion, and Florence Court, a riot of rococo plasterwork. Note that there are discounts on stays of more than one night. *Directions:* From Cavan take the Clones road. At the end of the speed limit turn right after the Jet petrol station. Go through Ballyhaise and Scothouse and the entrance to Hilton Park is on your left 1 km after the Clones Golf Club.

HILTON PARK
Owners: Lucy & Johnny Madden
Scotshouse
Clones
Co Monaghan, Ireland
Tel: (047) 56007, Fax: (047) 56033
www.karenbrown.com/ireland/hilton.html
6 en-suite rooms
Double: £98–£135, dinner £25
Open Apr to Sep, Credit cards: MC, VS
Country house

The charm of Greenhill House is Elizabeth Hegarty, who is exceptionally sweet and helpful. I very much enjoyed the late-evening conversation around the drawing room fire with a cup of tea and cakes, while James and Elizabeth and fellow guests were "putting the world to rights." All this after a 6:30 pm dinner that included a groaning dessert trolley where Elizabeth encouraged guests to try a bit of everything. Wine is not served. The beautiful farmhouse is lovingly decorated with antiques, and bouquets of fresh garden flowers add the finishing touches. Our bedroom (overlooking an immaculate garden) had everything: sightseeing information; a tray set with teapot, kettle, tea bags, coffee, and chocolate; hairdryer; television; and even a little box of After Eight mints by the bedside. Plump comforters top the beds and fluffy towels hang on the old-fashioned towel rail, all coordinating in shades of pink with the curtains and the carpet. Bedrooms in the attic have bathrooms tucked neatly under the eaves while other rooms have snug shower rooms, in what at first appears to be large fitted closets. It goes without saying that you should plan on staying here for several days. With Greenhill House as a base you can set off to explore the Antrim coast. *Directions:* From Co Donegal, take the N13 to Derry. Cross the Foyle Bridge and at Limavady take the A37 towards Coleraine, turn right on the A29 (Garvagh and Cookstown road) for 11 km, turning left on the B66 (Greenhill Road) and Greenhill House is on the right.

GREENHILL HOUSE
Owners: Elizabeth & James Hegarty
24 Greenhill Road, Aghadowey, Coleraine
Co Londonderry, BT51 4EU, Northern Ireland
Tel: (01265) 868241, Fax: (01265) 868365
www.karenbrown.com/ireland/greenhill.html
6 en-suite rooms
£24–£25 per person B&B, dinner £16
Open Mar to Oct, Credit cards: VS
Farmhouse B&B

Markree Castle, Charles Cooper's ancestral family home, is a fine example of a castle built as an impressive family home complete with battlements and turrets rather than as a fortification. From the entrance broad stone steps lead you into the impressive reception hall with its grand staircase rising to an enormous stained-glass window portraying a fanciful depiction of the family tree with Henry VIII center stage. The reception hall opens up to the central hall which rises through three stories to an elaborate wooden ceiling. This impressive room with its groupings of tables and chairs leads to several smaller sitting rooms and a bar. The elaborate plaster cherubs decorating the dining room all add to the castle-hotel ambiance. At the time of my visit (1996) the high-ceilinged principal bedrooms up the broad staircase were not as well decorated as they could have been but I appreciated their spaciousness—I much preferred the rooms at the top of the castle (lift access available). The castle is run in a more casual manner than the grander, more formal Irish castle hotels. Markree is in the heart of Yeats country with magnificent scenery all around. Golden sand beaches line the shore, while rugged mountains such as Knocknarea and Ben Bulben and placid lakes such as Lough Gill and Lough Arrow make for a marvelous variety of scenery. *Directions:* From Sligo take the N4 (Dublin road) for 11 km—Markree Castle is signposted to your left (1km).

MARKREE CASTLE
Owners: Mary & Charles Cooper
Collooney
Co Sligo, Ireland
Tel: (071) 67800, Fax: (071) 67840
E-mail: markree@iol.ie
www.karenbrown.com/ireland/markree.html
30 en-suite rooms
Double: £110–£120
Open all year, Credit cards: all major
Country house hotel

Ashford Castle was built over a period of 30 years by Lord Ardilaun in the 19th century. Incorporated into its castellated façade are the remains of the 13th-century de Burgo Castle and the original Ashford House, built in the style of a French château. This certainly was a sumptuous residence. In more recent years, Ashford has been renovated and luxuriously appointed to create one of Europe's premier castle hotels. The decor of the public rooms is lavish and opulent, the views across the lake stunning. This is a hotel that attracts kings and presidents—the billiard room was built for King George V (then the Prince of Wales) when he came to stay in 1905; for President Reagan's visit in 1984, a luxurious bed was commissioned. No meals are included in the quoted tariff. After a splendid dinner in one of the castle's two restaurants, you can enjoy Irish entertainment in the Dungeon Bar, take a stroll through the lakeside gardens, or saunter into the adjacent village of Cong. The setting on the shores of beautiful Lough Corrib—with its hundreds of islands, bays, and coves—is stunning. A nine-hole golf course and tennis courts are reserved for guests' use as is a health club with sauna, gym, and Jacuzzi. The Lough is famous for its fishing, and shooting for snipe and woodcock can be arranged. *Directions:* The castle is 43 km north of Galway on the shores of Lough Corrib.

ASHFORD CASTLE
Manager: Rory Murphy
Cong
Co Mayo, Ireland
Tel: (092) 46003, Fax: (092) 46260
E-mail: ashford@ashford.ie
www.karenbrown.com/ireland/ashford.html
83 en-suite rooms
Double: £165–£310,* Suite: £260–£440*
*breakfast not included, dinner £37
Open all year, Credit cards: all major
Luxury resort

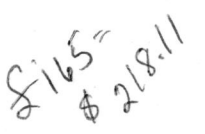

Maura and Michael Verling have long been collectors of antique furniture, and when Maura decided that she wanted to try her hand at bed and breakfast, they looked around for an old home to house their collection. They found the ideal spot, for Conna House, with its well-proportioned Victorian rooms and stripped-pine doors and floors, is the perfect backdrop for all her treasures. Toast your toes by the fire in the cluttered parlor and enjoy a drink with your hosts. Dinner is a hearty repast: on the night of my visit we had smoked salmon and salad, tomato soup, breast of chicken with fresh veggies, and dessert—concluded with Irish coffee by the fire. Conna House is a very casual place, and guests often wander into the farmhouse kitchen for tea and a chat round the pine table. Upstairs, the bedrooms are delightfully decorated in a less cluttered way than downstairs, and several have lovely old pine furniture. This is "horse country," with many opportunities for trekking and hunting. A half-hour drive brings you to the city of Cork. Midleton is the home of the Jameson whiskey distillery where you can watch a film on the making of Irish whiskey, then taste some samples and enjoy the craft and coffee shop. Nearby in Cobh, the Heritage Centre covers Irish emigration, the *Lusitania* (which sank offshore), and the *Titanic* (Cobh was its last port of call). *Directions:* From Fermoy take the Cork road (N8) through Rathcormac to the Bride River bridge: turn left and next left. The house is 10 km from the N8 on the right before you reach Conna.

CONNA HOUSE
Owners: Maura & Michael Verling
Conna
Co Cork, Ireland
Tel: (058) 59419, Fax: none
5 en-suite rooms
£25 per person B&B, dinner £20
Open all year, Credit cards: none
B&B

Cork has been up and coming for several years—its ancient buildings are receiving a face-lift, its stores are bustling, and, thanks to the new bypass, its streets are no longer clogged with traffic. Hayfield Manor, an oasis of calm just a mile from the heart of this lively metropolis, is a brand-new brick and yellow-painted hotel made to look like a dignified old *grande dame*, with much of the charm of an old building and none of the problems. The clubby bar has a no-smoking section and if you are not up for a formal country-house dinner in the gracious dining room, you can enjoy a light supper here. Relax in the library or the pretty residents' lounge or disport yourself at the leisure center with its swimming pool and well-stocked gym. Bedrooms are uniform in size and décor and have individually controlled air conditioning and heating. Walk into the city (20 minutes) for its wealth of shops but be sure not to miss the covered market with its stallholders selling everything from fish and vegetables to underwear and pots and pans. Farther afield lie Blarney, Kinsale, Midleton, and Cobh where you can take a spin around the vast expanse of Cork harbor. *Directions*: From the east go onto the one-way system following signs for city center, then university (brown sign) and Killarney. Pass Jury's Hotel, take the first left, trace the university grounds, go right, then immediately left and into Hayfield Manor's grounds. Best ask the hotel to send you a map.

HAYFIELD MANOR   New
Owners: Margaret & Joe Scally
Manager: Ewan Plenderleith
Perrott Avenue
Cork, Ireland
Tel: (021) 315600, Fax: (021) 316839
E-mail: hayfield@indigo.ie
53 en-suite rooms
Double: £150, Suite: £220–£330, dinner £30
Open all year, Credit cards: all major
Country house hotel

Seven North Mall, a 1740s townhouse beside the River Lee, is a perfect location for exploring the up-and-coming historic town of Cork. Up the narrow stairs, bedrooms are spotless and simply decorated in pleasing colors—request a room with a view of the river or, if you prefer spaciousness over view, opt for the "best room" that faces the back of the house. A ground-floor room is wheelchair friendly and often requested by guests who have difficulty with stairs. Angela Hegarty prides herself on the excellence of her breakfasts, discussing with guests the array of cooked dishes available following the freshly squeezed juice, fruit, and cereal—her scrambled eggs deserve a special mention. There is no shortage of places to walk to for dinner, from atmospheric pubs to delightful restaurants. Cork is easily explored on foot and the medieval quarter is becoming more of a destination now it is receiving extensive restoration. The Cobh Experience which traces the history of this historic port is accessible by train. A short drive finds you at Blarney with its famous castle and woolen mill. *Directions:* Arriving in Cork, follow the one-way system beside the River Lee (lots of lane changing) past five bridges. Pull in between the large black gates beside Number Seven to the car park. The car park is locked at night.

SEVEN NORTH MALL
Owner: Angela Hegarty
7 North Mall
Cork City, Ireland
Tel: (021) 397191, Fax: (021) 300811
E-mail: sevennorthmall@tinet.ie
7 en-suite rooms
£30 per person B&B
Closed Christmas, Credit cards: MC, VS
Guesthouse

Fergus View is a perfect stepping-off place for those arriving at Shannon airport and heading north, but stretch your visit to several nights so that you can explore the area. Fergus View was built as a teacher's residence at the turn of the century and Declan's grandfather was its first occupant. Continuing in his grandfather's footsteps, Declan is the principal of Corofin's school. Mary's farmhouse-style dinners are delicious and incorporate salad and vegetables from the large garden. The fire is lit in the little parlor and guests browse through the books and information on the area. Declan and Mary take great pride in their heritage and have compiled a booklet on the area, its history, and the points of interest. The snug little bedrooms (leave large cases in the car) all have Gaelic names inscribed on small plaques and are prettily decorated with pastel-painted walls and flowered drapes and bedspreads. Beds are orthopedic and all but one of the rooms have very tiny shower rooms (the other one has a large bathroom across the hall). Facilities are not designed for persons of large proportions. For an extended stay the Kellehers have an attractive, modern, self-catering cottage. The nearby Burren is most interesting, and the magnificent Cliffs of Moher are nearby. *Directions:* Shannon lies 37 km to the south. From the airport take the N18 to Ennis, the N85 towards Lisdoonvarna, turn first right to Corofin, then pass through the village, and the house is on your left after 3 km.

FERGUS VIEW
Owners: Mary & Declan Kelleher
Kilnaboy, Corofin
Co Clare, Ireland
Tel: (065) 37606, Fax: (065) 37192
E-mail: deckell@indigo.ie
www.karenbrown.com/ireland/fergusview.html
6 rooms, 5 en suite
£16–£18 per person B&B, dinner £15.50
Open Easter to Sep, Credit cards: none
B&B

Enniscoe House is the home of Susan Kellett—a descendant of the original family who settled this estate in the 1670s—her son, and their labrador Strider. Staying as her guest gives you a glimpse of what it was like to live in a grand country mansion—the old family furniture, portraits, books, and family memorabilia are yours to enjoy. The lofty rooms are decorated true to the Georgian period and all are in tiptop condition. The three front bedrooms, of enormous proportions, are reached by a grand elliptical staircase. Those in the older part of the house are less grand but just as lovely. I particularly enjoyed the old nursery with half-tester and twin beds, and comfortable chintz chairs drawn round the fireplace. Dinners by soft, flickering candlelight at little tables artfully arranged in the large dining room are a real treat. Tucked behind the house and farmyard, the barns have received a new lease of life, with farm machinery and local artifacts on display. The adjacent 2-acre vegetable garden produces organic vegetables. Personable fishery manager Barry Segrave offers help to anglers fishing Lough Conn for brown trout and salmon (*tel: 096-31853, fax: 096-31773*). Walk the forest and nature trail that goes through the woodlands past the forestry plantations and along the lake shore. There are great cliffs along the north coast, where the Stone-Age settlements at Céide Fields are being excavated. *Directions:* From Ballina take the N59 to Crossmolina, turn left in town for Castlebar, and the house is on the left after 3 km.

ENNISCOE HOUSE
Owner: Susan Kellett
Castlehill, Crossmolina
Co Mayo, Ireland
Tel: (096) 31112, Fax: (096) 31773
www.karenbrown.com/ireland/enniscoehouse.html
6 en-suite rooms
£44–£56 per person B&B
Open Apr to mid-Oct, Credit cards: all major
Country house

Joe Moffatt was born at Kilmurray House, but after leaving school he had to emigrate to England. Joe always dreamed of his home in Ireland and many years later he returned with his young wife, Madge, to the farm. The house was in need of repair and their first thought was to build a modern bungalow nearby, but thankfully they realized the potential in Kilmurray House and persevered in its restoration. When their home was complete, Madge decided to open it to guests. The bedrooms are decorated in bright colors with coordinating bedspreads and walls—four have small, older-style shower rooms and two have bathrooms across the hall. The downstairs bedroom is suitable for people who have difficulty with stairs. The dining-room tables are set with floral cloths for breakfast, the only meal served (there are several good places for dinner nearby). Joe is active in the local fishing club and enjoys planning outings for the avid fishermen who come to these parts to fish for brown trout and salmon. North Mayo is an interesting, though off-the-beaten-tourist-path area of Ireland. To the south lies Achill Island and to the north Yeats country. *Directions:* From Ballina go to Crossmolina, turn left in the town for Castlebar, pass the gates of Enniscoe House, and take the first turn to your right for the 3-km drive to the farm.

KILMURRAY HOUSE
Owners: Madge & Joe Moffatt
Castlehill
Crossmolina
Co Mayo, Ireland
Tel: (096) 31227, Fax: none
www.karenbrown.com/ireland/kilmurray.html
6 rooms, 4 en-suite
£16–£19 per person B&B
Open Apr to Sep, Credit cards: none
Farmhouse B&B

Culdaff House has been in the Mills family since 1642, and until 1948, when George's mother decided to remove the front wing, it was a grand mansion. After the remodel, the furniture was sold, though a heavy sea chest (which reputedly came from a Spanish Armada vessel) and an enormous pine kitchen table remain, and Frances has added a couple of traditional pieces. Frances has done a tremendous job of making what could well have been a "white elephant" into a comfortable home and whatever shortcomings remain are more than made up for by her outgoing and friendly personality. Family bedrooms (there are five children) are interspersed with guestrooms, and guests have the use of two large bathrooms—one on each floor. Bedrooms, like all of the house, are prettily papered and simply furnished. There's a comfortable sitting room for relaxing round the fire. Guests usually walk into the village to eat dinner. Culdaff has three very lively pubs where there's always plenty of entertainment. The Inishowen Peninsula is very pretty, with lots of ancient archaeological sites and quiet beaches. *Directions:* From Letterkenny take the N13 towards Derry to Bridgend where you turn north following signposts for Muff, Quigley's Point, Cardonagh, and Culdaff. Pass the village shops, bear left (beaches) and carry on straight into Culdaff House's driveway.

CULDAFF HOUSE
Owners: Frances & George Mills
Culdaff
Inishowen
Co Donegal, Ireland
Tel: (077) 79103, Fax: none
5 rooms sharing 2 bathrooms
£16 per person B&B
Open Mar to Dec, Credit cards: none
Farmhouse B&B

Iskeroon is the most hidden of the Hidden Ireland properties, yet it is just 4¼ kilometers from the popular Ring of Kerry. Reached by a precipitous lane that tumbles down to the sea and a narrow farm track, Iskeroon boasts the most spectacular view in Ireland—truly a hidden gem. Geraldine and David are the first family to call this home, for while the house was built in the 30s, it was previously used as holiday home. Snuggling into a sheltered spot, the long, low-lying house captures the sea view from every room, a view so enchanting that it takes you a while to realize that the house is also delightful with its three spacious bedrooms, living room, and dining room decorated in Mediterranean shades of yellow, blue, red, and green and furnished in a most attractive, unfussy way. Robes are provided for nipping across the hall to your private bathrooms. The garden tumbles down to a private jetty and guests are welcome to accompany Geraldine and David as they check their shrimp and lobster pots. David is also a certified diving instructor and his bay is an ideal place to learn to dive. Guests often take the boat from Bunavalla pier to the Skelligs, an absolute must of a trip if the weather is good. *Directions*: Derrynane is between Waterville and Caherdaniel. Find the Scarriff Inn (large and yellow) between these villages and take the road signposted Bunavalla Pier, all the way to the bottom, bearing left wherever there's a choice of roads. At the pier turn left, drive over the beach, through two white gateposts and you arrive at Iskeroon.

ISKEROON   New
Owners: Geraldine & David Hare
Derrynane, Caherdaniel
Co Kerry, Ireland
Tel & fax: (066) 75119
E-mail: iskeroon@iol.ie
3 rooms with private bathrooms
From £30 per person B&B, dinner £18
Closed Nov to Mar, Credit cards: MC, VS
Country house

Cleevaun has the advantage not only of an exquisite position facing the mouth of Dingle Bay, but also of being purposely built as a bed and breakfast, so each of the bedrooms has a modern en-suite shower or bathroom, telephone, and television. The weather was blustery and cool when we stayed but, inside, efficient central heating kept the house toasty and we appreciated the abundance of hot water in the shower and the luxury of towels hot from the heated towel rail. The decor is tasteful and uncluttered and several rooms have exquisite views across the fields to the bay. Guests are encouraged to come into the sitting room for a cup of tea and a slice of porter cake and to browse through an extensive collection of books and pamphlets on Ireland and the Dingle Peninsula in particular, which help you appreciate the beauty and folklore of the area. Pine tables and chairs are arranged to capture the lovely view of Dingle Bay from the adjacent dining room and guests enjoy a hearty breakfast before setting out to explore. In 1994 Cleevaun won the Galtee Breakfast of the Year award. It would be a pity to come so far and not experience the peace and tranquillity which the unspoiled scenery of this area has to offer, so allow plenty of time for meandering down narrow country roads and walking along deserted beaches. The peninsula is rich in historical remains, particularly beehive huts which were used as individual cells by ascetic monks in the earliest monasteries. *Directions:* Cleevaun is 2 km beyond Dingle town on the road to Slea Head.

CLEEVAUN
Owners: Charlotte & Sean Cluskey
Lady's Cross
Dingle, Co Kerry, Ireland
Tel & fax: (066) 51108
www.karenbrown.com/ireland/cleevaun.html
9 en-suite rooms
£22–£24 per person B&B
Open mid-Feb to mid-Nov, Credit cards: MC, VS
B&B

Doyle's Seafood Bar is famous the world over for excellent seafood. A small shop and pub built in 1790 house the famous bar with its flagstone floor and cozy arrangements of tables and chairs while the house next door offers delightful accommodation. The two houses are interconnected yet self-contained, so that guests can come and go to the bar and restaurant but will not have their peace disturbed when they are sleeping. You step from the street into the old-fashioned parlor with its pine floor, grandfather clock, and sofas drawn into seating areas—large umbrellas are close at hand to shelter you while bringing your luggage in, should it be raining. The eight spacious guestrooms here have en-suite bathrooms and are decorated in a comfortable, traditional style with 20th-century amenities such as television and phone. The two ground-floor rooms are ideal for anyone who has difficulty with stairs. Just up the road a courtyard of four little townhouses offers complete privacy. Each has its own entrance, a snug downstairs sitting room, and a bedroom and bathroom upstairs. After dinner inquire at the bar which of the many little pubs has traditional music that night and stroll along to join in the merriment. *Directions:* Dingle is a 2½-hour drive from Limerick. Turn right at the roundabout, right into John Street, and Doyle's is on your left. Parking is on the street.

DOYLE'S SEAFOOD BAR & TOWNHOUSE
Owners: Stella & John Doyle
John Street
Dingle
Co Kerry, Ireland
Tel: (066) 51174, Fax: (066) 51816
www.karenbrown.com/ireland/doyless.html
12 en-suite rooms
£34 per person B&B, dinner from £15
Open mid-Mar to mid-Nov, Credit cards: MC, VS
Restaurant with rooms

Places to Stay

Mary and John Curran built Greenmount House as a home for themselves and their small children then later expanded their moderately sized bungalow, adding a grand wing of eight luxurious rooms, a large sitting room, and additional accommodation for themselves and their family. Their top-of-the-line rooms are a delight: all have French windows opening onto a patio or balcony and are large enough to accommodate a spacious sitting area—the kind of rooms you want to spend time in. The considerably less expensive rooms, snug by comparison, are charmingly decorated. A conservatory breakfast room, prettily furnished with painted pine furniture, has a panoramic view across fields and Dingle's rooftops to the harbor. Mary prepares the most bountiful of breakfasts and tries to offer at least two fruit dishes, delicious mueslis, and yogurts as well as a cooked breakfast menu that includes not only the traditional breakfast but also fish and mushrooms in yogurt sauce. Breakfast is the only meal served. For dinner you can stroll down the hill into town where there are some particularly fine fish restaurants. Wander down to the harbor and watch the catch come in, window shop, and enjoy a pint in one of the many pubs. Explore the byways of the peninsula and if the weather is fine, take a trip to the Blasket Islands. *Directions:* Turn right at the roundabout in Dingle, next right into John Street, and continue up the hill to Greenmount House.

GREENMOUNT HOUSE
Owners: Mary & John Curran
Gortonora
Dingle
Co Kerry, Ireland
Tel: (066) 51414, Fax: (066) 51974
www.karenbrown.com/ireland/greenmounthouse.html
12 en-suite rooms
£17.50–£30 ~~~ person B&B
~~~~~ s, Credit cards: MC, VS

41

A long grassy lane tracing the fields leads to The Old Stone House, a farmhouse built in 1864 and purchased in 1990 by Becky and Michael O'Connor who forsook their native America to move here. Becky and Michael have done a lovely job of restoring the little house and keeping all of its cottagey flavor—the simple country antiques that furnish their home are those that came with the house. The spacious old kitchen, the heart of the house where family and friends gathered round the fire, is now the guests' sitting and breakfast room with a rustic chair and an old pine settle drawn up beside the fire. Old fiddles hung in a row upon the wall and aged bottles displayed in the window add to the old-world charm. Upstairs, one large and two small bedrooms share a bathroom. The tiniest bedroom is just large enough for its interesting old cot bed (where the children of the house slept). The Old Stone House comes with all the comforts of orthopedic beds, central heating, and hot showers. Becky and Michael are very knowledgeable about the wealth of history and archaeological sites of the Dingle Peninsula—they have a plentiful supply of books and maps which guests are welcome to study. Besides offering sailing in Dingle Bay or farther afield to the Skelligs and the Blasket Islands, Becky and Michael also arrange walking holidays of the Dingle Peninsula. *Directions:* The Old Stone House is 4 km beyond Dingle town on the road to Slea Head.

THE OLD STONE HOUSE
Owners: Becky & Michael O'Connor
Cliddaun, Dingle
Co Kerry, Ireland
Tel & fax: (066) 59882
E-mail: innkeeper@oconnor.ie
3 rooms, sharing 1 bathroom
£19–£22 per person B&B
Open all year, Credit cards: MC, VS
B&B

Set on a wooded, tidal island in Donegal Bay and joined to the mainland by a narrow causeway, St. Ernan's house was built in 1826 by John Hamilton, a nephew of the Duke of Wellington, for his wife. Over lunch here one day, Brian and Carmel O'Dowd decided that St. Ernan's was the kind of hotel they would like to own, so several years later when it came on the market they took the plunge and forsook their careers in banking and teaching to become hoteliers. From almost every one of the rooms you are treated to marvelous views across a mirrorlike span of water. In the lounge, window seats offer views across the water to the mainland and chairs are artfully arranged to provide numerous nooks for intimate after-dinner conversation. A four-course candlelit dinner, with choices for each course, is served in the dining room. The attractive bedrooms come in all shapes and sizes, with the larger view rooms commanding the highest prices. Be sure to enjoy the walk around this delightful little island. The center of bustling Donegal town is The Diamond, a market place surrounded by shops (Magees sells the famous tweed), a hotel, and some pubs. Beyond Donegal town lies the wild, rugged landscape that has made this county famous. *Directions:* From Sligo take the N15 towards Donegal and St. Ernan's is signposted to your left 2 km before you reach Donegal town.

ST. ERNAN'S HOUSE HOTEL
Owners: Carmel & Brian O'Dowd
Donegal
Co Donegal, Ireland
Tel: (073) 21065, Fax: (073) 22098
www.karenbrown.com/ireland/sternans.html
12 en-suite rooms
Double: £130–£170
Open Apr to Oct, Credit cards: MC, VS
Country house hotel

Sylvan Hill House has that essential ingredient that ensures that guests return again and again—welcoming hosts, Elise and Jimmy Coburn. Elise and Jimmy began taking guests into their delightful home as a means of paying for the installation of a very expensive damp course and they discovered that they loved taking guests from all over the world and all walks of life. Staying here is to become part of the family—if there are two guests, Elise and Jimmy eat with them round the little pine table in the sitting room or if there are more, they join them for dinner in the dining room. The price of dinner includes wine. Dining with guests affords the Coburns the opportunity to help them plan sightseeing forays as far away as the Antrim coast and as close as the craft shops in the local villages. Upstairs, a spacious twin-bedded room has an en-suite bathroom, while a snug double room has its shower cubicle in the room and an adjacent loo. A third bedroom is available for families who wish to have children share the bathroom with them. *Directions:* Leave the A1 (Belfast to Dublin road) at Dromore (just south of Belfast) and at the mini-roundabout (a painted circle in the road) take the Lurgan road for 1 km where you turn right opposite the factory cottages for the 2-km drive up the hill to Sylvan Hill House.

SYLVAN HILL HOUSE
Owners: Elise & Jimmy Coburn
76 Kilntown Road
Dromore BT25 1HS
Co Down, Northern Ireland
Tel & fax: (01846) 692321
3 rooms, 2 en suite
£22–£25 per person B&B, dinner £15
Open all year, Credit cards: none
B&B

The entrance to the Adams Trinity Hotel is off Dame Lane, a little lane that is hard to access though a maze of back streets in the heart of Dublin. I found it much easier to enter the hotel from the adjoining restaurant, The Mercantile, which fronts onto the main thoroughfare Dame Street. The Mercantile is a lively bar and eating establishment where patrons sit on broad balconies tiered beneath an ornate plasterwork ceiling—a perfect place for people-watching. In contrast to the hubbub of the restaurant, all is serene in the hotel. A lift takes you from the paneled lobby to your room which faces either Dame Lane or Dame Street—city views are the order of the day in this central Dublin location. I found the standard bedrooms to be small—just adequate for two people and their luggage. However, the superior rooms that I saw were much more appealing. I particularly enjoyed rooms 205, 208 (king-size bed), and 403. If you cannot afford to splurge on a larger room, request room 202, the largest of the standard rooms. The management and staff are young and friendly. *Directions:* Dame Street begins at the main gates of Trinity College and parallels the River Liffey. With Trinity College at your back the hotel is on your left before you reach Dublin Castle. See *Dublin Walking Tour* map for location.

ADAMS TRINITY HOTEL
Manager: Una Macdermot
28 Dame Lane
Dublin 2, Ireland
Tel: (01) 670 7100, Fax: (01) 670 7101
28 en-suite rooms
Double: £150 ~ 204.80
Open all year, Credit cards: all major
City hotel

What a treat to find a home-away-from-home atmosphere in the hurly-burly of central Dublin. Located just off St. Stephen's Green, this oasis of tranquillity in a bustling city gives you the opportunity to pop home to drop off your packages or take a break from sightseeing. A cozy fire enhances the homelike feel of the reception lounge with its comfortable grouping of sofas and chairs around a blazing fire. The majority of the bedrooms are on the larger side, each with a very small shower room tucked into a corner of the room. A couple of the bedrooms have more spacious bathrooms. All are pleasantly decorated in different color schemes and furnished with attractive antiques. A buffet breakfast is the only meal served in the below-stairs breakfast room. The receptionist is happy to bring tea or coffee to your bedroom for an additional charge. *Directions:* Harcourt Street leads from the southwestern corner of St. Stephen's Green and is on your left. Albany House has off the road parking. See *Dublin Walking Tour* map for location.

ALBANY HOUSE
Manager: Elaine Walsh
84 Harcourt Street
Dublin 2, Ireland
Tel: (01) 475 1092, Fax: (01) 475 1093
32 en-suite rooms
Double: £90–£100
Open all year, Credit cards: all major
B&B

Isolated by acres of fields and gardens, Belcamp Hutchinson is an oasis of country house elegance just 15 minutes' drive from Dublin airport, making this the ideal first or last night's stop if you are flying to or from Dublin. However, it is such an outstanding home and Doreen is such a gracious hostess, that you will want to stay for several days. You'll doubtless be greeted by Digger, the German Shepherd, who brings along his toys in the hope that you'll be ready for a game. You'll know it's time for the drawing room fire to be lit when Clyde, the Rhodesian Ridgeback, wanders in. Up the elegant staircase, the bedrooms are decorated in strong, dark, Georgian colors, each beautifully coordinated with lovely fabrics. Burgundy can be a twin or a king room and has a sofa bed that can accommodate a child. Wedgwood has a romantic four-poster bed. Wicker and Pine are spacious king-sized rooms. Blue is a spacious double, while Terra Cotta and Green are smaller rooms. Doreen always has three or four perfumes on the dresser and a variety of interesting magazines by the bedside. While the heart of Dublin is just a half-hour's drive away, she also suggests that guests not overlook Newgrange, Malahide Castle, and the village of Howth. *Directions:* Belcamp Hutchinson is just off the Malahide Road in the Dublin suburb of Balgriffin. Doreen will fax or mail you detailed directions. See *Dublin Walking Tour* map for location.

BELCAMP HUTCHINSON
Owners: Doreen Gleson & Karl Waldburg
Carrs Lane, Malahide Road
Balgriffin
Dublin 17, Ireland
Tel: (01) 846 0843, Fax: (01) 848 5703
www.karenbrown.com/ireland/belcamphutchinson.html
8 en-suite rooms
£38 per person B&B, dinner £23
Closed Christmas, Credit cards: MC, VS
Country house

Bewley's Café, an old-fashioned Dublin institution, has added a hotel behind its Westmorland Street café. The hotel entrance is on a quiet side street and an elevator whisks you to the upstairs lobby. A small, rather unmemorable sitting room beside the lobby is the hotel's only public room: the great attraction of the hotel is its very central location rather than its amenities. A maze of corridors and stairways leads to the bedrooms and the receptionist who showed me around had to pause on several occasions to orient herself. Bedrooms are plainly furnished and decorated in an almost identical masculine decor with green-and-rust carpet and rust-and-beige decor. All have television and telephone but very few have views (room 202 is an exception). There is no smoking in the second-floor bedrooms. I got lost on my first attempt to find the "back way" from the hotel to the café where a hearty old-fashioned breakfast is served by genteel waitresses. Another "back way" leads to The Bridge Street Bar and Grill, a trendy cellar-style restaurant and bar. The hotel has arranged a discounted overnight rate (6 pm to 9 am) in a nearby parking lot for guests' cars. *Directions*: Bewley's Hotel is located one block from O'Connell Bridge. Bewley's Café faces the main thoroughfare of Westmorland Street and the hotel entrance is just round the corner on Fleet Street. See *Dublin Walking Tour* map for location.

BEWLEY'S HOTEL
Manager: Colin Rafferty
19–20 Fleet Street
Dublin 2, Ireland
Tel: (01) 670 8122, Fax: (01) 670 8103
70 en-suite rooms
Double: £105–£140
Closed Christmas, Credit cards: all major
City hotel

Brimming with youthful enthusiasm, Helen Finnegan showed me round Butlers just days after it opened. This delightful townhouse hotel in the Victorian suburb of Ballsbridge, just a 25-minute walk from the heart of Dublin, is the brainchild of Helen and her husband George. They knew exactly what they wanted in a hotel, so when they had the spacious townhouse extended and refurbished they added all the extras such as individually controlled air conditioning and central heating. Helen and George have taken great pains to decorate the hotel in a contemporary, airy Victorian style and furnish it in an attractive, uncluttered Victorian way, in keeping with the age of the building. The bedrooms I saw were on the snug side but carefully thought out to provide plenty of room for luggage. Five high-ceilinged bedrooms accommodate four-poster beds (though I prefer the space offered by non-four-poster rooms). A short room service dinner menu is available. There is off-road parking to the front and rear of the house. It is an easy walk to the 6, 7, and 8 bus routes and a three-minute ride on DART (Dublin Area Rapid Transit) to the rear of Trinity College. *Directions*: Follow signs for South City till you come to Baggot Street which continues south into Pembroke Street and Lansdowne Road (do not turn right in front of Jury's Hotel). Butlers is on your left before you come to the Lansdowne Road Stadium. See *Dublin Walking Tour* map for location.

BUTLERS   New
Owners: Helen & George Finnegan
44 Lansdowne Road
Ballsbridge
Dublin 4, Ireland
Tel: (01) 667 4022, Fax: (01) 667 3960
19 en-suite rooms
Double: £123
Open all year, Credit cards: all major
Guesthouse

Ballsbridge, just southeast of Dublin proper, is noted for its Victorian charm. Just across from the British Embassy, the pebbledash, Edwardian-style home of Mary and Gerard Doody offers twelve guestrooms in a three-story extension overlooking their grassy garden. Guests are given a front-door key and come and go through Mary and Gerard's home where they have a hallway seating area with a blazing fire and a comfortable sitting room. Breakfast is the only meal served, but there is no shortage of delightful restaurants and pubs within walking distance. Bedrooms are spacious and splendidly kitted out with good reading lights, desk, phone, TV, and tea- and coffee-makings. Pastel-painted walls coordinate with attractive bedspreads and drapes and the rooms' uncluttered, tailored look is enhanced by fitted ash closets, bedheads, and bedside tables. While Merrion Road is a major thoroughfare, a quiet night's sleep is ensured by double-glazed windows. Two major attractions at the nearby Royal Dublin Society are the Agricultural Show in May and the Dublin Horse Show in August. A 15-minute bus ride brings you to the heart of Dublin. *Directions:* Follow signs for South City to Baggot Street which becomes Pembroke Road. Turn right in front of Jury's Hotel into Merrion Road, continue past the Royal Dublin Society showgrounds, and Cedar Lodge is on your left opposite the British Embassy. See *Dublin Walking Tour* map for location.

CEDAR LODGE
Owners: Mary & Gerard Doody
98 Merrion Road
Ballsbridge
Dublin 4, Ireland
Tel: (01) 668 4410, Fax: (01) 668 4533
www.karenbrown.com/ireland/cedarlodge.html
16 en-suite rooms
£32.50–£40 per person B&B
Open all year, Credit cards: all major
Guesthouse

The heart of Temple Bar with its trendy stores and vibrant nightlife is a most appropriate spot for Bono, of U2, and his business partners to open a luxury boutique hotel. Originally built in 1852, the hotel has been completely refurbished, keeping all the attractive architectural features such as oak paneling, wooden floors, and lovely old windows and adding a pleasing modern decor with uncluttered, simple lines. Relax in the peace and quiet of the study with its open fire, writing table, and wood-paneled walls or join the hubbub of the Octagon Bar with its crowded little alcoves. Bedrooms are decorated in natural tones and rich jewel colors, and double glazing ensures a quiet night's sleep. The hand-crafted beds are king-sized and rooms are equipped with satellite TV and fax/PC points. In keeping with the hotel's desire to provide guests with all the technology expected by a hotel in the '90s, cellular phones are available for hire. The location, overlooking the River Liffey on Dublin's "left bank," is perfect for exploring Dublin on foot. The hotel does not have a garage but valet parking is available if needed. *Directions:* Wellington Quay is on the south bank of the River Liffey—see *Dublin Walking Tour* map for location.

THE CLARENCE
Manager: Claire O'Reilly
6–8 Wellington Quay
Dublin 2, Ireland
Tel: (01) 670 9000, Fax: (01) 670 7800
50 en-suite rooms
Double: £175–£190, Suite: £400–£1,450*
*breakfast not included
Open all year, Credit cards: all major
City hotel

The Hibernian Hotel, a grand, redbrick building, was constructed as a nurses' residence at the turn of the century and underwent a complete transformation to open as a lovely townhouse hotel in 1993. It is decorated throughout in a clubby, traditional style, with every piece of furniture new, which detracts a little from the old-world atmosphere the hotel is striving to create. Be that as it may, this an absolutely charming Dublin hotel with its library and drawing room full of luxuriously upholstered sofas and chairs arranged around fireplaces, and its sunny conservatory restaurant serving traditional country house fare. The bedrooms are especially pleasing and equipped with everything from a full range of toiletries in the sparkling bathrooms to fax/modem point, hairdryer, TV, bowls of candies (licorice "allsorts"—my absolute favorite), and tea- and coffee-makings. The Hibernian Hotel is located on a quiet side street in the Victorian suburb of Ballsbridge, just a ten-minute stroll from St. Stephen's Green, making it an ideal base for exploring the city. *Directions:* Follow signs for South City. Cross the Baggot Street bridge into Baggot Street. Pass a row of shops on your left, turn left at the AIB bank, and the Hibernian Hotel is on your left. The hotel has a small car park. See *Dublin Walking Tour* map for location.

HIBERNIAN HOTEL
Manager: David Butt
Eastmoreland Place
Upper Baggot Street
Ballsbridge
Dublin 4, Ireland
Tel: (01) 668 7666, Fax: (01) 660 2655
www.karenbrown.com/ireland/hibernian.html
40 en-suite rooms
Double: £160–£180
Closed Christmas, Credit cards: all major
City hotel

Grand as life in Georgian Dublin may have been, it is surpassed at The Merrion, a dream of a hotel found in the heart of Georgian Dublin opposite Leinster House, home of Ireland's parliament. A few steps from bustling city streets and you are in vast drawing rooms enjoying traditional afternoon tea overlooking a tranquil expanse of garden watching the gardener manicure the box hedges. If you are in the mood for the most sophisticated of meals, adjourn to *Restaurant Patrick Guilbaud* (the only eatery in Ireland to command two Michelin stars) or enjoy more casual cuisine in The Mornington restaurant after letting your hair down over a few drinks in The Cellar Bar. The Tethra Spa is an aptly named spot to assist guests in recovering from the revelry of the night before—swimming in the pool, working out in the gym, or enjoying a massage. It costs a small fortune to stay in one of the elegant suites in the "old building," while more affordable accommodation is found in the deluxe garden wing whose most attractive rooms open up to views of the loveliest of gardens. A traditional hotel in the heart of this vibrant city—what more could you ask from a place to stay? Well worth a splurge! *Directions*: The Merrion is adjacent to Merrion Square, opposite Leinster House. Park in front of the hotel and the porter will take care of your car. See *Dublin Walking Tour* map for location.

THE MERRION   New
Manager: Peter MacCann
Upper Merrion Street
Dublin 2, Ireland
Tel: (01) 603 0600, Fax: (01) 603 0700
E-mail: info@merrionhotel.ie
145 en-suite rooms
Double: £210–£255*, Suite: £350–£810*
*breakfast not included
Open all year, Credit cards: all major
City hotel

Modern hotels are not usually included in this guide but I was so taken with the value for money and excellent location offered by the Mespil Hotel that I decided to include it. Sitting on a quieter side street beside the Grand Canal with its grassy verges and leafy trees, the Mespil Hotel sports a pleasing modern exterior which complements its attractive contemporary interior. Dark-green leather sofas and stylish light-wood furniture deck the public rooms. The lunchtime carvery becomes the bar in the evening when the spacious restaurant offers a short à-la-carte menu and always features one entrée as a very-good-value-for-money special of the day. Bedrooms come in two varieties—front and back—and two colors—burgundy and green. Front rooms face the canal (opt for one of these as it's a treat to have a view room in Dublin), while back rooms have slightly larger bathrooms. All are spacious enough to accommodate a seating area and two double beds. If you want just a little more luxury, request an executive room which comes with wallpaper, a dried-flower arrangement, and a futon sofa. *Directions:* Follow signs for South City to Baggot Street. Cross the canal, turn right, and the Mespil is on your left after 200 meters. The hotel has a private car park and there is plenty of off-road parking available. See *Dublin Walking Tour* map for location.

MESPIL HOTEL
Manager: Martin Holohan
Mespil Road
Ballsbridge, Dublin 4, Ireland
Tel: (01) 667 1222, Fax: (01) 667 1244
153 en-suite rooms
Double: £75–£95*
*breakfast not included
Open all year, Credit cards: all major
City hotel

The city of Dublin stretches inland through the vast acres of Phoenix Park and beyond to the prosperous, peaceful suburb of Castleknock. Here, on a quiet crescent of detached homes, you find Park Lodge, distinguished by its mock-Tudor façade and, in summer, a garden ablaze with flowers. Surprisingly, inside you find a lovely Regency-style decor designed to complement Eileen's enviable collection of antiques. Starched white linen cloths and napkins grace the breakfast table where tea is served in a silver pot. The sumptuous breakfast menu includes dishes such as baked trout and Irish smoked salmon with eggs as well as the traditional Irish breakfast. The three small double bedrooms and the larger family room (with a double and a single) have a sophisticated décor, with crisp cotton sheets on the beds and duvets topped with intricately crocheted white bedspreads. Three of the rooms have small en-suite shower rooms while the fourth has its private bathroom across the hall. For trips into the city the bus stop is a three-minute walk away. Being just 14 kilometers from Dublin airport (most of it motorway), Park Lodge is ideal for your first or last night in Ireland. *Directions*: Take the N3 exit off the M50 motorway. Turn towards the city center and at the roundabout first right, signposted Castleknock (Auburn Avenue). Turn left at the T-junction, first left on Deerpark Road, and third right on Deerpark Drive. Park Lodge is on your right. See *Dublin Walking Tour* map for location.

PARK LODGE New
Owners: Eileen & Patrick Kehoe
19 Deerpark Drive
Castleknock
Dublin 15, Ireland
Tel & fax: (01) 821 2887
3 en-suite rooms, 1 with private bath
£27.50–£30 per person B&B
Open Mar 1 to Oct 31, Credit cards: none
B&B

Dublin's residential areas were built during the 1860s and Ballsbridge emerged as a well planned suburb of wide, tree-lined streets with smart redbrick houses fronted by impressive gardens. More recent times have seen this fashionable suburb come to house diplomatic missions and commercial institutions, but fortunately the aura of a sedate residential area has been retained. On one of Ballsbridge's most attractive streets, Raglan Lodge offers visitors a quiet respite from the hustle and bustle of the city. This splendid, three-story Victorian is Helen's home and she works very hard to keep everything in apple-pie order. The large traditional sitting room with its stripped-pine floor has the feeling of a comfortable Victorian parlor. Downstairs is a cozy breakfast room with groupings of little tables and chairs. Breakfast is the only meal served but Helen has local restaurant menus on the hall table for guests' convenience. I particularly admired Room 1, a large ground-floor room with long, flowing drapes and tall ceilings with pretty cornices recalling the elegance of the Victorian era. Just round the corner is Jury's Hotel with its many restaurants and popular cabaret show. A long walk or a short stroll and a bus ride brings you into the heart of Dublin. *Directions:* Follow signs for South City to Baggot Street which becomes Pembroke Street, turn right on Raglan Road, and Raglan Lodge is on your left. There is plenty of off-the-road parking available. See *Dublin Walking Tour* map for location.

RAGLAN LODGE
Owner: Helen Moran
10 Raglan Road
Dublin 4, Ireland
Tel: (01) 660 6697, Fax: (01) 660 6781
www.karenbrown.com/ireland/raglan.html
7 en-suite rooms
£40–£50 per person B&B
Closed Dec 25–Jan 7, Credit cards: all major
Guesthouse

Just a few steps from St. Stephen's Green, the Russell Court Hotel has a perfect location for exploring Dublin on foot. The hotel has grown like Topsy over the years and has a rather amusing contrast of styles and decor. I continue to include it in this guide because of its location and friendly staff, and because it is good value for money for a city hotel. The spacious bedrooms, decorated in dark maroons and blues with dark-wood, traditional furniture, are located up and down small staircases (the tiny lift is suitable only for taking luggage to and from the rooms). Bathrooms are immaculate and on the whole very roomy. All the rooms have a very similar price, making rooms like 111 with its bed and a circular dais, 112 with its four-poster bed, and 300, a paneled attic room with separate living room and bedroom, surprisingly good value for money (the hotel does its best to give these larger rooms to guests who are staying several days). While there is a small traditional restaurant, guests often enjoy a barbecue in the beer garden (May to September) or a more casual meal in Dicey Riley's. Set up like an old-fashioned Irish shop, bar, and barn, this large room is decorated with an eclectic mixture of Irish bygones and is a lively place to visit in the evening. *Directions:* Harcourt Street leads from the southwestern corner of St. Stephen's Green and Russell Court Hotel is on your right. The hotel has secure, off-the-road parking. See *Dublin Walking Tour* map for location.

RUSSELL COURT HOTEL
Managers: John Killeen & Michael Flanagan
21–25 Harcourt Street
Dublin 2, Ireland
Tel: (01) 478 4066, Fax: (01) 478 1576
47 en-suite rooms
Double: £95*
*plus 12½% service
Closed Christmas, Credit cards: all major
City hotel

Irish nobility and country gentlemen needed to spend time in Dublin, so in 1824 the Shelbourne opened its doors to the gentry who did not have a residence in the city. Since day one, the Shelbourne has been "the" place to stay and today it remains as Dublin's deluxe hotel, suffused with the elegance of other eras, living up to its motto as "the most distinguished address in Ireland." The comings and goings of Dublin are reflected in the enormous gilt mirrors of the Lord Mayor's Lounge where people gather to enjoy a sophisticated afternoon tea. Traditional decor, good conversation, and the presence of Dublin characters combine to make the Horseshoe Bar a most convivial place. The very elegant dining room, No.27 The Green, provides equally elegant food, while the adjacent Shelbourne Bar provides an opportunity to soak up the friendly atmosphere over a relaxed drink. The newest addition, a jazzy bistro-style restaurant, The Side Door, serves mouthwatering Italian/Californian-style cuisine. Everything is delightful in the bedrooms, with a premium being charged for those with views of St. Stephens Green. This landmark historic hotel overlooks St. Stephen's Green, a refreshing oasis of greenery in the center of this bustling city. There is a full health and fitness center which includes a swimming pool. *Directions:* The Shelbourne Hotel is on the north side of St. Stephen's Green. Park in front of the hotel. See *Dublin Walking Tour* map for location.

SHELBOURNE HOTEL
Manager: Jean Ricoux
27 St. Stephen's Green
Dublin 2, Ireland
Tel: (01) 676 6471, Fax: (01) 661 6006
www.karenbrown.com/ireland/shelbourne.html
190 en-suite rooms
Double: £175–£227,* Suite: £325–£855*
*breakfast not included, plus 15% service
Open all year, Credit cards: all major
City hotel

Norah Brown so loves to cook that she not only provides dinners for her resident guests but regularly opens up her dining room to larger groups looking for that special dinner party. Norah uses fresh local ingredients and a great deal of culinary skill to create an exquisite evening repast. Ralph discusses the menu over drinks in the den and both he and Norah join their guests for coffee and conversation in the drawing room. Norah is an inveterate collector, filling every nook and cranny with collections of old china, pewter, stoneware, and fascinating bygones. Upstairs are the very comfortable, attractively decorated bedrooms, all of which have their own pretty bathrooms. If you are intensely interested in the production or are an avid collector of crystal, you can tour the nearby Tyrone crystal factory and see firsthand the hand-blowing and cutting of sparkling crystal. The National Trust has two properties close at hand: Ardress House, a 17th-century manor, and The Argory, an 1820s house with a lot of original furniture set in 300 acres of woodland. A half-hour drive brings you to the Ulster American Folk Park, a collection of historic cottages and buildings that tells the story of the great migrations of Ulster people to the New World. *Directions:* Take the M1 from Belfast to junction 15 where you take the A29 towards Armagh for 2 km to the left-hand turn to Grange. Turn immediately right and Grange Lodge is the first house on the right.

GRANGE LODGE
Owners: Norah & Ralph Brown
Grange Road
Dungannon
Co Tyrone, Northern Ireland
Tel: (01868) 784212, Fax: (01868) 723891
www.karenbrown.com/ireland/grange.html
5 en-suite rooms
£34.50 per person B&B, dinner £20
Closed Christmas & Jan, Credit cards: MC, VS
Country house

The summertime evening view from the Castle Murray House dining room is simply staggering. As the night slowly draws in on green fields that tumble to the sea and scudding clouds dapple the reddening sky, the sun slowly sinks behind the distant Slieve League, the highest sea cliffs in Europe. The food is as outstanding as the view and served in portions that satisfy even the heartiest of Irish appetites. Claire and Thierry Delcros, who hail from France, converted what was a nondescript farmhouse with a spectacular view into a restaurant with rooms. Claire is very French and has a cooler, more aloof personality than many Irish hostesses. Thierry has cooked at various hotels and restaurants in Ireland for some years now and earned quite a reputation for fine French cooking tailored to the Irish palate. The price of a meal is very reasonable, based on the cost of the main course, and there is an emphasis on fresh local seafood. Perhaps the best way to secure an often hard-to-come-by dinner reservation is to stay here, so that after an evening-long repast you can retire up the narrow pine staircase to one of the smart, tailored bedrooms with their tweedy carpet and matching drapes and bedspreads. If you are lucky, you will get one that captures the view across the bay. Between breakfast and dinner the rugged Donegal landscape is yours to explore. *Directions:* From Donegal take the N56 towards Killybegs. The left-hand turn to Castle Murray House is in Dunkineely.

CASTLE MURRAY HOUSE
Owners: Claire & Thierry Delcros
Dunkineely
Co Donegal, Ireland
Tel: (073) 37022, Fax: (073) 37330
www.karenbrown.com/ireland/castlemurray.html
10 en-suite rooms
£26–£30 per person B&B, dinner £18–£26
Open all year, Credit cards: MC, VS
Restaurant closed Mon & Tue in winter
Restaurant with rooms

Killaghtee House offers you spacious accommodation and the chance to enjoy your breakfast in an art gallery. Jackie and Robin came to County Donegal so that Robin could paint and they could have a gallery in their home. The thought of doing bed and breakfast never entered their heads until a local restaurateur asked them if they could take his overflow guests for a couple of nights. Jackie discovered she loved being a hostess so Robin was moved to a studio in an outbuilding and they relocated their living quarters to the attics. Displays of Robin's watercolors and oil paintings hang in the ground-floor gallery where guests enjoy breakfast amongst the art. Up the open-tread pine staircase guests have an airy sitting room with comfortable sofas drawn round the fire. There are books and pamphlets on the area and Jackie is always on hand to direct guests to her favorite places such as the Slieve League mountains which tumble into the sea and the beautiful countryside that surrounds the little harbor of Port. One of the bedrooms is very large and enjoys lovely sea views across the road and the fields. A smaller double room at the back of the house faces Robin's studio in the converted stables. As breakfast is the only meal served, guests usually dine at the nearby Castle Murray restaurant or the Bay View restaurant in Killybegs. *Directions:* From Donegal take the N56 towards Killybegs. Killaghtee House is on your right just beyond Dunkineely.

KILLAGHTEE HOUSE
Owners: Jackie & Robin Atkinson
Dunkineely
Co Donegal, Ireland
Tel: (073) 37453, Fax: (073) 37499
E-mail: atkin@iol.ie
www.karenbrown.com/ireland/killaghtee.html
2 en-suite rooms
£25 per person B&B
Open all year, Credit cards: MC, VS
B&B

There's an ends-of-the-earth feel to Enniscree Lodge set high on a hill overlooking the stark beauty of Glencree valley and the distant Wicklow mountains, yet it's only a half-hour drive from Dublin. Long ago the hotel was a farmhouse but several additions have obliterated its original exterior, leaving it with little external appeal. Once inside, the jarring architectural features are forgotten and everything is cozy and full of charm. A snug bar leads to the Mountain View restaurant where walls of windows frame the sky-wide view of moors and mountains. Bedroom are snug and comfortable, bathrooms are functional—decorated at a time when large tan-colored tiles were the fashion. Plan on arriving early in the afternoon to enjoy a tea of homemade scones in the cozy little sitting room. Josephine and Raymond are young and enthusiastic about their little hotel which they purchased in 1996. Walking, particularly along the nearby Wicklow Way, is a great attraction. Just a few kilometers away lie the attractive village of Enniskerry and Powerscourt Gardens. A little farther afield lies the oh-so-picturesque monastic settlement of Glendalough. *Directions:* From Dublin take the N11, exiting the dual carriageway at Enniskerry. Go straight through the village into the Glencree valley and Enniscree Lodge is on you right after 7 km.

ENNISCREE LODGE
Owners: Josephine & Raymond Power
Glencree Valley
Enniskerry
Co Wicklow, Ireland
Tel: (01) 2863542, Fax: (01) 2866037
www.karenbrown.com/ireland/eniscree.html
10 en-suite rooms
Double: £80–£85
Open all year, Credit cards: all major
Family hotel

Grace and Padraig's families have farmed around Fivealley for as long as anyone can remember. After remodeling their Georgian farmhouse, keeping all the lovely old aspects and adding all the modern conveniences, Grace set about filling it with a melange of antiques: gilt Napoleonic furniture with raspberry taffeta upholstery in the sitting room; painted Austrian country furniture in one bedroom; Victorian in another; and an antique pine famine hutch in the country kitchen. From crisp white cotton sheets to authentic Victorian bathrooms, Grace believes in giving her guests quality. The land roundabout is known as Ely O'Carroll Country, a diverse landscape that goes from the River Shannon to the Slieve Bloom mountains through gently undulating farmland. At its center lies the nearby town of Birr with its Georgian homes and grand castle. The ruins of the monastic settlement of Clonmacnois cast their spell on all who visit—an ideal day out is to combine the monastic ruins with a ride on the West Offaly Railway which takes visitors to the heart of a peat bog to see how Ireland's "brown gold" is harvested. The Slieve Bloom mountains offer walks in wooded valleys of singular beauty. *Directions*: From Birr take the N52 toward Tullamore for 8 km (sadly, Fivealley is not signposted though it appears on maps) where you turn right (signposted Rath)—Parkmore Farmhouse is on your left after 1km.

PARKMORE FARMHOUSE   New
Owners: Grace & Padraig Grennan
Fivealley, Birr
Co Offaly, Ireland
Tel: (0509) 33014, Fax: (0509) 333054
3 rooms, 1 en suite
£23–£25 per person B&B, dinner £18
Closed Christmas, Credit cards: none
Farmhouse B&B

Olive and Paddy O'Gorman have a troop of children (six) and a relaxed, easy-going attitude to life. They welcome guests to the newly converted wing of their commodious farmhouse nestled in the pretty Nire Valley, an off-the-beaten-tourist-path area of Ireland noted for its beautiful scenery. Olive finds it no problem at all to juggle her family and a houseful of guests, chatting to them over a cup of tea and home-made cake, feeding them scrumptious dinners and copious breakfasts, packing tempting lunches, and arranging for them to go walking with a knowledgeable local guide. Guests come to this quiet corner of County Waterford to walk the Comeragh mountains and experience the very best of Irish farmhouse hospitality. If the outdoor pursuits of fishing, pony-trekking, and walking are not your cup of tea, you can drive to Lismore, Cashel, or over the Vee, returning in time for dinner and a visit to one of the local pubs for a drink and a chat with locals or perhaps (more often in the summer months) a late-night Irish music session. Bedrooms are as neat as new pins, attractively decorated, and each sporting a snug en-suite shower room. *Directions*: From Clonmel or Dungarven follow the R672 to Ballymacarbry. The little village of Four-Mile Water is signposted to your right just before you reach Ballymacarbry if you are coming from Clonmel or just after to your left if you are coming from Dungarven.

GLASHA   New
Owners: Olive & Paddy O'Gorman
Four-Mile Water, Via Clonmel
Co Waterford, Ireland
Tel & fax: (052) 36108
5 en-suite rooms
£20 per person B&B, dinner £15
Open all year, Credit cards: MC, VS
Farmhouse B&B

Richard's family received the Kilrush estate as a land grant from Charles II in 1660 and until this grand home was built in the 1820s his forbears occupied the tower house, the small castle that stands in the garden. This is a home of vast rooms which Sally and Richard make feel remarkably homey. Up a grand sweep of staircase, guests can choose from the Yellow Room, a vast twin-bedded room overlooking the castle (my favorite), the very spacious Pink Room with its large white wrought-iron bed, or the coziness of Uncle Arthur's Room, named because to Richard it will always be Uncle Arthur's room. The wallpaper in the drawing room has celebrated its centenary, while that in the dining room went up when the house was built—just about the time the dining room furniture was moved in. Richard is happy to discuss the colorful family history and his love for this rural part of Ireland over dinner with his guests. The delightful town of Freshford is a half-hour drive from Kilkenny, with its castle and many fine old buildings, and Cashel, with its famous rock. Cahir Castle and the Swiss Cottage are a popular day trip while garden lovers are directed to the peaceful Lutyens garden in nearby Balinakill. *Directions*: From the N8, Cork to Dublin road, turn left in Johnstown towards Freshford and Kilkenny and Kilrush is on your right after 10 km.

KILRUSH HOUSE   New
Owners: Sally & Richard St. George
Freshford
Co Kilkenny, Ireland
Tel: (056) 32236, Fax: (056) 32588
3 en-suite rooms
£45 per person B&B, dinner £25
Open Apr to Sep, Credit cards: all major
Country house

Stay awhile with Dee and Mark Keogh at Norman Villa, their tall Victorian townhouse just a 15-minute walk from the center of Galway city. Norman, as he is fondly referred to, is a delightful fellow, decorated in sunny colors and full of antiques, his walls hung with contemporary Irish art, and with broad plank-and-slate floors underfoot. Each very attractive bedroom sports a lovely antique bed—the most spacious, room 4, is large enough to accommodate two double beds. Each bedroom offers interesting artwork, antiques, books, and snug shower facilities unobtrusively disguised as cupboards, which gives the maximum amount of space to the bedroom. Breakfast is the only meal served round the long pine tables in the dining room but there is no shortage of places to walk to for dinner. The evening often concludes with a nightcap at the adjacent pub. Dee and Mark highlight maps for exploring the sea coast and Burren of County Clare, the wonderful wilds of Connemara, or for taking a day trip to the Aran Islands. Leave your car in the secure car park and explore Galway on foot. *Directions*: Follow signs for Salthill and then Lower Salthill. Norman Villa is next to P.J. Flaherty's pub. Avoid getting lost by having one of the Keoghs' maps with you.

NORMAN VILLA   New
Owners: Dee & Mark Keogh
86 Lower Salthill
Galway, Ireland
Tel & fax: (091) 521131
5 en-suite rooms
£30 per person B&B
Open all year, Credit cards: MC, VS
Guesthouse

Castle Leslie was built as an impressive home rather than a fortification at the insistence of Constance Leslie who came here as a young bride from London in 1878. Sammy grew up here and now makes her childhood home a paying concern. Do not expect to find a reception desk on arrival but a welcoming oak-panelled hall, log fire and complimentary tea in the vast Drawing Room. Also do not expect to find formality and stand-offishness—it's a casual, rather haphazard kind of a place and Sammy exhibits a rather offbeat, tongue-in-cheek sense of humor in her decor. Directions pinned to the front door indicate that first you should ring the bell, second press the intercom, and, failing that, yell and scream. Sammy and her partner Ultan are young and enthusiastic, which gives a buzz to the place. Take a step back in time and opt for one of the master bedrooms which offer lovely family furniture, spaciousness, a faded elegance and views of the lake and gardens. There are no TV's or phones and the only concession the 20th century is lots of hot water and heating. Sammy is the chef and trained in Switzerland. Guests dine at their own table in the grand dining room and make themselves at home round the fire in the drawing room. If you tire of walks round the 1,000-acre estate and views of Glaslough lake, there are endless sightseeing possibilities in nearby Northern Ireland as well as the Republic. *Directions:* Castle Leslie is a 1½-hour drive from Belfast airport and 2 hours from Dublin airport. The village of Glaslough is between Armagh and Monaghan.

CASTLE LESLIE
Owners: Sammy Leslie & Ultan Bannon
Glaslough
Co Monaghan, Ireland
Tel: (047) 88109, Fax: (047) 88256
E-mail: ultan@castle-leslie.ie
13 en-suite rooms
Double: £116–£136
Open Apr to Oct, Christmas, & weekends, Credit cards: MC, VS
Country house hotel

Look no further—this is **it**: an idyllic Irish pub off the beaten tourist path with country-cozy bedrooms, good chat with locals in the old-world bar, and wonderful food in the intimate little restaurant. You'll be so captivated by the place that you'll want to base your Irish holiday here—the challenge is how far can you tour in a day and be back in time for Ken's delicious dinner? (Waterford of crystal fame, Cashel with its castle, and the coastal villages of Dungarven, Ardmore, and Ballycotton are all realistic possibilities.) Three lovely, well-kitted-out little bedrooms lie upstairs (leave your large suitcases in the car). Soak in the claw-foot tubs, admire the country antiques, and relax in the little guest sitting room or over a drink in the bar. The pub's snugness, its plethora of country memorabilia, and its proximity to the road make it unsuitable for young children. Ken and Kathleen are extremely patient and welcoming—given a few years, I feel confident that their hospitality and the old-world Irishness of what they offer in this little country pub will put this quiet part of Ireland on the map. Go before it gets too crowded! *Directions*: Take the N25 (Waterford to Cork road) to Lismore, pass the castle, and as you leave the town bear right at the Toyota dealership for the 4-km drive to Glencairn where Buggy's Glencairn Inn, fronted by a cottage garden, is on the right.

BUGGY'S GLENCAIRN INN   **New**
Owners: Kathleen & Ken Buggy
Glencairn, Tallow
Co Waterford, Ireland
Tel & fax: (058) 56232
3 en-suite rooms
£24 per person B&B, dinner £20
Closed Christmas, Credit cards: MC, VS
Inn

Desmond, the 29th Knight of Glin's demesne is a 400-acre farm and the late-18th-century castle which stretches along the banks of the River Shannon. Staying here affords you the opportunity to live luxuriously—the house is a real beauty, full of exquisite furniture, family portraits, and beautiful artifacts. It is all very grand but not at all stuffy, for your host is Bob Duff, a gregarious New Zealander who ensures that you are well taken care of and well fed. He will give you a tour of the house with lots of suitably embellished stories. If you are passionate about art, literature, furniture, or books, be sure to ask if the Knight is in residence, for Desmond is happy to meet with guests when he is at home. The castle is open to the public during May and June but when you stay here it is yours to enjoy. Sip tea in the grand drawing room or curl up with a good book in the oh-so-comfortable sitting room. Bedrooms range from large and luxurious with extra-large bathrooms and dressing rooms to small and ordinary. Depending on guests' wishes, you dine either with fellow guests or at separate tables. Ballybunion golf course is close at hand. For something different, Bob can arrange for a helicopter to wing you to the Cliffs of Moher for a picnic (he packs a champagne lunch). *Directions:* From Limerick take the N69 towards Tralee for 50 km to Glin. At the end of the village turn left following the estate's wall to the castle entrance.

GLIN CASTLE
Owners: Olda & Desmond FitzGerald
Manager: Bob Duff
Glin
Co Limerick, Ireland
Tel: (068) 34173, Fax: (068) 34364
www.karenbrown.com/ireland/glin.html
6 en-suite rooms
Double: £220–£260, dinner £27.50
Open all year, Credit cards: all major
Country house hotel

This dazzling, three-story Regency house, formerly the dower house of the Courtown estate, has an atmosphere of refined elegance created by vivacious hostess, Mary Bowe and her delightful daughter Margaret. Mary has great charm and energy—during our stay she chatted with guests before dinner, made the rounds during dinner, and was back again at breakfast checking up to make certain that everything was perfect. The house is full of antiques, classic pieces that transport you back to the days of gracious living in grand houses. While we especially enjoyed our large, twin-bedded room with impressive, well-polished furniture, elegant decor, and a grand bathroom, I found the other bedrooms equally attractive. Six prized units are the ultra-luxurious, gorgeously decorated, extravagantly priced, State Rooms tucked away in a separate ground-floor wing: request the Print Suite, Stopford, Georgian, or French. Dinner is served in the ornate Gothic conservatory dining room—all greenery and mirrors. The food is a delight—superb French and Irish dishes. This is one of the few hotels in Ireland where it is appropriate to dress for dinner. An atmosphere of formal extravagance prevails: it is very much Mary Bowe's personal vision of a country house. *Directions:* Marlfield House is 88 km from Dublin. Take the N11 south to Gorey and as you enter the town turn left, before going under the railway bridge, onto the Courtown Road: the house is on your right after 2 km.

MARLFIELD HOUSE
Owners: Mary, Margaret, & Ray Bowe
Courtown Road, Gorey
Co Wexford, Ireland
Tel: (055) 21124, Fax: (055) 21572
19 en-suite rooms
Double: £165, Suite: £250–£450
E-mail: marlf@iol.ie
Closed Dec & Jan, Credit cards: all major
Country house hotel

If you enjoy horse-riding, you will be happy to learn that Collette and Tillman Anhold offer the experienced rider week-long riding vacations at their farm. It has the most magnificent position overlooking vast stretches of empty golden beaches and little green islands, while at its back rise the rugged Ben Bulben mountains. On arrival, Collette sees that you are settled into one of the snug, pine-paneled bedrooms, then it's off to the stables to meet your fine Irish hunter. Your four-legged friend is yours to ride just when and where you want to—along unspoiled beaches, through green mountain forests, and along a cross-country course jumping walls and wooden fences. You are expected to look after him by feeding, grooming, and tacking up. Collette provides a hearty breakfast and a full four-course dinner, serving it to guests seated around the large dining-room table. A spirit of happy camaraderie prevails as guests gather in the evening around the fire in the large stone fireplace to have horsey conversations. If you wish to range farther afield, Tillman can also arrange seven-day treks on the Sligo Trail and fourteen-day treks on the Donegal Trail where overnight accommodation is provided in traditional farmhouses. As you will not need a car for your holiday, it is suggested that you take the train to Sligo where a transfer will be organized. *Directions:* Grange is north of Sligo on the road to Donegal. Horse Holiday Farm is on your left.

HORSE HOLIDAY FARM
Owners: Collette & Tillman Anhold
Grange
Co Sligo, Ireland
Tel: (071) 66152, Fax: (071) 66400
6 en-suite rooms
£650 per person per week*
*Dinner, B&B, & horse
Open Apr to Nov, Credit cards: none
B&B with stables

Temple, which is almost at the geographic center of Ireland, was home to Declan's grandparents who were farmers hereabouts. While Declan still keeps a small herd of sheep, he and Bernadette concentrate more on tourism, offering cycling and walking holidays and relaxation weekends with classes in yoga, massage, aromatherapy, and shiatsu. A fire is lit in the cozy parlor in the evening and it is here that guests relax after dinner round the long dining-room table where they often dine on lamb from the farm and vegetables and fruit from the huge organic vegetable garden. Bedrooms are delightful: one fresh and flowery with a brass-and-wrought-iron bed, another enormous, home to a grand draped metal-and-brass bed, and the Bishops room all dark polished wood—the room was built for an elderly bishop who retired here to live with his relatives. Downstairs is a family room with a separate child's room colorfully decorated in a gay nursery print. Guests can borrow bikes and Bernadette has lots of tourist information on this often-neglected part of Ireland. The bog train, a small train that chugs you through a vast bogland while a guide explains its history and management, is popular with guests. Just down the road in Killbeggan is Locke's whiskey distillery, while the Clonmacnois monastic ruins and round tower overlooking the River Shannon are a half-hour's drive away. *Directions:* Temple is about 1 km off the N6 midway between Dublin and Galway, between Horseleap and Moate. The house is well signposted.

TEMPLE
Owners: Bernadette & Declan Fagan
Horseleap
Moate
Co Westmeath, Ireland
Tel & fax: (0506) 35118
E-mail: horsehol@iol.ie
4 en-suite rooms
£28–£30 per person B&B, dinner £18
Open Mar to Oct, Credit cards: MC, VS
Farmhouse B&B

Virginia creeper, wisteria, and roses cover the exterior of Berryhill, a small-scale manor house perched high on the side of the valley overlooking the River Nore. Built by George's ancestors in the 1780s, the house received a much-needed face-lift a few years ago when George and his wife Belinda moved into the family home, adding modern plumbing and wiring along with a light-hearted sense of fun in the decorating. The bedrooms—Frog, Pig, and Elephant—are subtly themed. My problem was to decide which one to choose: Pig with its claw-foot tub gracing the bathroom and grandfather clock in the sitting nook; Frog with its terrace overlooking the garden and cozy sitting room overlooking the valley; or Elephant with the opportunity to sink into a bubble bath by the flicker of firelight. Make yourself at home in the drawing room and enjoy a drink from the honesty bar. If you are staying for several nights, Belinda is happy to prepare a light supper for you but there is no shortage of excellent places to eat within a short driving distance. Dog lovers will be happy to know that the Dyers have seven adorable dogs of various breeds and sizes. You can happily spend your days exploring the craft trail and visiting medieval Kilkenny and the Waterford glass factory. *Directions*: From Thomastown take the R700 for 8 km to Inistoge. Go through the village, cross the bridge, bearing right, take the next left (Craignamanagh Rd), first right, then second left.

BERRYHILL   New
Owners: Belinda & George Dyer
Inistoge
Co Kilkenny, Ireland
Tel & fax: (056) 58434 or (087) 461532
3 en-suite rooms
£35 per person B&B
Open Apr to Oct, Credit cards: MC, VS
Country house

Glenlohane is a lovely Georgian home of spacious but not overly grand rooms, sitting in beautiful, parklike grounds. It is a comfortable house, full of attractive things—lovely antiques, furnishings, fires, and rooms in cheerful colors. Hosts Desmond and Melanie—the tenth generation of the family who built the house—are most welcoming and their dogs are friendly but not intrusive. Enjoy tea by the fire in the drawing room, play a tune on the grand piano, and immerse yourself in the charm of it all. Return at night to this lovely haven to recount your adventures to Desmond over dinner—while Melanie prepares the delicious food, Desmond often eats with guests, hosting them Irish-house-party style. Garden lovers are directed to Anne's Grove gardens at Castletownroche and Garinish Island with its grand Italianate gardens. Glenlohane is also a working farm of three hundred acres with cattle, sheep, horses, and hens, as well as barley, wheat, and oats. Outdoor activites are very much a part of life, including riding, fishing, horse shows, carriage driving, rough shooting, and agricultural shows. *Directions*: From Kanturk take the R576 toward Mallow. Very soon, bear left at religious monument towards Buttevant on R580. Take the first right at Sally's Cross towards Ballyclough. Glenlohane is the first residential entrance on the left after 2½ kilometers—the house does not have a sign.

GLENLOHANE   New
Owners: Melanie & Desmond Sharp Bolster
Kanturk
Co Cork, Ireland
Tel: (029) 50014, Fax: (029) 51100
4 en-suite rooms
£45–£50 per person B&B, dinner £25
Open all year, Credit cards: MC, VS
Country house

The Irish name for Kenmare, *An Neidin*, means "the little nest," which is a good description of this attractive town nestling beside the Kenmare river at the foot of some of Ireland's most spectacular scenery. Kenmare's two wide main roads are lined with bustling shops. On a quieter side street, Hawthorne House offers visitors an attractive guesthouse with an especially gracious hostess, Mary O'Brien. Inside, the old house has received a complete face-lift with light pine replacing all the old woodwork and doors. The contemporary decor is light and attractive. The bedrooms Derrynid, Neidin, and Dromore are superior rooms (well worth the extra cost), having the additional facilities of a spacious sitting area, color television, hairdryer, bottled spring water, and flowers. Standard rooms are snug in size—not the place for huge suitcases. Breakfast is the only meal served since Kenmare has a plethora of restaurants and pubs—Mary will happily make dinner reservations for you. Mary's favorite sightseeing excursion is to Garinish Island where her husband proposed to her. Guests often drive around the Ring of Kerry, competing with coaches for views that are much overrated. Rides to Bantry and Killarney provide stunning vistas. *Directions:* Kenmare is about a three-hour drive from Shannon on the N71 between Killarney and Bantry. Hawthorne House is next to the Park Hotel. A large car park provides safe, off-the-road parking.

HAWTHORNE HOUSE
Owners: Mary & Noel O'Brien
Shelbourne Street
Kenmare
Co Kerry, Ireland
Tel: (064) 41035, Fax: (064) 41932
www.karenbrown.com/ireland/hawthorne.html
8 en-suite rooms
£19–£23 per person B&B
Closed Christmas, Credit cards: MC, VS
Guesthouse

The Park Hotel began life in 1897 as the Great Southern Hotel Kenmare to provide a convenient overnight stop for railway travelers en route to or from the Ring of Kerry. The furnishings are those of a hotel of the late Victorian or Edwardian age—almost every piece of furniture is antique, some of it massive, but somehow in keeping and much of it very valuable. Owner Francis Brennan's charm, humor, and professionalism all infect his young staff. Guests are greeted by a blazing coal fire which casts its glow towards the cozy bar and lounge, and you sit down at a partners' desk to register before being shown to your room. Such touches give a small-hotel feeling to this large hotel. Exquisite accommodations are provided in nine very luxurious and very pricey suites with splendid views out over the Kenmare Bay. Bedrooms in the main hotel are large and pleasant, those in the newer wing uniform in size, all with big-city prices. The cooking is excellent and has been awarded a Michelin star. The menu offers some tempting choices and the cellars offer a fine selection of wines. The Park Hotel provides programs for the Christmas and New Year holidays. Adjacent to the hotel is an 18-hole golf course and the hotel also arranges golfing programs at Killarney, Ballybunion, and Waterville. *Directions:* Kenmare is about a three-hour drive from Shannon on the N71 between Killarney and Bantry.

PARK HOTEL
Owner: Francis Brennan
Kenmare, Co Kerry, Ireland
Tel: (064) 41200, Fax: (064) 41402
E-mail: phkenmare@iol.ie
www.karenbrown.com/ireland/parkhotel.html
49 en-suite rooms
Double: £220–£312, Suite: £360–£430, dinner £39
Open Apr to Nov, Christmas, & New Year
Credit cards: all major
Luxury resort

Kenmare is one of my favorite Irish towns, and how appropriate that several of my favorite bed and breakfasts are located here, amongst them Sallyport House. Janie Arthur returned home after working for 15 years in California to help her brother, John, convert the family home into a luxurious bed and breakfast, decorating it in an uncluttered, sophisticated style. Return in the evening to chat round the fire in the drawing room or curl up in one of the comfortable chairs in the less formal sitting area with its exposed stone wall and photographs of Kenmare at the turn of the century. Breakfast is the only meal served—for dinner, it's a two-minute walk into town. The bedrooms are delightful, each furnished with antiques and accompanied by a large luxurious bathroom. Muxnaw has views of Muxnaw mountain and deep window seats; Ring View looks out to the Kenmare river; Reen a Gross has an American king-sized four-poster bed; The Falls has a view of the pretty garden. It's delightful to stroll along the riverbank, through the park, and back through the town. You can spend several days exploring the Beara Peninsula, Ring of Kerry, and lakes of Killarney. *Directions:* Kenmare is about a three-hour drive from Shannon on the N71 between Killarney and Bantry. From Bantry, Sallyport House is on your right just after you cross the bridge. From Killarney, follow Bantry signposts through Kenmare and Sallyport House is on your left before you come to the bridge.

SALLYPORT HOUSE
Owners: Janie & John Arthur
Kenmare
Co Kerry, Ireland
Tel: (064) 42066, Fax: (064) 42067
www.karenbrown.com/ireland/sallyport.html
5 en-suite rooms
£35–£40 per person B&B
Open Apr to Oct, Credit cards: none
B&B

After visiting Shelburne Lodge, I can understand why I was showered with readers' letters urging me to visit and praising not only the high quality of the decor but also the delicious breakfasts. The building, a Georgian farmhouse, is lovely and the grounds with their lawns, herb garden, and tennis court are very attractive but it is the interior that is outstanding. The polished wooden floors gleam and lovely antiques grace the sitting room and hallway. Each lovely bedroom is accompanied by a luxurious bathroom—Maura Foley went into such detail when she restored the house that she chose a different color scheme for each bathroom. Kenmare has some excellent restaurants (look out, Kinsale!) and Packies (named for Uncle Packie who used to run a grocery business here) is one of the best—it offers a lively, informal atmosphere and your hostess Maura as chef (advance reservations are a must). Maura also helps her sister Grainne at The Purple Heather, a great venue for lunch or snacks. After dinner wander into one of Kenmare's many pubs—there's entertainment and music to suit all tastes. Kenmare is ideally placed for touring the Ring of Kerry and the prettier Beara Peninsula as well as for visiting several historic houses and gardens including Muckross House and Derrynane House, home of the famous Daniel O'Connell. *Directions:* Kenmare is about a three-hour drive from Shannon on the N71 between Killarney and Bantry. Shelburne Lodge is on the R569 (Cork road) opposite the golf club.

SHELBURNE LODGE
Owner: Maura O'Connell Foley
Kenmare
Co Kerry, Ireland
Tel: (064) 41013, Fax: (064) 42135
www.karenbrown.com/ireland/shelburnelodge.html
8 en-suite rooms
£30–£40 per person B&B
Open mid-Apr to early Oct, Credit cards: MC, VS
B&B

Apparently Dunromin's former owner was an insurance agent who had traveled all over Ireland, so when he bought this house, he changed its name from Whittington Cottage to reflect his circumstances, "done roaming." Just a narrow strip of garden separates the house from the busy main road so there's lots of traffic noise, but Dunromin is one of the few listings in this book that is within easy walking distance of bus and rail transportation. Guests have a snug sitting room where Valerie provides a carefully compiled book detailing the many attractions of the town and leaflets for guests to take. She discusses the merits of the various restaurants and pubs and has sample menus on hand. Traditional Irish music is a feature of the local pubs, but as it does not start until very late in the evening, guests often ask Tom for a couple of tunes on his accordion and he is always happy to oblige. Upstairs, Tom has done an excellent job of fitting small shower rooms into the bedrooms and Valerie has made the little rooms very pretty with attractive wallpaper, drapes, and bedcovers. A ten-minute walk brings you to the picturesque heart of town with its many fine old buildings, including beautifully painted shops and pubs with hand-crafted signs. Kilkenny Castle is definitely worth a visit. *Directions:* From Carlow take the N10 to Kilkenny. At the first roundabout follow signs for the city center and you will find Dunromin on your right after 1 km.

DUNROMIN
Owners: Valerie & Tom Rothwell
Dublin Road
Kilkenny
Co Kilkenny, Ireland
Tel & fax: (056) 61387
www.karenbrown.com/ireland/dunromin.html
4 en-suite rooms
£16 per person B&B
Closed Christmas, Credit cards: MC, VS
B&B

Killarney is a pleasant town to visit after the crowds of daytime visitors have departed. Staying at Earls Court gives you the opportunity to go sightseeing out of town during the day, return in the evening for a cup of tea, and then walk into town for dinner. Emer and Ray built the house a few years ago and while the style outside is very modern, the inside is very traditional, for Emer is a great collector of lovely English and Irish antiques—guests sign in at a writing desk once owned by President Cearbhaill O'Dalaigh. All but two of the absolutely delightful bedrooms have balconies with views of the distant mountains across the trees and all have lovely antique furniture, queen-sized beds, bathrooms with power showers, satellite TV, and phones. Many also have an extra single bed and two bedrooms have an interconnecting door, making them ideal for families. Earls Court makes an excellent base for exploring this popular part of Kerry and there's enough sightseeing to keep you busy for a week. Golfers are spoiled for choice, with Killarney, Waterville, Dooks, Tralee, and Ballybunion being the most popular courses. *Directions*: Arriving from Cork on the N22, take a left-hand turn 1km before the first roundabout in Killarney (or go to the roundabout and retrace your steps, taking the first right). Proceed for 2 km past a slew of bed and breakfasts and Earls Court is on your right. Emer and Ray have an excellent map on their brochure.

EARLS COURT   New
Owners: Emer & Ray Moynihan
Woodlawn Junction
Killarney, Co Kerry, Ireland
Tel: (064) 34009, Fax: (064) 34366
10 en-suite rooms
£30–£40 per person B&B
Open mid-Feb to mid-Nov, Credit cards: MC, VS
Guesthouse

Kathleen O'Regan-Sheppard possesses boundless energy, taking great pride in keeping her house in tiptop condition, planning improvements (heated cupboards for golfers to dry their bags and boots are her latest innovation), working with the hotel keepers association, and being a wife and mother. Kathleen is especially proud of her collection of contemporary watercolors by local artists. Guests enjoy the large lobby parlor, often gathering here with friends after dinner. The upstairs sun room/library is a particularly inviting place to curl up with a book. The bedrooms are of the highest standards, all furnished in antique pine, with orthopedic beds, tea- and coffee-makings, telephones, hairdryers, and color televisions. Those in the newer wing enjoy especially large bright bathrooms. A hearty breakfast, with plenty of vegetarian choices, is the only meal served. Recommendations are made for nearby restaurants for dinner. A measure of Kathleen's success is that over 50% of her guests are repeat visitors. Whether viewed from a boat or a pony and trap, the lakes of Killarney are beautiful but in summer the town can get very crowded. Enjoy Muckross House and Ross Castle but be sure to allow time (on a fine day) to drive through the Gap of Dunloe. *Directions:* Kathleen's Country House is situated in the countryside a 3-km drive from Killarney on the N22, Tralee road.

KATHLEEN'S COUNTRY HOUSE
Owner: Kathleen O'Regan-Sheppard
Tralee Road
Killarney
Co Kerry, Ireland
Tel: (064) 32810, Fax: (064) 32340
www.karenbrown.com/ireland/kathleens.html
17 en-suite rooms
£25–£40 per person B&B
Open late-Mar to mid-Nov, Credit cards: all major
Guesthouse

This traditional farmhouse in the rich farmlands of County Cork is run by Margaret Browne who is becoming increasingly famous as one of Ireland's leading chefs and has published a popular cookbook, "Through My Kitchen Window." This is a most professional operation and Margaret has had the house altered to incorporate her growing endeavors: all the bedrooms have smart, en-suite bathrooms, the dining room has been extended to accommodate non-guests, and a sunny conservatory and hard tennis court have been built for guests' enjoyment. Yet this remains very much a working farm where you wander across the garden to explore the farmyard and watch the cows coming home to be milked. There is a particularly pretty sitting room all decked out in shades of green with Victorian sofas. Bedrooms are named after local rivers and all are attractively decorated with well-chosen antique furniture, wallpaper, and fabrics—two have six-foot beds. The same care goes into the feeding of her guests—Margaret uses only the finest local meats, fish, and vegetables. The nearby fishing port of Youghal (pronounced yawl) is famous for its delightful old buildings, medieval streets, and having had Sir Walter Raleigh as its mayor. The Midleton Jamestown Heritage Centre tells the history of Irish whiskey production. Cobh (pronounced cove) has an interesting maritime museum. *Directions:* Killeagh is on the N25 between Youghal and Cork. Turn at The Old Thatch Tavern, then after 1 km turn right: Ballymakeigh House is on your right after 1 km.

BALLYMAKEIGH HOUSE
Owners: Margaret & Michael Browne
Killeagh
Co Cork, Ireland
Tel: (024) 95184, Fax: (024) 95370
www.karenbrown.com/ireland/ballymakeighhouse.html
6 en-suite rooms
£25–£30 per person B&B, dinner £22.50
Open Feb to Oct, Credit cards: VS
Farmhouse B&B

As newlyweds, Philomena and her husband John put in an exceedingly low bid on a very tumbledown Woodlands Farmhouse and it was many years before she found out why their offer had been accepted. To hear why and enjoy intriguing tales of gold sovereigns, cursed families, and arranged marriages, you will have to go and stay and ask Philomena for an after-dinner story session. What started out as a simple bed and breakfast has now grown into a very professional guesthouse and restaurant business. Guests have a cozily cluttered parlor with an eclectic assortment of chairs, from stately Victorian to modern leather. The parlor opens up to an expansive dining room lit by two grand crystal chandeliers which overlooks the lovely back garden. The front garden is even more impressive: a grand sweep of lawn with shrubs and trees going down to the river and the tennis court. All the smartly decorated bedrooms enjoy garden views and range in size from large family rooms to snug twins—all have electric blankets and small en-suite shower or bathrooms with hairdryers. The nearby beaches are particularly attractive. In Wexford you can visit Wexford Heritage Park or Johnstown Castle Agricultural Museum. To the north lies the Vale of Avoca where you can visit the hand-weavers. *Directions:* Woodlands Farmhouse is signposted on the N11 between Arklow (10 km) and Gorey (6 km). Woodlands is just before the village of Killinierin, 2 km west of the N11.

WOODLANDS FARMHOUSE
Owner: Philomena O'Sullivan
Killinierin, Gorey
Co Wexford, Ireland
Tel & fax: (0402) 37125
www.karenbrown.com/ireland/woodlands.html
6 en-suite rooms
£20 per person B&B, dinner £16
Open Mar to Oct, Credit cards: MC, VS
Guesthouse

Flemingstown House, an 18th-century farmhouse, is just an hour's drive south of Limerick and Shannon airport, a quiet countryside world away from the hustle and bustle of the cosmopolitan area. Walk round the farm, watch the cows being milked, and chat with Imelda as she works in her spacious kitchen, for the two things that Imelda loves are cooking and taking care of her guests. It would be a shame to stay and not eat, for Imelda prepares tempting meals in which, following the starter and soup, there is a choice of meat or fish as a main course and always three or four desserts and farm cheeses made by her sister and her husband. The intricate stained-glass windows of the conservatory-style dining room were made by the same artist as those in the local church. Upstairs, the low-ceilinged bedrooms are snug in size, and come with a variety of twin and double combinations that can accommodate families of all sizes. The decor is simple and attractive, with painted walls and matching bedcovers and drapes, and each room has a small shower room. Nearby Kilmallock has the ruins of two friaries and the remains of its fortified wall weaving through the town. Imelda's guests often use her home as a base for touring counties Limerick, Tipperary, Kerry, and Cork. *Directions:* From Limerick take the N20 (Cork road) for 40 km and turn left to Kilmallock (10 km). From Kilmallock take the Kilfinane road (R512) for 3 km and the house is on your left.

FLEMINGSTOWN HOUSE
Owner: Imelda Sheedy-King
Kilmallock
Co Limerick, Ireland
Tel: (063) 98093, Fax: (063) 98546
E-mail: keltec@iol.ie
5 en-suite rooms
£20–£22.50 per person B&B, dinner £17
Open Feb to Oct, Credit cards: VS
Farmhouse B&B

Scilly is the quiet side of Kinsale (no frantic hunting for a parking spot) and just a ten-minute stroll into town. Yet why go into Kinsale, for Scilly has everything you need: atmospheric pubs, The Spaniard and The Spinnaker, an excellent restaurant, Man Friday's, and Geraldine and Denis O'Connor's welcoming accommodation with its breathtaking views. Denis is passionate about golf and not only is he happy to make golfing reservations for guests, but he is also glad to escort players of all abilities (they can provide clubs)—there are three courses in Kinsale. All O'Connors' four bedrooms have spectacular water views up the river to Charles Fort and down to Kinsale's sailboat-filled harbor. I was awed by the view from the two rooms at the top of the house (4 and 5) and preferred them to the more spacious accommodation offered by rooms 2 and 3 simply because it is a joy to open your eyes in the morning to panoramic water views (in rooms 2 and 3 you have to step beyond the bedroom to the sunroom to admire the 180-degree vista). Bedrooms offer good big beds but plain, rather functional décor. Guests come as visitors and leave as friends—you'll regret it if you stay only one night! *Directions*: Arriving in Kinsale, follow the harbor to the east which brings you into the district of Kinsale known as Scilly. O'Connors is opposite The Spaniard pub—there is off-road parking to the rear.

O'CONNORS   New
Owners: Geraldine & Denis O'Connor
Hill House, Scilly
Kinsale, Co Cork, Ireland
Tel: (021) 773222, Fax: (021) 773224
E-mail: ocbb@iol.ie
4 en-suite rooms
£38–£48 per person B&B
Closed Christmas, Credit cards: all major
B&B

This tall Georgian townhouse has a perfect downtown Kinsale location opposite the sailboat-filled harbor. Here you are at the heart of town, the only problem being finding a place to park your car for the duration of your stay. This is a tall, skinny house with steep staircases, so remember everything you need from the car on the first journey. The higher you go, the better the view but the more stairs you tackle (a drawback for some). Bedrooms are spick-and-span and tastefully decorated. Each has a phone and TV and all but one family room have bathrooms with showers over the tub. Rooms at the front enjoy harbor views and if you want "the" view, request Room 9, an attic room, bearing in mind the climb to your aerie (it's the honeymoon suite and the most expensive room in the house). This is not a place for lots of owner attention, though I have always found the staff very polite. Michael, a master chef, cooks a delicious breakfast. The location at the very heart of this most attractive harbor town is ideal: you can stroll round the shops perusing the restaurant menus as you go (Kinsale has a much-vaunted reputation as the gourmet dining capital of Ireland) or take a bracing walk along the yacht-filled harbor or along the cliffs of the Old Head of Kinsale. *Directions:* Follow the main road into Kinsale (Pearse Street)—the Old Bank House is on the right next to the post office. Parking is on the street which is well lit.

OLD BANK HOUSE
Owners: Marie & Michael Riese
Pearse Street
Kinsale
Co Cork, Ireland
Tel: (021) 774075, Fax: (021) 774296
9 en-suite rooms
£40–£55 per person B&B
Closed Christmas, Credit cards: all major
B&B

Beyond the yacht-filled harbor, the narrow streets of Kinsale terrace upwards to high ground. Here you find The Old Presbytery, a narrow house on the end of a terrace. Owners Noreen and Philip McEvoy moved here from West Clare where Philip was a chef at a seafood restaurant and Noreen ran a guesthouse. Philip now concentrates his culinary efforts on breakfast, offering everything from traditional Irish fare to crepes filled with fruit. The breakfast room, warmed by a blackened, wood-burning stove, is the old kitchen and has been extended into a sunny conservatory. Up the narrow stairs Victorian brass beds topped with crisp, embroidered white cotton quilts decorate the attractive bedrooms, the most spacious being a large room whose zip-and-link beds can either be twins or king-sized. Another most attractive larger room has its own private entrance up a steep iron stairway. Both the larger rooms' bathrooms have lovely old-fashioned claw-foot tubs. Please be aware that this is a small house—leave large suitcases in the car. *Note:* Philip and Noreen have plans to extend their home adding larger rooms where breakfast will not be included in the tarrif. They hope to have everything completed by July 1998. *Directions:* Go straight up the main street in Kinsale (Pearse Street) to the end, turn left, first right, and first right, and The Old Presbytery is the first house on the right. The Old Presbytery has a large yard for off-road parking.

THE OLD PRESBYTERY
Owners: Noreen & Philip McEvoy
43 Cork Street
Kinsale
Co Cork, Ireland
Tel & fax: (021) 772027
www.karenbrown.com/ireland/oldpresbytery.html
9 en-suite rooms
£20–£30 per person B&B
Closed Christmas, Credit cards: none
B&B

In the north corner of Kinsale harbor is a wooded promontory on which there is a village within the town called Scilly. Here, commanding the most idyllic views of the yacht-speckled harbor, Charles Fort, and the encircling green hills, is Scilly House Inn, the home of Karin Young and Bill Skelly. Karin hails from California and Bill from Ireland and, loving both places, they divide their time between the two. Decorated in an uncluttered, luxurious style, their home makes the most of the views across the lawns and gardens down to the water. From the ground-floor garden room with its shaded balcony overlooking the harbor to the luxurious suite with its glassed-in porch capturing glorious views, the bedrooms are a delight (one bedroom does not have a view, and another is tucked in an adjacent cottage), decorated in a trim, sophisticated style. Breakfasts are another treat with fresh fruit, scrambled eggs with smoked salmon, and fluffy omelets on the menu. Dinner is available for parties of more than six people. The adjacent pub, The Spaniard, with its low-beamed bars and stone-flagged floors is worth a visit. Walk along the harbor shore into Kinsale or set your sights on Charles Fort where William Penn's father once worked as governor of Kinsale. *Directions:* Follow the road that fronts the harbor to the east which brings you into the district of Kinsale known as Scilly and Scilly House is on your right.

SCILLY HOUSE INN
Owners: Karin Young & Bill Skelly
Scilly, Kinsale
Co Cork, Ireland
Tel: (021) 772413, Fax: (021) 774629
www.karenbrown.com/ireland/scillyhouseinn.html
7 en-suite rooms
£45–£67.50 per person B&B, dinner £30
Open Apr 21 to Oct, Credit cards: all major
No-smoking house
Country house

Absolute oohs and ahs for this lovely, centrally located Queen Anne townhouse which occupies a position on a former busy quay. After suffering years of neglect, this architectural gem was beautifully restored under the loving care of Eamonn McKeown, who lives just up the road. His mother, Eileen, resides at Sovereign House, preparing delicious breakfasts served in the dining room and giving guests expert advice on where they should eat their other meals (never an easy choice in this town so noted for its restaurants). Up the grand staircase you come to the billiard room and the Ormonde Suite with its queen-sized four-poster bed placed between the tall windows looking out over Kinsale's rooftops. Up another flight of stairs are three spacious guestrooms under the eaves—Elizabethan has an en-suite shower, while the other rooms have more spacious bathrooms with claw-foot tubs. All the rooms have TV and phone. The hurly-burly of Kinsale is on your doorstep and Eileen or Eamonn are always available to point you in the right direction for explorations farther afield. *Directions*: Arriving from Cork, go straight up the main street, turn right at the Blue Haven, bear left with the road, and directly left into a long, narrow car park. Sovereign House is at the end of the car park on your right, behind a tall stone wall. You can pull up directly in front of the house if you cannot find designated parking in this busy little town.

SOVEREIGN HOUSE   *New*
Owners: Eileen & Eamonn McKeown
Newmans Mall
Kinsale, Co Cork, Ireland
Tel: (021) 772850, Fax: (021) 774723
4 en-suite rooms
£45–£50 per person B&B
Closed Christmas, Credit cards: all major
B&B

When the British built this army complex in 1800, they could never have imagined that it would serve for many years as the village school and more recently become a delightful restaurant that, fortunately for the traveler, offers accommodation. Pine tables and chairs and a massive dresser filled with pretty pottery give the restaurant a country air which extends up the steep pine staircase to the attractive little bedrooms set under the sloping roof. All the bedrooms have an antique pine dresser or table, and a tea and coffee tray. You order your breakfast the night before so that it is ready for you at the time of your choosing. Breakfast service ends at 10 am and last orders for dinner are 9 pm, but beyond that, there is a great deal of flexibility about when lunch, afternoon tea, and dinner are served. A large sign on the front of the building states that Mitchells does not cater to children—best be forewarned. Margaret and Jerry have purchased the lovely watermill opposite and are planning on additional accommodation here—I'm sure it will be charming. The remains of the monastic city of Glendalough with its round tower and seven churches is just down the road and there are spectacular gardens and houses to visit nearby. *Directions:* From Dublin take the N11 to Kilmacanogue where you turn right for Glendalough. Eight km after Roundwood, as you enter Laragh, bear right to Mitchells.

MITCHELLS OF LARAGH
Owners: Margaret & Jerry Mitchell
The Old Schoolhouse
Laragh, Glendalough
Co Wicklow, Ireland
Tel & fax: (0404) 45302
5 en-suite rooms
£19.50 per person B&B, dinner £18.50
Closed Jan, Credit cards: all major
Restaurant with rooms

Delphi Lodge with its surrounding estate was for centuries the sporting estate of the Marquis of Sligo. This wild, unspoilt, and beautiful valley with its towering mountains, tumbling rivers, and crystal-clear loughs was acquired in 1986 by Jane and Peter Mantle. Fortunately for those who have a love of wild, beautiful places, they have restored the Marquis's fishing lodge and opened their home to guests who come to walk, fish for salmon, relax, and enjoy the camaraderie of the house-party atmosphere. In the evening Peter often presides at the head of the very long dinner table (guests who catch a salmon take the place of honor) and guests enjoy a leisurely meal and lively conversation. A snug library and an attractive drawing room are at hand and guests often spend late-night hours in the billiard room. Bedrooms are all furnished in antique and contemporary pine, several having large comfortable armchairs and views to the peaceful lake. Such is the popularity of the place that it is advisable to make reservations well in advance to secure a summer booking. Four deluxe, self-catering cottages are also available on the estate. *Directions:* Leenane is between Wesport and Clifden on the N59. From Leenane go east towards Westport for 5 km, turn left and continue along the north shore of Killary harbor towards Louisburgh for 10 km. Delphi Lodge is in the woods, on the left after the adventure center.

DELPHI LODGE
Owners: Jane & Peter Mantle
Leenane
Co Galway, Ireland
Tel: (095) 42211, Fax: (095) 42296
E-mail: delfish@iol.ie
www.karenbrown.com/ireland/delphi.html
12 en-suite rooms
£40–£55 per person B&B, dinner £28
Closed Christmas & New Year, Credit cards: MC, VS
Country house

Rosleague Manor is a lovely Irish hotel—a comfortable country house hotel overlooking Ballinakill Bay and an ever-changing panorama of wild Connemara countryside. This is a quiet, sparsely populated land of steep hills, tranquil lakes, and grazing sheep, where narrow country lanes lead to little hamlets. Anne Foyle is much in evidence making certain that guests are well taken care of. The hotel is beautifully furnished with lovely old furniture and the lounges are cozy with their turf fires and comfortable chairs. The garden-style conservatory is a popular place for before- or after-dinner drinks. Bedrooms are most attractive. I prefer those with views to the loch and find the newer rooms a little too contemporary for my taste—they also have unexciting views of a gravelled car park. The dining room is my favorite room in the house: tall windows frame the view and lovely old tables and chairs are arranged in groupings on the polished floor. There is an à-la-carte menu as well as the fixed-price menu which offers four or five choices for each course. Dishes vary with the seasons and include a wide selection of locally caught fish and Connemara lamb. This is a peaceful place to hide away and a well located base for exploring the ruggedly beautiful countryside of Connemara. *Directions:* Take the N59 from Galway to Clifden then turn right at the church for the 10-km drive to Rosleague Manor.

ROSLEAGUE MANOR
Owner: Anne Foyle
Letterfrack, Connemara
Co Galway, Ireland
Tel: (095) 41101, Fax: (095) 41168
www.karenbrown.com/ireland/rosleague.html
20 en-suite rooms
Double: £80–£160, dinner £28
Open Easter to Nov, Credit cards: all major
Country house hotel

Standing on the shores of Lough Eske, a 20-minute drive from Donegal and overlooking some of Ireland's prettiest scenery, Ardnamona House is the place to visit if you have an interest in rhododendrons and azaleas. Without a doubt, Amabel and Kieran Clarke's 40 acres of grounds contain some magnificent specimens from giant trees (many over 100 years old) to small bushes. Until Kieran (a piano tuner by profession) gave me a short tour of their property, I was unaware that there were so many varieties of rhododendrons and azaleas. Upon arrival I was greeted by an effusive Amabel and Debbie the donkey who wanders the grounds and searches out guests, hoping for a pat and a treat. Guests enjoy a cozy sitting room and a little conservatory overlooking the lough. In the evening guests dine together round the long dining-room table at 8:30 pm to a set three-course meal. Upstairs the five very attractively decorated bedrooms are priced according to size and whether their little bathroom is en suite or down the hall. The rhododendrons are at their peak during April and May, the azaleas at their peak in May. Donegal town bustles and parking can be a problem but the effort of finding a space is worth it. The scenery is rugged and beautiful, the roads quiet and narrow. *Directions:* From Donegal town take the N15 towards Letterkenny for 5 km to a small signpost that indicates a left turn to Harvey Point Hotel. Follow this road for 11 km and Ardnamona's driveway in on your right.

ARDNAMONA HOUSE
Owners: Amabel & Kieran Clarke
Lough Eske
Co Donegal, Ireland
Tel: (073) 22650, Fax: (073) 22819
www.karenbrown.com/ireland/ardnamona.html
5 rooms, 3 en suite
£35–£45 per person B&B, dinner £18
Open Feb to Oct, Credit cards: MC, VS
Country house

Kilkenny is a most attractive, historic town, and there is no more perfect a base for exploring its many charms than Blanchville House, a 15-minute drive away. Acres of farmland give this handsome Georgian home seclusion. You'll know you've arrived when you see a tall square church-tower-like folly—in days gone by it was equipped with clocks and bells. Inside Blanchville House, tall-ceilinged, generously proportioned rooms are the order of the day, and Monica is particularly proud of having several pieces of furniture that were made for the house. One of these is the glorious half-tester bed that graces the principal bedroom. Apparently Sir James Kearny, a great eccentric, was fond of waxing and singeing his mustache, an operation he performed in his bed. One day, while practicing this routine, he set fire to the bedding and narrowly escaped burning the house down. There's a portrait of Sir James in the drawing room which has the lovely wallpaper hung in 1823: guests enjoy a drink here before going in to dine together round the long polished table. County Kilkenny is particularly lovely and Monica can give you a tourist map which directs you to a great many craft shops. *Directions:* Leave Kilkenny on the N10 (Carlow to Dublin road) and Blanchville House is signposted to your right after The Pike pub, 5 km out. Pass over the railway crossing, turn left at Connly's pub, and the house is on your left after 1 km.

BLANCHVILLE HOUSE
Owners: Monica & Tim Phelan
Dunbell
Maddoxtown
Co Kilkenny, Ireland
Tel (056) 27197, Fax: (056) 27636
www.karenbrown.com/ireland/blanchville.html
6 rooms, 5 en suite
£27.50–£32.50 per person B&B, dinner £22.50
Open Mar to Oct, Credit cards: MC, VS
Country house

If you are seeking a romantic interlude on a gracious country estate, you can do no better than to choose Longueville House, whose size takes your breath away. Set on a hill overlooking the River Blackwater, this elegant country house offers you the very best of Irish hospitality. It was built by one of the O'Callaghan's ancestors, who was spurred on to grander things by a sum of money he received for supporting the British Act of Union. The icing on the cake is that the O'Callaghan clan is dedicated to making certain that you enjoy your stay: Jane, Michael, and daughter-in-law Aisling make certain you are well cared for while William ensures that you are well fed. William is blessed with the fact that Longueville is almost completely self sufficient. Vegetables, salmon, lamb, and herbs—even a few bottles of wine—come from the estate. The dining room in soft shades of pink is a picture, while the adjacent library provides a snug place to dine. Each and every bedroom is beautifully decorated and accompanied by a splendid modern bathroom. Below stairs is a large games room with a full-size billiard table. The nearby River Blackwater offers salmon and trout fishing for guests. There are several 18-hole golf courses within easy reach of Longueville—Mallow, Killarney, Cork, and Tralee and the links at Ballybunion. *Directions:* The hotel is located on the N72, 5 km west of Mallow on the Killarney road. Shannon airport is 85 km away.

LONGUEVILLE HOUSE
Owners: Aisling, Jane, Michael, &
  William O'Callaghan
Mallow
Co Cork, Ireland
Tel: (022) 47156, Fax: (022) 47459
www.karenbrown.com/ireland/longuevillehouse.html
21 en-suite rooms
Double: £134–£164
Open mid-Feb to-Dec 20, Credit cards: all major
Country house hotel

Standing amidst hundreds of acres of parkland, a half-hour drive from Dublin, Moyglare Manor was built in 1770 as an elegant country mansion. A refined air still pervades the hotel as you step into a world of opulence, where elegant Victorian antiques are flanked by old-fashioned sofas and chairs covered in fabrics that coordinate with the wallpaper and draperies. There's a cluttered, over-furnished look to the drawing room, and whenever I have visited, there has always been a buzz of conversation as groups draw their chairs round the fire or gather in convivial clusters. The dining room occupies three small rooms, so there is always an intimate atmosphere. Bedrooms are delightful, all beautifully furnished with many lovely Victorian antiques. The suites are especially large and opulent. Sightseeing attractions within a half-hour drive include Castletown House, Russborough House (with its collection of world-famous paintings including the only Vermeer in private hands apart from H.M. The Queen's), and Glendalough, the 6th-century monastic site founded by St. Kevin with its round tower, ruined churches, and high cross. *Directions:* From Dublin take the N4 to Maynooth. Keep right at the Catholic church—the 2-km drive to Moyglare Manor is well signposted.

MOYGLARE MANOR
Owner: Norah Devlin
Manager: Shay Curran
Maynooth
Co Kildare, Ireland
Tel: (01) 6286351, Fax: (01) 6285405
E-mail: moyglare@iol.ie
16 en-suite rooms
Double: £150, Suite: £360, dinner £25.
Closed Christmas, Credit cards: all major
Country house hotel

Beth and Ken Sherrard bought Glenview House over 30 years ago as little more than a shell and worked very hard to restore it, using authentic materials and antiques whenever possible, creating a comfortable family home. Now the children are grown, guests occupy the family's bedrooms. The names of former occupants are on the doors, and family pictures, photo albums, and stuffed toys remain. If you want to languish in a huge tub or drench yourself from a plate-sized shower head, request the room with the Jules-Verne-like, Victorian shower/tub combination—operating instructions essential. If you want wonderful views and lots of space, request Mum and Dad's room with its king-size bed and panoramic view of the wooded valley. Downstairs is a small wheelchair-accessible double room whose bathroom also provides a home for a wide variety of sporting equipment. In the evening, guests help themselves to drinks from the little honesty bar and enjoy them either on the sheltered patio or in the spacious drawing room with its chairs drawn up cozily by the fire. Beth is happy to provide a three-course dinner. "Must visits" include the whiskey distillery in nearby Midleton and the maritime museum in Cobh. *Directions:* From Midleton take the L35 towards Fermoy for 4 km to a forested area. Take the first left and go immediately right up the hill. Glenview House is the first on the left.

GLENVIEW HOUSE
Owners: Beth & Ken Sherrard
Ballinaclasha
Midleton
Co Cork, Ireland
Tel & fax: (021) 631680
www.karenbrown.com/ireland/glenview.html
4 en-suite rooms
£30–£30 per person B&B, dinner £20
Open all year, Credit cards: all major
Country house

Amongst the scattered modern holiday cottages and retirement homes surrounding the village of Miltown Malbay, a popular Irish holiday destination, you find a traditional Irish farmhouse that is now a welcoming guesthouse, restaurant, and cookery school operated by Rita Meade. Rita offers cookery courses for adults, teenagers, and children and the heart of the house is the kitchen with its large central island designed for day-long cooking classes. Two small rooms have been combined and extended with a conservatory to serve as a guest sitting and dining room filled with pine tables and chairs and decorated with an old pine dresser. The country theme is continued in the bedrooms with their pine furniture and old iron beds topped with colorful quilts. All bedrooms have televisions and compact shower rooms and three rooms have a double and a single bed. There is a small ground-floor double-bedded room for those who have difficulty with stairs. The nearby Cliffs of Moher are a great attraction but one guest used Berry Lodge as a base for visiting Bunratty Folk Park, Craggaunowen Megalithic Centre, the Aran Islands, exploring the Burren, and sailing to Scattery Island. *Directions:* From Ennis (on the Limerick to Galway road) take the N85 for 32 km to Miltown Malbay. Turn left at the Y in the center of the village and Berry Lodge is just near the second left turning after you pass the caravan park and cross the bridge.

BERRY LODGE
Owner: Rita Meade
Annagh
Miltown Malbay
Co Clare, Ireland
Tel & fax: (065) 87022
www.karenbrown.com/ireland/berry.html
5 en-suite rooms
£18–£20 per person B&B, dinner £18.50
Closed Jan 6 to mid-Feb, Credit cards: MC, VS
B&B

When Nancy Malone and her young family moved to Vesey Place in the 1970s the terrace of Regency-style homes was in a sad state of disrepair—theirs was one of the first families to see the potential in these grand homes where residents once enjoyed afternoon tea on silver service in their private park. Today the terrace has achieved a total face-lift and is considered quite the most prestigious address in the little seaside village of Monkstown overlooking Dublin Bay. Staying here is a delightfully peaceful alternative to the hubbub of Dublin. A six-minute walk finds you at the DART station from where a fifteen-minute ride takes you to Trinity College (it's also just a few minutes' drive to the Dun Laoghaire car ferry terminal for Holyhead, Wales). All the lovely old features of this house built in 1840 remain intact and Nancy's attractive antiques add to the ambiance. Nancy has cleverly tucked a small shower room into the corner of each of the apeallingly decorated bedrooms. Breakfast is the only meal served—freshly squeezed orange juice and fresh fruit precede a cooked breakfast though I suggest opting for Nancy's muesli with honey and fruit as an alternative. *Directions:* From Dublin take the N11 and follow signs for Dun Laoghaire. Pass through Monkstown (a big Gothic church and cluster of shops). At the next traffic lights turn right into York Road then first right into Vesey Place.

CHESTNUT LODGE
Owner: Nancy Malone
2 Vesey Place
Monkstown
Co Dublin, Ireland
Tel: (01) 2807860, Fax: (01) 2801466
4 en-suite rooms
£30–£35 per person B&B
Open all year, Credit cards: MC, VS
B&B

Roundwood House is situated near Mountrath in a scenic spot at the foot of the Slieve Bloom mountains. The house was built in the 1730s for Anthony Sharp upon his return from America. He attached this elegant Palladian home to his grandfather's simple Quaker cottage which still remains at the back of the house. Roundwood House had pretty much fallen into disrepair by the time it was purchased in the 1970s by the Georgian Society whose careful restoration is being continued by Rosemarie and Frank Kennan who forsook the corporate life of IBM. The gray appearance of the outside of the house belies its colorful interior—bright white and blue for the hall and bold yellows, blues, and reds for the bedrooms—all done in true Georgian style to give a dramatic impact to the lovely, high-ceilinged rooms. Bathrooms and central heating are the only visible 20th-century modifications. Collections of books and paintings and beautiful antique furniture combine with the friendliness of your hosts to make this a most inviting place to stay. There is no need to worry about bringing children along because a portion of the top floor of the house is a nursery with plenty of toys and games to keep children amused for hours. *Directions:* Take the N7 from Dublin to Mountrath and follow signs for the Slieve Bloom mountains which will bring you to Roundwood House 5 km out of town.

ROUNDWOOD HOUSE
Owners: Rosemarie & Frank Kennan
Mountrath
Co Laois, Ireland
Tel: (0502) 32120, Fax: (0502) 32711
E-mail: roundwood@tinet.ie
10 en-suite rooms
£38 per person B&B, dinner £23
Closed Jan, Credit cards: all major
Country house

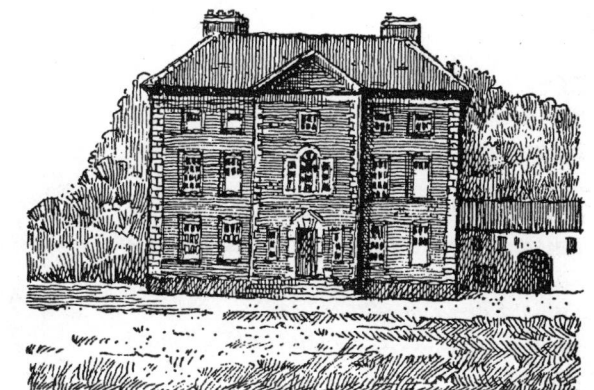

A crooked little lane winds you up the hill to Crookedwood House, a 200-year-old rectory that sits at the crest of the hill overlooking Lough Derragh (the lake of the oaks) where mythology has it that the children of Lir were turned into swans. It's a lovely spot almost in the center of Ireland—a delightful place to unwind and enjoy good food and a warm welcome. Noel is one of Ireland's noted chefs and the recent addition of guestrooms means that diners now also have an agreeable place to lay their heads. Gather by the fire in the reception sitting room and study the menu before going below stairs to the restaurant which is divided into intimate nooks in several whitewashed cellars. The bedrooms are not as imaginative as the food—each has identical decor with matching drapes and bedspreads, reproduction furniture, and an immaculate modern bathroom: more Hilton than Irish county house. The center of Ireland with its quiet roads, low hills, and warren of lakes is a delight to explore (see other Mullingar listings). *Directions:* From Dublin take the Sligo Road (N4). When you are on the Mullingar bypass, exit for Castlepollard, following this road for 10 km to Crookedwood where you turn right by The Wood pub. Crookedwood House is on your right after 2 km.

CROOKEDWOOD HOUSE
Owners: Julie & Noel Kenny
Crookedwood, Mullingar
Co Westmeath, Ireland
Tel: (044) 72165, Fax: (044) 72166
www.karenbrown.com/ireland/crookedwood.html
8 en-suite rooms
Double: £90–£100, dinner £23
Closed 2 weeks in Jan, Credit cards: all major
Restaurant with rooms

Lough Owel Lodge is a modern house set between Lough Owel and a quiet country road that runs into Mullingar. While the house has no architectural distinction, this is a tranquil country spot where you can cycle down quiet roads, stroll the shores of Lough Owel, and generally enjoy the peace and quiet of the center of Ireland. Aideen and Martin Ginnell find that the house works really well for raising a family of four children and providing bed and breakfast, for it is divided into two parts, the front being for guests and the back for their family. I particularly appreciated the large car port which sheltered me from the rain as I arrived. A large sitting room with comfortable sofas and floor-to-ceiling windows offering views of the garden and lake leads into the dining room with its lovely old table and chairs. Upstairs, the most spacious room has an enormous, almost 2-meter-square bed. A family suite consists of a small double bedroom leading to a small twin-bedded room and a large bathroom. A smaller double room has a lovely family-heirloom half-tester bed and small bathroom. Guests often wander down to the lough, enjoy a game of tennis, and make use of the children's game room. Tullynally Castle, Carrickglass Manor, Belvedere House, Fore Abbey, and Athlone Castle are within an hour's drive. *Directions:* Take the N4 from Dublin towards Sligo. After passing the third exit for Mullingar, Lough Owel Lodge is signposted to your left after 1 km.

LOUGH OWEL LODGE
Owners: Aideen & Martin Ginnell
Cullion
Mullingar
Co Westmeath, Ireland
Tel & fax: (044) 48714
www.karenbrown.com/ireland/loughowel.html
5 en-suite rooms
£18–£19 per person B&B, dinner £14
Open Mar to Dec, Credit cards: MC, VS
B&B

Readers' letters praise the warmth of welcome, delectable food, quality of the house, and the utter charm of this country house in the center of Ireland. I totally concur, for a stay at Mornington House with Anne and Warwick, the fifth generation of his family to call this home, is also something I find completely delightful. The O'Haras have an easy way of making guests feel at home. They chat with them in the drawing room after dinner and put a lot of trouble into helping them with their activities and sightseeing in this unspoiled region of Ireland with its lakes, canals, and gently undulating countryside—well off the beaten tourist path. Anne is a talented cook, producing delicious dinners and outstanding breakfasts. Families are welcome and children can be served an early tea. The two front bedrooms are enormous: one has a large brass bed sitting center stage which requires a climb to get into it, while the other has a Victorian double bed and shares the view across the peaceful grounds. The third bedroom, a twin-bedded room, looks out to the side garden and the woods. The oldest wing of the house contains two smaller bedrooms overlooking the kitchen garden. *Directions:* From Dublin take the Sligo Road (N4). When you are on the Mullingar bypass, exit for Castlepollard and follow this road for 10 km to Crookedwood where you turn left by The Wood pub. After 2 km turn right and Mornington House is on your right after 1 km.

MORNINGTON HOUSE
Owners: Anne & Warwick O'Hara
Mornington, Multyfarnham, Mullingar
Co Westmeath, Ireland
Tel: (044) 72191, Fax: (044) 72338
E-mail: morning@indigo.ie
www.karenbrown.com/ireland/morningtonhouse.html
5 rooms, 4 en suite
£32.50 per person B&B, dinnner £20
Open Apr 4 to Oct, Credit cards: AX, VS
Country house

Dromoland Castle is a spectacular, albeit very expensive, place to spend either your first or last night's stay if you are flying into or out of Shannon airport. Before it became a luxury hotel in 1963, Dromoland Castle saw almost 400 years as the ancestral home of the O'Brien clan. Now it is the luxurious sister hotel of the prestigious Ashford Castle. Jacket and tie for gentlemen are required after 7 pm in the elegant, formal dining room and the book-lined bar where guests often settle after dinner to join in the singing of popular Irish ballads. The sumptuous, ornate drawing room is an ideal haven for morning coffee and afternoon tea. Up the grand staircase are found the hotel's premier rooms and luxurious suites and a portrait gallery of past incumbents of the estate. Smaller cozy rooms are located round a courtyard in the castle's oldest part (1736) and have the same lavish amenities: robes, slippers, masses of toiletries, fruit bowl, and a decanter of Irish Mist. Treat yourself to a leisurely breakfast in bed or order dinner from the extensive room service menu (breakfast is not included in the room rates)—the hotel prides itself on its impeccable service. Fishing, horse riding, and bird shooting can be arranged nearby, and tennis courts and Dromoland's golf course are here for you to use. Nearby Bunratty Castle and Folk Park is well worth a visit. *Directions:* The Dromoland estate is on the N18, Ennis to Limerick road, 13 km north of Shannon airport.

DROMOLAND CASTLE
Manager: Mark Nolan
Dromoland, Newmarket-on-Fergus
Co Clare, Ireland
Tel: (061) 368144, Fax: (061) 363355
73 en-suite rooms
Double: £221–£268, Suite: £319–£452**
**breakfast not included*
Open all year, Credit cards: all major
Luxury resort

When Lord Inchquin sold Dromoland Castle in 1963, he moved five minutes up the hill to Thomond House, a large Georgian-style mansion. Now it is home to his nephew Conor O'Brien (the present Lord Inchquin and head of the O'Brien chieftancy) and his family—and what a lovely home it is, with its high-ceilinged rooms looking out through tall windows to the surrounding countryside. Guests enjoy a comfortable drawing room, take breakfast in the dining room, and watch television in the library. A sweeping staircase leads to the upper gallery and bedrooms which are all elegantly kitted out and offer views of the parkland or the adjacent castle. Additional bedrooms are found on the ground floor. Dinner, incorporating farm-fresh ingredients, is served every evening except Sundays. Alternatively, you might want to walk down to Dromoland Castle for a superb formal meal or drive a few kilometers to Durty Nelly's and enjoy casual fare in this traditional Irish pub. Readers' letters overwhelmingly state that they feel they receive a courteous, aloof reception at Thomond House. A stay here is expensive—the only competition is next-door Dromoland Castle! Guests often play golf on the neighboring Dromoland course or roam over the 1,000-acre estate, while farther afield lie the dramatic Cliffs of Moher and the Burren with its rocky landscapes. *Directions:* The Dromoland estate is on the N18, Ennis to Limerick road, 13 km north of Shannon airport. The entrance to Thomond House is south of Dromoland Castle.

THOMOND HOUSE
Owners: Helen & Conor Inchquin
Dromoland
Newmarket-on-Fergus
Co Clare, Ireland
Tel: (061) 368304, Fax: (061) 368285
www.karenbrown.com/ireland/thomondhouse.html
8 en-suite rooms
Double: £130–£170, dinner £30
Closed Christmas, Credit cards: all major
Country house

Newport House, an old Virginia-creeper-covered mansion set amidst gardens overlooking the River Newport, presents a welcoming picture to visitors to the town of the same name. I soon learned that the pursuit of fish is the main reason for staying here since Newport House has the exclusive fishing rights to the adjacent river and Lough Beltra West. In the morning the front hallway is a hive of activity, with ghillies waiting to escort guests for a day of fishing. Wicker picnic hampers are packed with sandwiches, soup, salad, boiled eggs, and porter cake. It's a very traditional country house where an old-fashioned house party atmosphere prevails. After registering their catch in the fishing log, guests exchange fishy tales over dinner and in the bar—a perfect end to an angler's day! The spacious sitting room is less formal than the grand dining room which is presided over by a larger-than-life portrait of Hugh O'Donnel (the last O'Donnel to own the house). First-class food is an important feature here: fish is always included on the menu and Newport House's own salmon cured with whisky is divine. A magnificent sweeping central staircase leads up to the gallery where sunlight cascades through the rooftop dome. Two very special bedrooms have enormous four poster beds—others are more ordinary, while bathrooms are by and large of the dated variety. This formal country house hotel reposes between Achill Island and the mountains of Mayo. *Directions*: Newport is on the N59 between Westport and Achill Island.

NEWPORT HOUSE
Owners: Thelma & Kieran Thompson
Newport
Co Mayo, Ireland
Tel: (098) 41222, Fax: (098) 41613
18 en-suite rooms
Double: £118–£145 Four Poster: £167, dinner £30
Closed mid-Oct to mid-Mar, Credit cards: all major
Country house hotel

Isolated by a tall hedge of cypress trees, Creacon Lodge and its exquisite rose garden look for all the world like a little bit of England transported to Ireland. The inside is just as charming as out for Josephine Flood, your stylish hostess, has everything in decorator-perfect order. Enjoy a drink in the bar, a meal in the handsome dining room or listen to music in the sitting room with its comfy sofas and chairs arranged around the fire. Up a narrow flight of stairs, the little bedrooms with their sloping ceilings are tucked under the roof and their tiny, floor-level windows offer glimpses of the garden. Each bedroom is equipped with TV and direct-dial phone. I loved the rooms in the house, all decorated in light, bright decor with attractive fabrics and wallpapers—a particular favorite is Peach, a ground-floor room named for the color of its decor. Across the courtyard are three bedrooms in the cottage and two in a little gatehouse. The staff is especially friendly and helpful. With advance notice, Josephine is happy to provide an early breakfast for those sailing on the morning ferry (Creacon Lodge is only a 40-km drive from Rosslare harbor). Ten minutes away is the John F. Kennedy Park. The nearby Hook Peninsula with its secluded coves has the oldest lighthouse in Europe. *Directions:* From Wexford take the N25 New Ross to Cork road. Just before reaching New Ross turn left on the R733 signposted John F. Kennedy Park (do not take the first left for JFK Park). After 5 km turn left for Creacon Lodge.

CREACON LODGE HOTEL
Owner: Josephine Flood
Creacon Lower, New Ross
Co Wexford, Ireland
Tel: (051) 421897, Fax: (051) 422560
www.karenbrown.com/ireland/creacon.html
10 en-suite rooms
£30–£40 per person B&B
Open all year, Credit cards: MC, VS
hotel

A cottage, a church, and Hanora's Cottage Guesthouse nestle beside the tumbling River Nire in this delightfully wild and isolated spot on the edge of the Comeragh mountains. The house is of modern, rather boxy, construction with a tidy sitting room and a restaurant downstairs, and upstairs, an array of small color-coordinated bedrooms with soft-pastel walls and matching drapes, bedcovers, and towels. Each bedroom has TV, hairdryer, tea- and coffee-makings, and a small shower room. The nicest accommodation is offered by the more spacious room 8 whose bathroom contains a Jacuzzi tub. Son Eoin (pronounced Owen) offers a set, four-course dinner with lots of choices for starters and main courses. Packed lunches, maps, and directions are available for walks that range from leisurely woodland rambles to challenging hill hikes. Try to plan your stay to include a Saturday so you can accompany Seamus and CJ, the family dog, on their ramble and hear stories of the folklore and history of the rocky, heather-clad Comeraghs. If you're not worn out by walking, visit the local pubs that offer music and dancing. *Directions:* From Clonmel or Dungarvan, follow the R672 as far as Ballymacarbry village where you turn left into the Nire Valley at Melody's Lounge Bar. Travel 5.6 km: Hanora's is beside the church just before the stone bridge.

HANORA'S COTTAGE GUESTHOUSE
Owners: Mary & Seamus Wall
Nire Valley
Via Clonmel
Co Waterford, Ireland
Tel: (052) 36134, Fax: (052) 36540
www.karenbrown.com/ireland/hanoras.html
8 en-suite rooms
£30–£35 per person B&B, dinner £20
Open all year, Credit cards: MC, VS
Guesthouse

Guests at Currarevagh House (pronounced "Curra-reeva") find themselves entering a world reminiscent of the turn of the century. Tranquillity reigns supreme and things are done the good old-fashioned way at Currarevagh House. However, do not be afraid that you will be deprived of central heating and private bathrooms, for this is not the case. Bedrooms are all priced the same. If you book well in advance, you may be able to secure room 1, 2, or 3 in the old house or room 16 in the new wing with its lake views. Try to arrive by 4:30 pm when tea and cakes are served—you will then have enough time for a brisk walk to make room for a delicious dinner at 8 pm. A gong announces dinner and while there are no choices, the helpings are of generous proportions. A tempting breakfast buffet of cold meats, cheeses, and traditional cooked breakfast dishes is spread on the sideboard and the hotel is happy to pack you a picnic lunch for your day's excursion. It's all very old-fashioned and un-decorator perfect, but I must admit that I thoroughly enjoyed it—the Hodgsons really do manage to create the illusion of being back in Victorian times. Harry can arrange for fishing on the adjacent Lough Corrib, the second-largest lake in Ireland, a haven for fishermen. *Directions:* From Galway take the N59 to Oughterard, turn right in the center of the village, and follow the lake shore for the 6-km drive to the house.

CURRAREVAGH HOUSE
Owners: June & Harry Hodgson
Oughterard, Connemara
Co Galway, Ireland
Tel: (091) 552312, Fax: (091) 552731
www.karenbrown.com/ireland/currarevaghhouse.html
15 en-suite rooms
Double: £100–£106*
*plus 10% service
Open Apr 9 to Oct 25, Credit cards: none
Country house hotel

The Narrows, named for the narrow body of water it overlooks, sits on the sea front in the small port of Portaferry with its traditional shops, pubs, and market square. Brothers Will and James Brown were brought up in one of the tall townhouses that makes up their guesthouse and when the adjacent house came up for sale, they and their wives, Sara and Melanie, decided to purchase it, amalgamating the two buildings into a guesthouse and restaurant. While the building is traditional, the decor is fresh and modern, with country-pine furniture throughout. All the bedrooms have water views and similar decor, with twin or double beds topped with plump duvets, coir (coconut matting) covering the floors, and attractive watercolors decorating the walls. The Browns have built their guesthouse to be wheelchair friendly, so all of the modern shower rooms have level-deck showers and there is a ramp into the herb and flower garden found on a high terrace off the back verandah. Sara is in charge of dinner and offers a set three-course menu with choices for each course. Mount Stewart, a fascinating 18th-century house, and its beautiful gardens are a big attraction as is Castle Ward, a 280-acre country estate on the banks of Strangford Lough. *Directions:* From Belfast take the A20 through Newtownards to Portaferry and turn left along Shore Road when you reach the water.

THE NARROWS
Owners: Sara & Will, Melanie, & James Brown
8 Shore Road
Portaferry BT22 1JY
Co Down, Northern Ireland
Tel: (012477) 28148, Fax: (012477) 28105
E-mail: the.narrows@dial.pipex.com
www.karenbrown.com/ireland/narrows.html
13 en-suite rooms
£29 per person B&B
Open all year, Credit cards: all major
Family hotel

On John's retirement the Deanes demolished the holiday cottage they owned on this site and in its place built Croaghross, a stylishly modern building which captures the stunning views of Ballymastocker Strand, one of Donegal's loveliest beaches. While the house is of modern design, the interior is very traditional and furnished with antiques. Relax in the comfortable sitting room and enjoy breakfast and dinner in the elegant dining room. Three bedrooms capture the view (a double, a twin-bedded, and a family room) and each has French windows opening up to private patios. Another very spacious twin-bedded room is specially equipped for wheelchair access, and has one of the best handicapped bathrooms that I saw in Ireland. (I have not quoted rates for the additional very small double-bedded room.) For longer stays there is a three-bedroomed cottage at the far end of their flower-filled garden. Guests often play golf on Portsalon golf course which runs beside the beach. Enjoy spectacular ocean views as you drive round the Fanad Peninsula or traveling farther afield to visit the beautiful gardens and castle in Glenveagh National Park. *Directions:* From Donegal, take the N56 to Letterkenny and on the outskirts of the town look for the T72, signposted for Ramelton and Rathmullen. Cross the bridge in Ramelton and turn left for Portsalon (25 km from Letterkenny). At the crossroads in Portsalon take the Fanad road for 1 km and just before the golf club (right) take a left-hand turn up a narrow lane to Croaghross.

CROAGHROSS
Owners: Kay & John Deane
Portsalon
Co Donegal, Ireland
Tel & fax: (074) 59548
E-mail: jkdeane@iol.ie
www.karenbrown.com/ireland/croaghross.html
5 en-suite rooms
£20–£30 per person B&B, dinner £15
Open mid-Mar to Sep, Credit cards: MC, VS
B&B

Bernhard had always dreamed of owning a castle with a long drive leading up to it—he settled instead for the long driveway leading not to a castle but to St. David's, his "little piece of heaven," and the vast expanse of Lough Derg. Bernhard hails from Austria, and while most of his staff comes from the Continent, St. David's is a quintessentially Irish country house hotel. Welcoming cups of tea, conversation by the fire, walks, and fishing set the pace of life here. Sumptuous fabrics adorn all of the rooms, giving grandeur to the place. Bernhard is both the host and the chef, moving seamlessly from his role as host to the kitchen and back into the dining room. His set menu depends on his inspiration and offers several choices of excellent Irish country house fare for each of the four courses. Five of the bedrooms are on the ground floor—lake views are reserved for the upstairs rooms. I was able to see only two of the upstairs bedrooms, both of which have very snug shower rooms, but Bernhard assured me that all the other rooms have larger bathrooms or shower rooms. I am told that Bernhard's lavish Christmas decorations are a sight to behold. Guests often visit Bunratty, Portumna Castle and forest park with its walks along the lake, and Birr Castle with its lovely gardens. *Directions*: From Nenagh take the N52 (signposted Borrisokane and Birr), turn first left for Puckane, pass the church, bear left by the grotto, turn first right, and follow the lane to St. David's.

ST. DAVID'S   **New**
Owner: Bernhard Klotz
Puckane, Nenagh
Co Tipperary, Ireland
Tel: (067) 24145, Fax: (067) 24388
10 en-suite rooms
Double: £120–£170, dinner £35
Closed Jan to Mar, Credit cards: all major
Country house hotel

Ardeen was an especially welcome haven after we explored the Donegal coast on a particularly gloomy, wet summer's day. This attractive Victorian house was once the town doctor's home. Anne Campbell and her husband had always admired Ardeen's airy rooms and large riverside garden, so when it came up for sale, they jumped at the opportunity to call it home. Breakfast around the large dining-room table is the only meal that Anne prepares, though she is happy to offer advice on where to eat in Ramelton. Guests can plan their sightseeing from the warmth of the sitting room. Upstairs, a sunny yellow double room faces the water and has a lovely en-suite shower room. A twin room enjoys a small shower room and the pretty peach double and an additional twin room share a large bathroom. The adjacent stable has been converted to a snug holiday cottage with an exposed stone living room, attractive kitchen, and two attic bedrooms. Ardeen is an ideal base for exploring the Donegal coastline and visiting Glenveagh National Park and the Glebe Art Gallery with its fine collection of Irish paintings. *Directions:* If you are arriving from Donegal, take the N56 to Letterkenny and on the outskirts of the town look for the T72, signposted for Rathmullen. It's an 11-km drive to Ramelton. When you reach the river turn right, following the bank, and Ardeen is on your right.

ARDEEN
Owner: Anne Campbell
Ramelton
Co Donegal, Ireland
Tel: (074) 51243, Fax: none
5 rooms, 3 en suite
£17–£18.50 per person B&B
Open Easter to Oct, Credit cards: AX, VS
B&B

Rathmullan House has a perfect setting amidst acres of lovingly tended gardens which slope down to a sandy beach, with views of the mountains across Lough Swilly. This large, rambling country house is decorated in a variety of styles from Egyptian (in the new wing), through traditional country house, to Bedouin in the dining pavilion where vast meters of fabric have been gathered across the ceiling to give a tentlike appearance. A three- or four-course dinner is offered with enough selections in each course to satisfy the most discerning diner. After dinner, coffee is served in the coffee lounge. Most spacious, attractive accommodation with large balconies is offered in the large rooms above the Egyptian baths (saltwater swimming pool, sauna, and steam room). Bedrooms in the main house are a mixed bunch, varying from a snug attic under the eaves to large bedrooms with bay windows that have views to the lough. Downstairs is a convivial cellar bar. A 10% service charge is added to your bill. Adjacent to the hotel is a complex of holiday cottages. Rathmullan is a particularly attractive village and there are some spectacular drives round the Fanad Peninsula. Inland lie Glenveagh National Park and the Glebe Art Gallery. Directions: From Donegal town take the N15 to Ballybofey, then the N56 to the outskirts of Letterkenny, through Ramelton, and follow the shores of Lough Swilly through Rathmullan. The house is on your right as you leave the village.

RATHMULLAN HOUSE
Owners: Robin & Bob Wheeler
Rathmullan, Letterkenny
Co Donegal, Ireland
Tel: (074) 58188, Fax: (074) 58200
20 en-suite rooms
Double: £85–£135*
*plus 10% service
Open Mar to Nov, Credit cards: all major
Country house hotel

"There is nothing which has yet been contrived by man by which so much happiness is produced as by a good inn"—Hunters Hotel has adopted Samuel Johnson's words as a creed and they certainly describe it. Dating back to the 1720s, the hotel retains its old-world charm with creaking wooden floorboards, polished tile floors, old prints, beams, ancient sofas covered in old-fashioned chintz, and antique furniture. The Gelletlie family have owned the inn since 1820, and now Tom and Richard Gelletlie (the fifth generation) ably assist their mother, Maureen. There is a delightful feeling of another age which endures in the tradition of vast, Sunday roast lunches (1 pm prompt: book ahead) and afternoon teas of oven-fresh scones and strawberry jam—a particularly delightful feast when enjoyed in the garden on a warm summer's afternoon. You can sleep in bedrooms that kings have slept in—the king of Sweden has paid several visits. I loved my room 12a with its pretty double iron-and-brass bedstead and light, airy decor. Be sure to request a room with a view of the flower-filled gardens stretching beside the hotel down to the River Vartry. Some of the country's most interesting gardens and houses are a short drive away: Powerscourt with its grand gardens, Mount Usher with its informal gardens, and Avondale House, the home of Charles Stewart Parnell with its wooded parklands. *Directions*: Take the N11 from Dublin to Rathnew and turn left in the village for the 1-km drive to Hunters Hotel.

HUNTERS HOTEL
Owners: The Gelletlie family
Rathnew
Co Wicklow, Ireland
Tel: (0404) 40106, Fax: (0404) 40338
16 en-suite rooms
Double: £105–£110, dinner £25
Closed Christmas, Credit cards: all major
Inn

Tinakilly House maintains the purpose for which it was designed—gracious living. The house was built in the 1870s by Captain Robert Halpin, the commander of the ship *Great Eastern* which laid the first telegraph cable connecting Europe to America. Tinakilly House's ornate staircase is reputed to be a copy of the one on this ship. Whether or not this is true is a matter of conjecture, but the captain certainly spared no expense when he built this classical house with its fine, pitch-pine doors and shutters and ornate plasterwork ceilings. Bee and William Power bought the house as a family home, but found the cost of restoration and its size too unmanageable, so decided to open it as a luxurious country house hotel. They have done a splendid job, extending the home and adding rooms that fit in perfectly, furnishing the house with appropriate Victorian furniture, and adding a welcoming charm to the place. Five of the bedrooms have four-poster beds, while all twelve junior suites and the three admiral's suites have breathtaking sea views. Rooms tucked into the original attics are snug and country-cozy and proportionately less expensive. There are some lovely walks on the grounds and Tinakilly is an ideal countryside base for exploring Dublin, Glendalough, and the Wicklow mountains. *Directions:* From Dublin take the N11 (Wexford road) to Rathnew village. Turn left, towards Wicklow, and the entrance to the hotel is on your left as you leave the village.

TINAKILLY HOUSE
Owners: Bee & William Power
Rathnew
Co Wicklow, Ireland
Tel: (0404) 69274, Fax: (0404) 67806
E-mail: wpower@tinakilly.ie
41 en-suite rooms
Double: £132–£160, Suite: £210
Open all year, Credit cards: all major
Country house hotel

Coopershill, built in 1774, has always been home to the O'Hara family and offers the best of both worlds—the luxury of a country house hotel and the warmth of a home. Continuing a tradition begun by Joan O'Hara, Lindy and Brian welcome guests to their lovely home through the massive front door into the stove-warmed hall whose flagged floor is topped by an Oriental rug, and where rain gear hangs at the ready. Beyond lies a parade of lovely rooms tastefully decorated and beautifully furnished with grand, antique furniture, much of which is as old as the house itself. All but three of the bedrooms have the original four-poster or half-tester beds, but, of course, with modern mattresses. All the bedrooms are large and have private bathrooms, though one is across the hall. Ancestors' portraits gaze down upon you in the dining room, set with tables to accommodate individual parties. After an excellent dinner, guests chat round the fire over coffee. Secluded by 500 acres of farm and woodland, there are many delightful walks, and since no shooting is allowed, wildlife is abundant. There's a tennis court, and boating and trout and coarse fishing are available on the River Arrow which flows through the property. There is enough sightseeing beyond the estate to justify spending a whole week here. *Directions:* From Dublin take the N4 to Drumfin (18 km south of Sligo). Turn right towards Riverstown and Coopershill is on your left 1 km before the village.

COOPERSHILL
Owners: Lindy & Brian O'Hara
Riverstown
Co Sligo, Ireland
Tel: (071) 65108, Fax: (071) 65466
www.karenbrown.com/ireland/coopershill.html
8 rooms, 7 en suite
£47–£52 per person B&B, dinner £25
Open Apr to Oct, Credit cards: all major
Country house

Margaret and Dick Johnson have been used to a house full of children, for between them they have nine. Dick has retired as the local vet and now that their family is grown, Margaret has redecorated bedrooms, added shower rooms, and opened their delightful old home to guests. Creaking polished pine floors are topped with rugs, rooms are furnished with antiques, and guests are welcomed as friends. Guests have a comfortable sitting room where they can chat round the fire and relax after dinner round the large oval table. Dinner might be a mackerel soufflé, beef bourguignon with salad and new potatoes, and, for dessert, cheese or profiteroles with raspberry sauce. All but the small single bedroom (bathroom down the hall) have snug en-suite shower rooms. The front bedrooms, a twin and a double, offer the most spacious quarters with lots of room for suitcases and a writing table and chair. Ballyteigue House is about an hour-and-a-half drive from Shannon airport. Margaret finds that guests often use this countryside base for taking day trips to Cashel and Killarney, an hour and a half away. Closer at hand lie Adare (the prettiest village in Ireland) and Bunratty with its interesting folk park. *Directions:* Traveling south on the N20, go through Croom, through a crossroads 7 miles on called O'Rourke's Cross, and take the next right, signposted for Ballyteigue House. Pass Rockhill church and Ballyteigue House is on your right after 500 meters.

BALLYTEIGUE HOUSE
Owners: Margaret & Dick Johnson
Rockhill
Bruree
Co Limerick, Ireland
Tel & fax: (063) 90575
www.karenbrown.com/ireland/ballyteigue.html
5 rooms, 4 en suite
£18–£20 per person B&B, dinner £16
Closed Christmas, Credit cards: MC, VS
Farmhouse B&B

Smugglers Creek Inn is a lively pub sitting high above Rossnowlagh beach, the vast sandy expanse that is reputedly the best surfing beach in Ireland. It's an energetic place where there's always a background of Irish music—on Friday and Saturday evenings there's often a traditional music session which starts at 10 pm and finishes at midnight. Pine benches, chairs, and tables, and a cozy fire flanked by a blackened kettle combine with nautical memorabilia to create an inviting ambiance. An identical menu is available in the bar, conservatory, or quaint little dining room (no smoking). Lots of emphasis is given to seafood, but there are steaks and even sausage and chips for children. Upstairs, the bedrooms are cottagey in size, furnished with old pine, and each accompanied by either a spotless modern shower or bathroom. I particularly enjoyed the three front bedrooms with their wide ocean views. Good roads quickly speed you into Donegal town where Magees is famous for its tweeds and parking is hard to come by. A picturesque day trip takes you to Marble Arch Caves and Florence Court, an 18th-century mansion famous for its ornate ceilings. *Directions:* Rossnowlagh is on the coast between Donegal and Ballyshannon. Smugglers Creek Inn is about 8 km north of Ballyshannon on the coast road, signposted from the country road that runs out of sight of the beach.

SMUGGLERS CREEK INN
Owner: Conor Britton
Rossnowlagh
Co Donegal, Ireland
Tel: (072) 52366, Fax: none
5 en-suite rooms
£25–£35 per person B&B
Open all year, Credit cards: MC, VS
Inn

In summer, the driveway of Rosturk Woods is lined with wild red fuchsias which lead you to the low white house hugging a vast expanse of firm, sandy beach on the shores of Clew Bay. Home to Louisa and Alan Stoney and their young family (Alan grew up in the imposing castle next door, while Louisa's parents live up the road), the house has the feel of an old cottage, though it is only a few years old. Bedrooms have stripped-pine doors and several have pine-paneled, sloping ceilings. There's a lot of old pine furniture, antique pieces, and attractive prints and fabrics. The house cleverly divides so that a wing of two or three large bedrooms, a living room, and a kitchen can be closed off and used as self-catering accommodation (with the option of dinner being served). Dinner is available with advance notice though guests often walk to a little restaurant down the road. Louisa can sometimes direct you to nearby places where traditional Irish music is played. You can hire a boat for a full- or half-day trip on Clew Bay. In contrast to the lush green fields and long sandy beaches that hug Clew Bay, a short drive brings you to the wilder, more rugged scenery of Achill Island. To the south lie Newport and Westport. *Directions:* From Westport take the N59 through Newport towards Achill Island. Before you arrive in Mulrany, cross the Owengarve river and after 500 meters turn left into the woodland to Rosturk Woods.

ROSTURK WOODS
Owners: Louisa & Alan Stoney
Rosturk, Mulrany
Co Mayo, Ireland
Tel & fax: (098) 36264
E-mail: stoney@iol.ie
www.karenbrown.com/ireland/rosturk.html
3 en-suite rooms
£22.50–£27.50 per person B&B, dinner £20
Open Mar to Dec, Credit cards: none
B&B

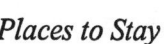

Ballymaloe House is a rambling, 17th-century manor house built onto an old Norman keep surrounded by lawns, a small golf course kept cropped by grazing sheep, and 400 acres of farmland. Run by members of the extended Allen family, Ballymaloe has established a reputation for outstanding hospitality and superb food, yet everything is decidedly simple and homey. Guests gather before dinner in the lounge to make their selections from the set menu which offers four or five choices for each course. The bedrooms in the main house come in all shapes and sizes, from large and airy to cozy and paneled. Several ground-floor rooms have been designed to take wheelchairs. Surrounding a courtyard, the smaller stable bedrooms offer country-cottage charm, sprigged-flowered wallpaper, and beamed ceilings for those on the upper floor. Most unusual accommodations are in the doll-sized gatekeeper's cottage which is just large enough to have a bathroom on the ground floor and a ladder to the twin-bedded room above, with its tiny, log-burning fireplace. Perhaps the most famous of the Allen clan is Darina Allen who came here to learn cooking, married son Tim, then founded Ballymaloe Cookery School in the courtyard of her nearby home. Her brother Rory O'Connell is head chef at Ballymaloe House. *Directions:* Ballymaloe is signposted from the N25 (Cork to Waterford road). Ballymaloe is 3 km beyond Cloyne on the Ballycotton Road.

BALLYMALOE HOUSE
Owners: The Allen family
Shanagarry
Midleton
Co Cork, Ireland
Tel: (021) 652531, Fax: (021) 652021
www.karenbrown.com/ireland/ballymaloehouse.html
30 en-suite rooms
Double: £125–£150
Closed Christmas, Credit cards: all major
Country house hotel

The Morrisseys are the first family to live at Carrigahilla House since it closed its doors as a convent. Margaret, an enthusiastic gardener, has transformed over 3 acres of grounds into gardens (open to the public) ranging from a wildflower meadow to a formal rose garden. There are five guestrooms, all with small en-suite shower rooms. Three smaller bedrooms are either doubles or twins. I really enjoyed the largest bedrooms, the Nuns' Parlor and the Nuns' Visitors' Room, which have grander furniture and the most lovely views of the gardens. The beautifully furnished drawing room is a delightful place to relax, though on warm days guests prefer to wander through the plant-filled conservatory to the patio beside the formal garden—a delightful spot to enjoy afternoon tea. The restaurant is always open for guests and on Friday and Saturday evenings to outside diners—Vincent is the chef. The seaside village of Stradbally is very picturesque as is the drive between here and Tramore, a coastal village near Waterford where touring the world-famous crystal factory is a must. Vincent is happy to outline walks in the nearby Comeragh mountains or plan a day's round-trip drive to include a visit to Kilkenny, Cashel, and Lismore. *Directions:* From the N25 (Cork to Waterford road) turn south at Griffin's garage (just west of Kilmathomas) and continue for 6½ km where you follow signposts for Carrigahilla House, just behind the large Catholic church on the outskirts of the village.

CARRIGAHILLA HOUSE
Owners: Margaret & Vincent Morrissey
Stradbally
Co Waterford, Ireland
Tel & fax: (051) 293127
www.karenbrown.com/ireland/carrighilla.html
5 en-suite rooms
£22–£28 per person B&B, dinner £20–£25
Open Mar to Dec, Credit cards: MC, VS
B&B

Riverrun House looks for all the world like an old farmhouse, when in fact it was built just a few years ago using a traditional farmhouse design with old windows, doors, and roof slates. The delightful deception continues inside where old-fashioned doors, deep skirting boards, and a traditional fireplace add appeal to the little sitting room. Bedrooms are charming, plainly and unfussily decorated, and all have sparkling modern bathrooms with showers. Two downstairs rooms have farmhouse half-doors and private patios. End rooms are larger. For dinner guests can walk the few yards to Paddy's Pub or The Derg. Riverrun House has a tennis court and bikes for guests to borrow—there's no shortage of quiet country lanes. You can hire a boat for the day and enjoy Lough Derg. Farther afield lies Bunratty Castle and Folk Park, and Clonmacnois, the 6th-century monastic settlement on the Shannon river. *Directions:* Nenagh is on the N7, Limerick to Dublin road. Leave the main road in Nenagh and travel through Borrisokane and Ballinderry to Terryglass. Riverrun House is opposite the bridge in the village.

RIVERRUN HOUSE
Owners: Lucy & Tom Sanders
Terryglass
Nenagh
Co Tipperary, Ireland
Tel: (067) 22125, Fax: (067) 22187
www.karenbrown.com/ireland/riverrun.html
6 en-suite rooms
£22.50 per person B&B
Open all year, Credit cards: AX, VS
B&B

Not only is Tir Na Fiúise the perfect place to stay to experience rural Ireland, it also has the most vivacious of young owners in Inez and Niall Heenan. While Niall farms organically and Inez is the principal of a Gaelschool (a school where Irish is the language of instruction), they both have time to give of themselves enthusiastically to their guests, encouraging them to take a guided walk around the farm, cycle the quiet lanes, try their hands at fishing from their boat on the lough, visit the Sunday market, and join in village activities. Bedrooms are simply decorated and neat as new pins, four with en-suite showers and one with its bathroom next door. The lovely parlor is the perfect place to relax and enjoy a welcoming pot of tea and homemade scones and jam. A feast of a breakfast is served until noon. The Heenans have converted the barns just down the lane into one- and two-bedroomed self-catering cottages for those who wish to stay for a week. If you must rush off to tourist spots, Bunratty Folk Park is an hour-and-a-half's drive away (as is Shannon airport). Closer at hand is the ancient monastic settlement of Clonmacnois and Birr Castle with its gardens and telescope. *Directions*: Nenagh is on the N7, Limerick to Dublin road. Leave the main road in Nenagh and travel through Borrisokane and Ballinderry to Terryglass. The lane that leads to Tir Na Fiúise (1 km on your left) is opposite the bridge in the village.

TIR NA FIÚISE   **New**
Owners: Inez & Niall Heenan
Terryglass, Nenagh
Co Tipperary, Ireland
Tel & fax: (067) 22041
E-mail: nheenan@tinet.ie
5 rooms, 4 en suite
£20 per person B&B
Open Easter to Oct, Credit cards: MC, VS
Farmhouse B&B

As you enter the Mount Juliet estate, you may catch glimpses of pheasants feeding along the driveway or see riders enjoying a pony trek through the 1,500-acre walled estate. A narrow, mellow-stone bridge takes you across the River Nore to the heart of Ireland's premier luxury resort. Guests need not travel beyond the estate's boundaries, for here you can enjoy swimming, relaxing at the spa and leisure centre, tennis, croquet, archery, clay-pigeon shooting, fishing for salmon and trout along the Nore, and riding along kilometers of idyllic park and woodland trails. Golfers can sharpen up their game at the David Leadbetter Golf Academy before taking on the magnificent Jack-Nicklaus-designed championship golf course. With lawns tumbling down to the river and overlooking fenced pastures and vast woodlands, Mount Juliet was built as a grand home for the Earls of Carrick in the 1760s. Its numerous rooms have received a complete and elegant revamping to provide quiet lounges, distinguished dining, clubby bars, a parade of deluxe bedrooms, and two superlative suites. More casual accommodation and dining is available in Hunters Yard, a stableyard-like complex beside the golf clubhouse. *Directions:* Thomastown is on the Kilkenny to Waterford road. The 5-km drive to the hotel is signposted from the center of town.

MOUNT JULIET
Manager: Stan Power
Thomastown
Co Kilkenny, Ireland
Tel: (056) 24455, Fax: (056) 24522
54 en-suite rooms
Double: £150–£295, Suite: £300**
**breakfast not included*
Open all year, Credit cards: all major
Luxury resort

Margaret and Tony are very proud that they are only the fourth family to own Tullaghan House, the oldest home in western Ireland (1750). The Hollands saw Tullaghan's "for sale" sign, went to take a peek, and on impulse bought the house. It came complete with many lovely old features and Margaret and Tony have gone to pains to keep the old-fashioned feel of the house while adding modern plumbing and heating, and decorating the home from top to bottom. The downstairs rooms are now a restaurant and Tony has turned his hand to cooking. Upstairs, guests have a little sitting room and all the double-bedded bedrooms are attractively, though not elaborately, decorated. All have small televisions and snug, modern shower rooms. Tullaghan's vast estates are long gone and the old road between Sligo and Donegal, now a quiet lane, runs up against the back of the house, while the new main road runs along the bottom of the front garden. It's a convenient place to stay for exploring Yeats country and a 25-kilometer drive finds you in either Donegal or Sligo. Margaret is passionate about Lissadell House which is very near to her family home. Walk through the fields to the nearby beach and up to Bundoran, a bucket-and-spade-brigade seaside town. Additional walks lead you through the bogs and into the mountains. *Directions:* Tullaghan House is on the N15 midway between Donegal and Sligo.

TULLAGHAN HOUSE
Owners: Margaret & Tony Holland
Tullaghan
Co Leitrim, Ireland
Tel: (072) 41515, Fax: (072) 43999
6 en-suite rooms
£25 per person B&B
Open all year, Credit cards: MC, VS
B&B

Ardtara, a grand home with well-proportioned rooms and lovely stained-glass windows, was built as a home in 1856 by the Clark family who owned the village linen mill. With a downturn in the Clark family fortunes, the gates were shut and for many years the house lay sleeping until it received a new lease of life, opening as a jewel of a country house hotel in 1994. Modern plumbing, central heating, and deluxe bathrooms with luxurious showers over the tubs have been added. A great many of the 16 fireplaces have been converted to open gas fires which give the house a cheerful warmth and means that all but one of the bedrooms has a cozy fireplace. Lovely antiques grace all the rooms and guests enjoy a drink in one of the gracious sitting rooms before dinner in the impressive dining room with its hunting frieze and ceiling almost covered by an enormous glass skylight. This is a perfect location for taking a day-long trip along the lovely Antrim coast and visiting the famous Giant's Causeway. Derry town is just an hour's drive away and guests often enjoy taking a guided walk around the city walls. *Directions:* From Belfast take the M2 motorway to the A6 (Derry road). After Castledawn take the A29 Coleraine road and just beyond Maghera turn right, signposted Upperlands and Kilrea. Go through the village of Upperlands and the hotel is signposted to your left.

ARDTARA COUNTRY HOUSE
Owner: Maebeth Fenton
Manager: Mary Braslin
8 Gorteade Road
Upperlands BT46 5SA
Co Londonderry, Northern Ireland
Tel: (01648) 44490, Fax: (01648) 45080
8 en-suite rooms
Double: £110–£150, dinner £25
Closed Christmas, Credit cards: all major
Country house hotel

Waterford Crystal is **the** reason that tourists come to Waterford and a grand place to stay is with Barbara, Leslie, and Charlie Brown at their delightful guesthouse on a peaceful side street just a few minutes' walk from the heart of this busy city. Leslie has a quiet, welcoming way also found in Charlie, his faithful golden Labrador. Charlie must be the most photographed dog in Ireland—Leslie just has to say, "photograph" and Charlie poses on cue. He'll be happy to take you for a walk around town and has been known, when he senses that he has won a guest's heart, to curl up on the sofa with him in the TV room. Upstairs are four attractive twin- or double-bedded rooms, each accompanied by a snug shower room (one is across the hall). The most spacious quarters are at the top of the house—a large pine-paneled room with extra beds for children. Leslie often directs guests in the evening to an excellent show of Irish dancing, music, and singing held in the lovely old City Hall (Thursdays, Saturdays, and Sundays May to October). Stay for several days: venture along the pretty coastal road to Dungarven and take the little ferry across Waterford harbor to explore the Hook Peninsula. *Directions*: Arriving in Waterford from the north, cross the river, follow the road along the quay, pass the Tower Hotel on your left, and at the second set of traffic lights turn left into South Parade. Brown's is on your right after 700 meters.

BROWN'S   *New*
Owners: Barbara & Leslie Brown
29 South Parade
Waterford
Co Waterford, Ireland
Tel: (051) 870594, Fax: (051) 871923
E-mail: browns@twe.iol.ie
4 rooms, 3 en suite
£22 per person B&B
Closed Christmas & New Year, Credit cards: MC, VS
Guesthouse

This 200-acre dairy and cattle farm is a delight for adults and children alike: as well as farm activities there are pony rides (on a leading rein) and tennis courts. Such is the popularity of the place that people who came as children are now returning with their children. Whenever David Kent is not occupied with farm matters, he loves to talk to visitors and discuss the farm and what to do and see in the area—the Waterford crystal factory is a big draw. Margaret is one of those people who shows her appreciation of her guests by feeding them lavishly. She delights in the preparation of dishes using meat from the farm and homegrown fruits (strawberries, raspberries, gooseberries, apples, and rhubarb, to name but a few) and vegetables—her specialty is her homemade ice cream. Her bountiful breakfasts have won her national awards. Guests are served after-dinner coffee in the lounge and often linger for discussions around the fireside. Upstairs, the bedrooms are delightfully decorated. Four spacious en-suite rooms have spanking new bathrooms and three have extra beds, making them ideal for family accommodation. Two small twin rooms are perfect for children and share a shower room. *Directions:* To find the house, take the road from Waterford toward Dunmore East. Three km after passing the regional hospital, take the left fork toward Passage East. Foxmount Farm is signposted on the right 500 meters from the Maxol garage.

FOXMOUNT FARM
Owners: Margaret & David Kent
Dunmore East Road
Waterford
Co Waterford, Ireland
Tel: (051) 874308, Fax: (051) 854906
www.karenbrown.com/ireland/foxmountfarm.html
6 rooms, 4 en-suite
£20–£23 per person B&B, dinner £17
Open Mar to Oct, Credit cards: none
Farmhouse B&B

The owner's plans for Clonard House, begun in 1783, showed a grand three-story structure, but skirmishes with the British continually interrupted construction and depleted funds so he got no farther than the second floor, leaving the grand central staircase to curve into the ceiling. The massive front door opens to a smiling welcome from Kathleen Hayes who takes a great interest in her guests and pride in her home. I particularly admired her traditional, high-ceilinged sitting room with its peach-colored walls and traditional chairs covered in soft colors that coordinate with the draperies and carpet. Crisp white tablecloths top the little tables in the attractive dining room where guests enjoy traditional breakfasts and hearty dinners. The bedrooms are all appealingly decorated and have TVs, en-suite showers, and hairdryers. The five bedrooms that face the front of the house, while smaller in size, offer lovely views across farmland to the distant sea. Being just a short drive from Rosslare, Clonard House is ideal for your first or last nights in Ireland if you are arriving by ferry. Sightseeing attractions nearby include the Irish National Heritage Park, Wexford, and Johnstown Castle garden and agricultural museum. *Directions:* From Rosslare travel 13 km towards Wexford, make a left at the first roundabout (N25), left at the second roundabout on to the R733, and immediately left to Clonard House.

CLONARD HOUSE
Owners: Kathleen & John Hayes
Clonard Great
Wexford
Co Wexford, Ireland
Tel: (053) 47337, Fax: (053) 43141
www.karenbrown.com/ireland/clonard.html
9 en-suite rooms
£21 per person B&B
Open Easter to mid-Nov, Credit cards: MC, VS
Farmhouse B&B

Youghal (pronounced "you all" with an American southern drawl), a workaday fishing port, is beginning to flaunt its historic past: drab, gray buildings are being restored, empty shopfronts are coming to life, and, standing amongst them, Aherne's old-world pub exterior is decked out in shiny new paint. Aherne's pub, in the Fitzgibbon family since 1923, includes a seafood restaurant and bedrooms. There's an old-world, traditional atmosphere in the bars where you can enjoy a pint with the locals and an array of tempting bar food. The restaurant specializes in locally caught seafood and the menu changes daily, depending on what is fresh and available. In the guests' sitting room, a cozy fire is flanked by comfortable sofas and a coffee table stacked with books on all things Irish. Three ground-floor bedrooms offer easy access, with one specially equipped for wheelchairs. I particularly enjoyed the upstairs rooms which have little balconies facing the courtyard. If you want privacy, request one of the suites in the adjacent townhouse. All guestrooms have attractive decor, antique furniture, and large firm beds, each accompanied by an immaculate bathroom. Stop by the Visitors' Centre and pick up a map which directs you on a walking tour of the walled port. *Directions:* Youghal is between Waterford and Cork on the N25. Aherne's is on the main street in town.

AHERNE'S
Owners: Gaye, Kate, John, & David Fitzgibbon
163 North Main Street
Youghal
Co Cork, Ireland
Tel: (024) 92424, Fax: (024) 93633
E-mail: ahe@iol.ie
www.karenbrown.com/ireland/ahernes.html
12 en-suite rooms
Double: £120
Open all year, Credit cards: all major
Restaurant with rooms

Key Map

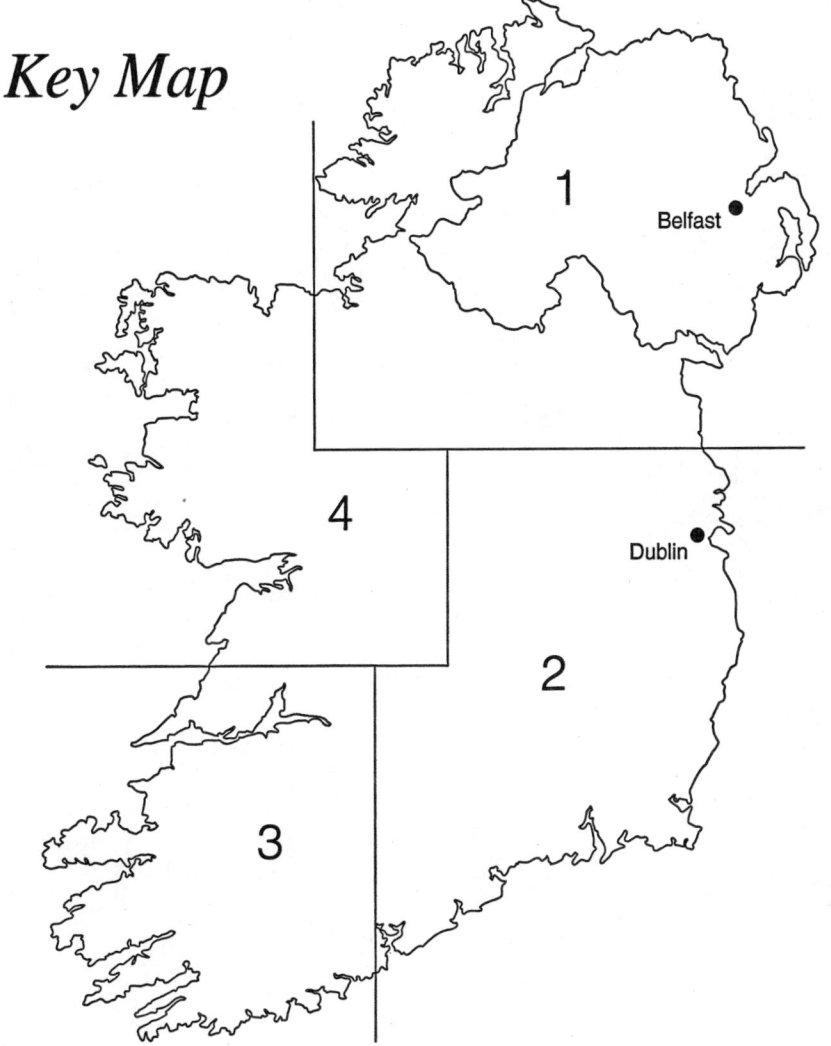

Belfast

Dublin

1

4

2

3

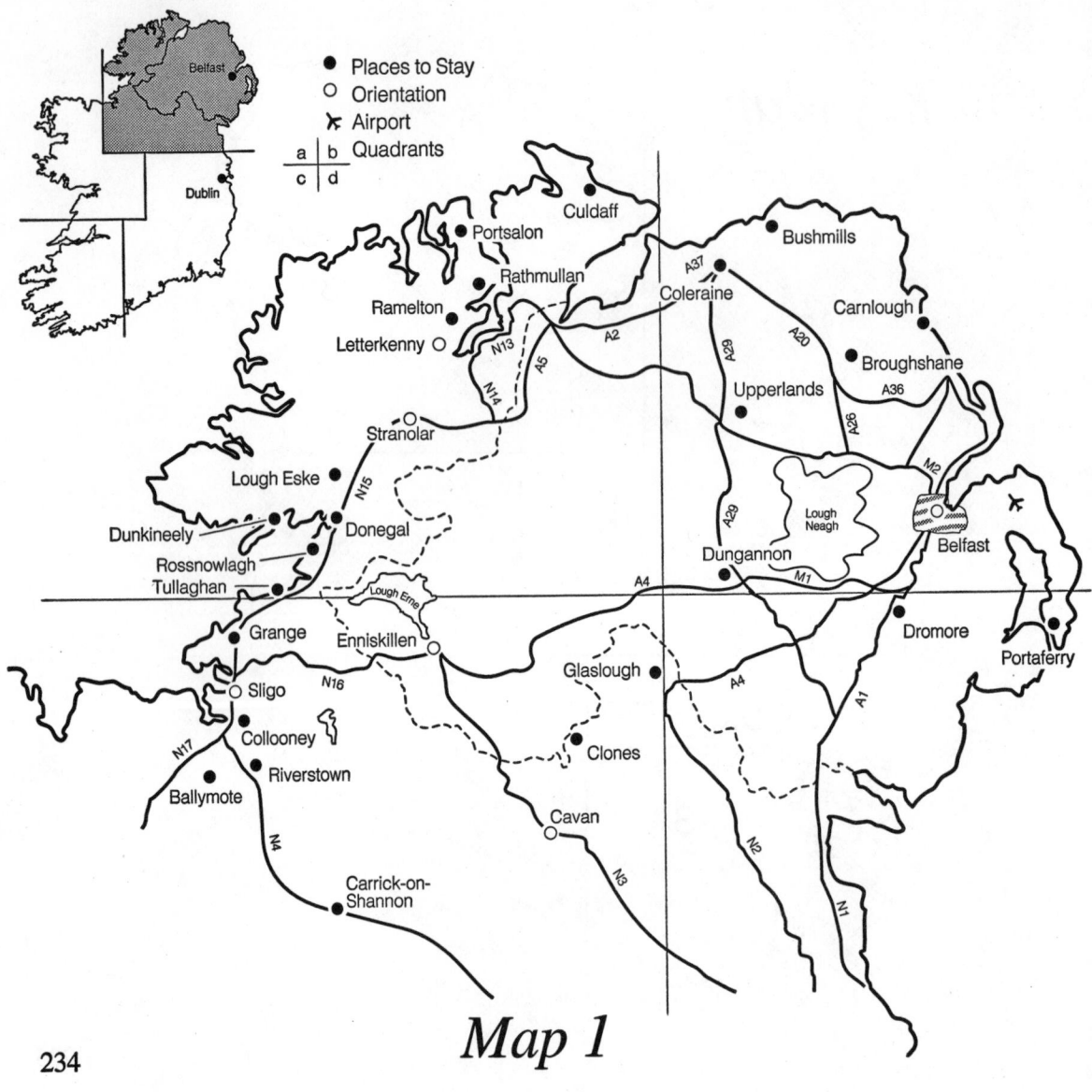

Map 1

Map 2

235

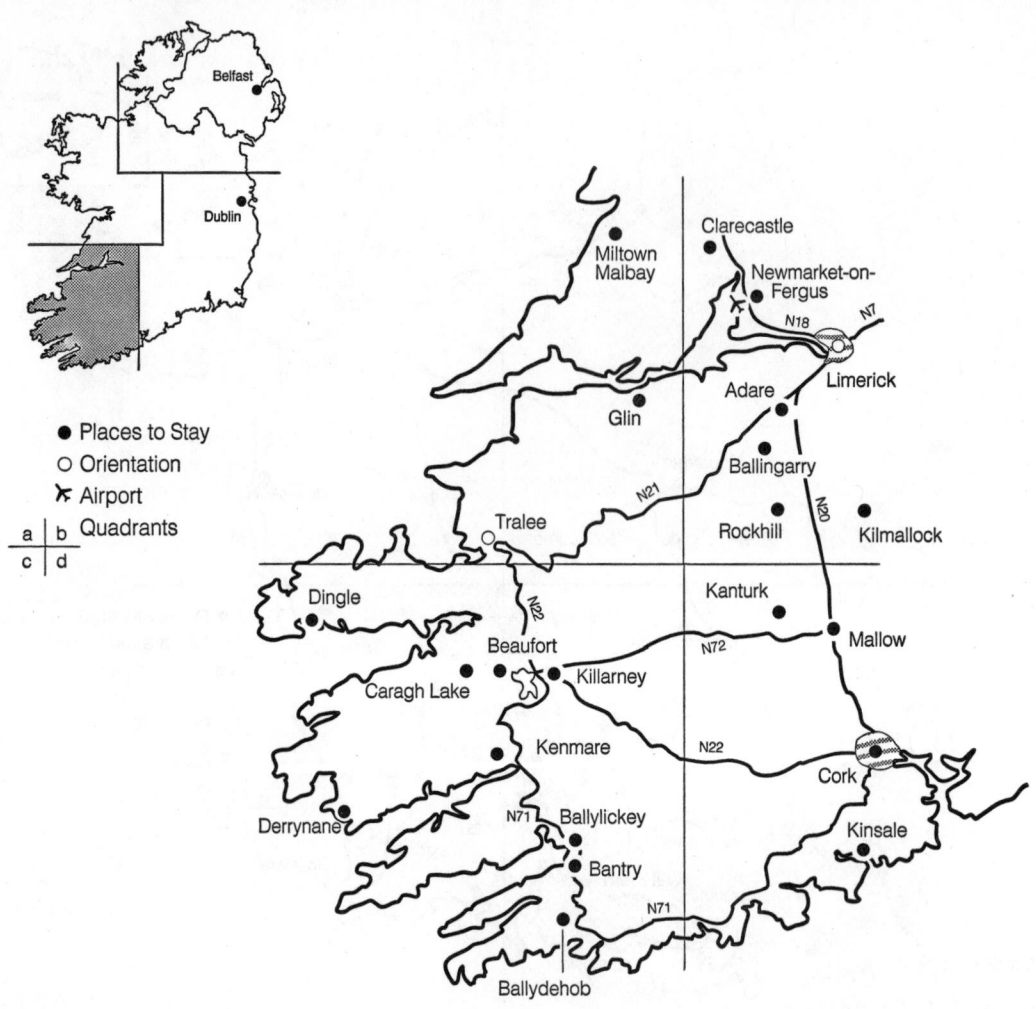

Belfast

Dublin

● Places to Stay
○ Orientation
✈ Airport

a	b
c	d

Quadrants

Clarecastle

Miltown
Malbay

Newmarket-on-
Fergus

N18

N7

Adare

Limerick

Glin

Ballingarry

N21

N20

Rockhill

Kilmallock

Tralee

Kanturk

Dingle

N22

Mallow

Beaufort

N72

Caragh Lake

Killarney

Kenmare

N22

Derrynane

N71

Ballylickey

Cork

Kinsale

Bantry

N71

Ballydehob

Map 3

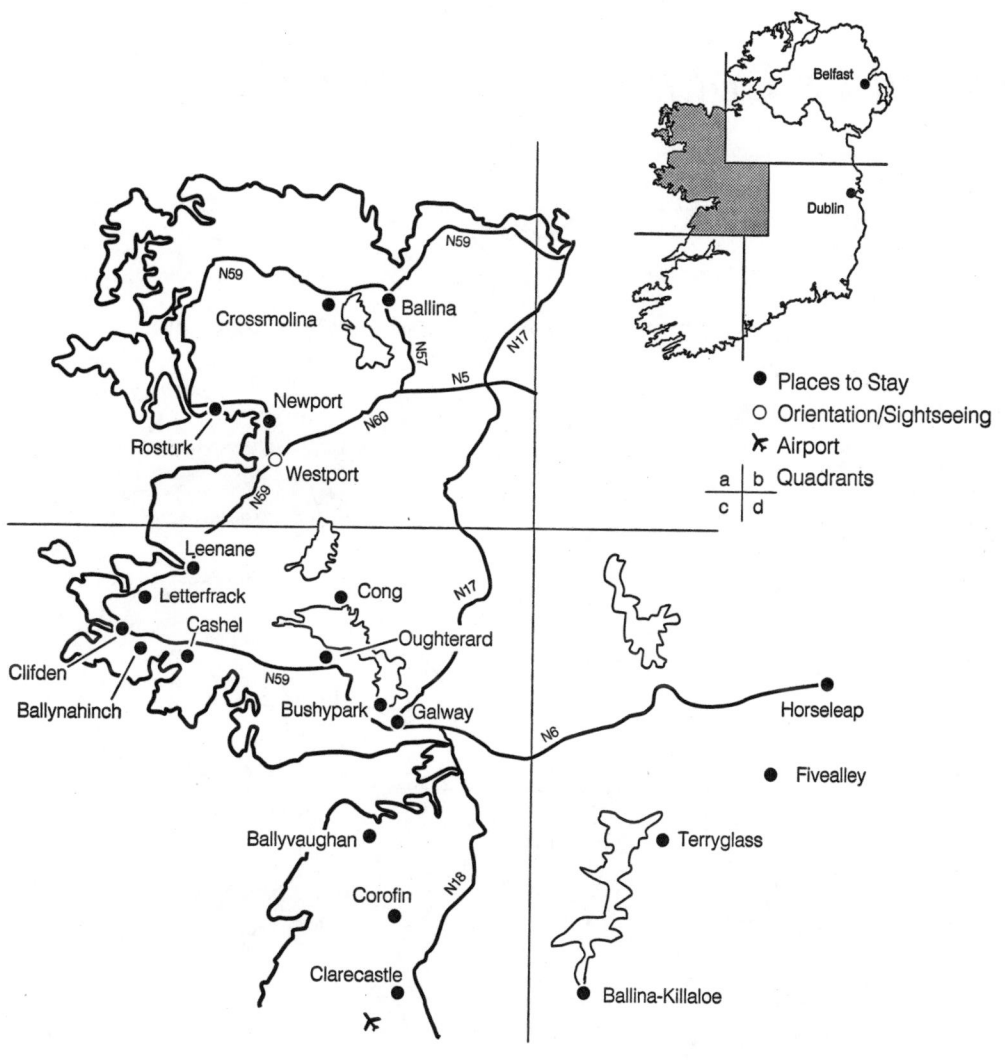

Belfast

Dublin

● Places to Stay
○ Orientation/Sightseeing
✈ Airport
a | b   Quadrants
c | d

N59

N59

Crossmolina   ● Ballina

N57

N5

N17

● Newport

N60

Rosturk

○ Westport

N59

● Leenane

● Letterfrack   ● Cong

N17

Cashel

Clifden   ● Oughterard

Ballynahinch

N59

Bushypark   ● Galway

N6   ● Horseleap

● Fivealley

Ballyvaughan ●

● Terryglass

Corofin ●

N18

Clarecastle ●

✈

● Ballina-Killaloe

Map 4

237

Ireland's Counties

ATLANTIC
OCEAN

Donegal

Londonderry

Antrim

Tyrone

Down

Fermanagh

Armagh

Sligo

Monaghan

Mayo

Leitrim

Cavan

Louth

Roscommon

Longford

Meath

Westmeath

Galway

Offaly

Dublin

Kildare

Wicklow

Laois

IRISH SEA

Clare

Carlow

Tipperary

Kilkenny

Wexford

Limerick

Waterford

Kerry

Cork

Places to Stay by County

County Antrim
Broughshane, Dunaird House
Bushmills, The Bushmills Inn
Carnlough, Londonderry Arms

County Carlow
Bagenalstown, Kilgraney House
Borris, Lorum Old Rectory

County Clare
Ballyvaughan, Gregans Castle
Clarecastle, Carnelly House
Corofin, Fergus View
Miltown Malbay, Berry Lodge
Newmarket-on-Fergus, Dromoland Castle
    Thomond House

County Cork
Ballydehob, Lynwood
Ballylickey, Sea View House Hotel
    Manor House
Bantry, Bantry House
    Dunauley
Castlelyons, Ballyvolane House
Conna, Conna House
Cork, Hayfield House
    Seven North Mall
Killeagh, Ballymakeigh House

Kinsale, O'Connors
    Old Bank House
    The Old Presbytery
    Scilly House Inn
    Sovereign House
Mallow, Longueville House
Midleton, Glenview House
Shanagarry, Ballymaloe House
Youghal, Aherne's

County Donegal
Culdaff, Culdaff House
Donegal, St. Ernan's House Hotel
Dunkineely, Castle Murray House
    Killaghtee House
Lough Eske, Ardnamona
Portsalon, Croaghross
Rathmullan, Rathmullan House
Ramelton, Ardeen
Rossnowlagh, Smugglers Creek Inn

County Down
Dromore, Sylvan Hill House
Portaferry, The Narrows

County Dublin
Dublin, Adams Trinity Hotel
    Albany House
    Belcamp Hutchinson

County Dublin (cont.)

Dublin, Bewley's Hotel
    Butlers
    Cedar Lodge
    The Clarence
    Hibernian Hotel
    The Merrion
    Mespil Hotel
    Park Lodge
    Raglan Lodge
    Russell Court Hotel
    Shelbourne Hotel
Monkstown, Chestnut Lodge

County Galway

Bushypark, Killeen House
Ballynahinch, Ballynahinch Castle
Cashel, Cashel House
Clifden, Mal Dua
    The Quay House
    Rock Glen Hotel
Galway, Norman Villa
Leenane, Delphi Lodge
Letterfrack, Rosleague Manor
Oughterard, Currarevagh House

County Kerry

Beaufort, Beaufort House
Caragh Lake, Caragh Lodge
    Glendalough House
Derrynane, Iskeroon

Dingle, Cleevaun
    Doyle's Bar & Townhouse
    Greenmount House
    The Old Stone House
Kenmare, Hawthorne House
    Park Hotel
    Sallyport House
    Shelburne Lodge
Killarney, Earls Court
    Kathleen's Country House

County Kildare

Maynooth, Moyglare Manor

County Kilkenny

Castlecomer, Wandesforde House
Freshford, Kilrush House
Kilkenny, Dunromin
Maddoxtown, Blanchville House
Thomastown, Mount Juliet

County Laois

Abbeyleix, Preston House
Mountrath, Roundwood House

County Leitrim

Carrick-on-Shannon, Glencarne House
    Hollywell
Tullaghan, Tullaghan House

County Limerick

Adare, Adare Manor
    Dunraven Arms

County Limerick (cont.)
Adare, Glenelg House
      Sandfield House
Ballingarry, Echo Lodge
Glin, Glin Castle
Kilmallock, Flemingstown House
Rockhill, Ballyteigue House

County Londonderry
Coleraine, Greenhill House
Upperlands, Ardtara Country House

County Mayo
Ballina, Ashley House
Cong, Ashford Castle
Crossmolina Enniscoe House
      Kilmurray House
Newport, Newport House
Rosturk, Rosturk Woods

County Monaghan
Clones, Hilton Park
Glaslough, Castle Leslie

County Offaly
Fivealley, Parkmore Farmhouse

County Sligo
Ballymote, Temple House
Collooney, Markree Castle
Grange, Horse Holiday Farm
Riverstown, Coopershill

County Tipperary
Ballina Killaloe, Waterman's Lodge
Bansha, Bansha House
Cashel, Ardmayle House
Puckane, St David's
Terryglass, Riverrun House
      Tir Na Fiúse

County Tyrone
Dungannon, Grange Lodge

County Waterford
Annestown, Annestown House
Cappoquin, Richmond House
Four-Mile-Water, Glasha
Glencairn, Buggy's Glencairn Inn
Nire Valley, Hanora's Cottage Guesthouse
Stradbally, Carrigahilla House
Waterford, Brown's
      Foxmount Farm

County Westmeath
Horseleap, Temple
Mullingar, Crookedwood House
      Lough Owel Lodge
      Mornington House

County Wexford
Ballymurn, Ballinkeele House
Bunclody, Clohamon House
Gorey, Marlfield House
Killinierin, Woodlands Farmhouse

County Wexford (cont.)
New Ross, Creacon Lodge Hotel
Wexford, Clonard House

County Wicklow
Arklow, Plattenstown House
Ballinaclash, Whaley Abbey
Enniskerry, Enniscree Lodge
Laragh, Mitchells of Laragh
Rathnew, Hunters Hotel
        Tinakilly House

Members of Hidden Ireland 1998

Listed alphabetically by house

Ardnamona House, Lough Eske
Ballinkeele House, Ballymurn
Ballyvolane House, Castlelyons
Bantry House, Bantry
Beaufort House, Beaufort
Blanchville House, Maddoxtown
Carnelly House, Clarecastle
Clohamon House, Bunclody
Delphi Lodge, Leenane
Enniscoe House, Crossmolina
Glendalough House, Caragh Lake
Glenlohane, Kanturk
Hilton park, Clones
Iskeroon, Derrynane
Kilgraney House, Bagnelstown
Kilrush House, Freshford
Lorum Old Rectory, Borris
Mornington House, Mullingar
The Quay House, Clifden
Roundwood House, Mountrath
Sovereign House, Kinsale
Temple House, Ballymote
Thomond House, Newmarket-on-Fergus

Members of Ireland's Blue Book 1998

Listed alphabetically by house

Aherne's, Youghal
Ballylickey Manor House, Ballylickey
Ballymaloe House, Shanagarry
Caragh Lodge, Caragh Lake
Cashel House, Cashel
Coopershill, Riverstown
Crookedwood House, Crookedwood, Mullingar
Currarevagh House, Oughterard
Doyle's Bar & Townhouse, Dingle
Enniscoe House, Crossmolina
Glin Castle, Glin
Gregans Castle, Ballyvaughan
Hunters Hotel, Rathnew
Longueville House, Mallow
Marlfield House, Gorey
Moyglare Manor, Maynooth
Mustard Seed at Echo Lodge, Ballingarry
Newport House, Newport
Park Hotel, Kenmare
Rathmullan House, Rathmullan
Rosleague Manor, Letterfrack
St. David's, Puckane
St. Ernan's House Hotel, Donegal
Tinakilly House, Rathnew

Index

S

Sally Gap, 31
Sallyport House, Kenmare, 178
Sandfield House, Adare, 90
Scariff Inn, 47
Scilly House Inn, Kinsale, 189
Sea View House Hotel, Ballylickey, 100
Seanachie, 35
Seven North Mall, Cork, 134
Shanagarry
    Ballymaloe House, 222, 244
Shelbourne Hotel, Dublin, 159, 22
Shelburne Lodge, Kenmare, 179
Shell House, 35
Shopping (Introduction), 9
Sightseeing (Introduction), 18
Skellig Michael, 49
Skibbereen, 43
Slea Head, 55
Slea Head Drive, 54
Slieve League Cliffs, 77
Sligo, 70, 73
    County Museum, 73
Smugglers Creek Inn, Rossnowlagh, 220
Sneem, 47
Sovereign House, Kinsale, 190, 243
St. David's, Puckane, 213
St. Ernan's House Hotel, Donegal, 144, 244
Stradbally, Co Kerry, 57
Stradbally, Co Waterford
    Carrigahilla House, 223
Sylvan Hill House, Dromore, 145

T

Tarbert Ferry, 57
Teilean, 77
Telin, 77
Temple House, Ballymote, 101, 243
Temple, Horseleap, 173
Terryglass
    Riverrun House, 224
    Tir na Fiúise, 225
The Clarence, Dublin, 152
The Mustard Seed at Echo Lodge, Ballingarry, 97
The Narrows, Portaferry, 211
The Old Presbytery, Kinsale, 188
The Old Stone House, Dingle, 143
Thomastown
    Mount Juliet, 226
Thomond House, Newmarket-on-Fergus, 206, 243
Thoor Ballylee (Yeats's Home), 63
Timoleague, 43
Tinakilly House, Rathnew, 217, 244
Tir na Fiúise, Terryglass, 225
Torc Waterfall, Killarney, 51
Torr Head, 83
Tory Island, 79
Tralee, 57
Tramore, 34
Tranarossan Bay, 79
Tullaghan
    Tullaghan House, 227
Tullaghan House, Tullaghan, 227
Twelve Bens Mountains, 65

U

Upperlands
    Ardtara Country House, 228
Urlingford, 37

V

Vale of Avoca, 33
Valencia Island
    Skellig Heritage Centre, 50
Vee, The, 36

W

Wandesforde House, Castlecomer, 122
Waterford, 34
    Brown's, 229
    Foxmount Farm, 230
    Waterford Crystal Factory, 34
Waterman's Lodge, Ballina Killaloe, 95
Waterville, 47
Way of St. Brendan, 57
Westport, 68
    Clew Bay Heritage Centre, 68
Wexford
    Clonard House, 231
Whaley Abbey, Ballinaclash, 96
Whitehead, 83
Whitepark Bay, 82
Woodlands Farmhouse, Killinierin, 184

Y

Youghal, 35, 41
    Aherne's, 232, 244
    Heritage Centre, 41

SHARE YOUR REVIEWS WITH US

We greatly appreciate first-hand evaluations of places in our guides. Your critiques are invaluable to us. To keep current on the properties in our guides, we keep a database of readers' comments.

Please list your comments about properties you have visited. We welcome accolades, as well as criticisms.

Name of hotel or b&b _____ Town _____ Country _____
Comments:

Name of hotel or b&b _____ Town _____ Country _____
Comments:

Your name _____ Street _____ Town _____ State _____
Zip _____ Country _____ Tel _____ e-mail _____ date _____

Please send report to: Karen Brown's Guides, Post Office Box 70, San Mateo, California 94401, USA
tel: (650) 342-9117, fax: (650) 342-9153, e-mail: karen@karenbrown.com, www.karenbrown.com

SHARE YOUR DISCOVERIES WITH US

Outstanding properties often come from readers' discoveries. We would love to hear from you.

Please list below any hotel or bed & breakfast you discover. Tell us what you liked about the property and, if possible, please include a brochure or photographs so we can share your enthusiasm. We keep a permanent database of all of your recommendations for future use. Note: we regret we cannot return photos.

Owner _____ Hotel or B&B _____ Street _____

Town _____ Zip _____ State or Region _____ Country _____

Comments:

Your name _____ Street _____ Town _____ State _____

Zip _____ Country _____ Tel _____ e-mail _____ date _____

Please send report to: Karen Brown's Guides, Post Office Box 70, San Mateo, California 94401, USA
tel: (650) 342-9117, fax: (650) 342-9153, e-mail: karen@karenbrown.com, www.karenbrown.com

KB Travel Service

Quality * Personal Service * Great Values

- Staff trained by Karen Brown to help you plan your holiday
- Special offerings on airfares to major cities in Europe
- Special prices on car rentals with free upgrades
- Countryside mini-itineraries based on Karen Brown's Guides
- Reservations for hotels, inns, and B&Bs in Karen Brown's Guides

For assistance and information on service fees contact:

KB Travel Service

16 East Third Avenue
San Mateo, California, 94401, USA
tel: 800-782-2128, fax: 650-342-2519, email: kbtravel@aol.com

For additional information on places in the Karen Brown's Guides, visit the following websites:
www.karenbrown.com and www.innsandouts.com

✈ UNITED AIRLINES

is the

Preferred Airline

of

Karen Brown's Guides

and

Karen Brown Travel Services

Seal Cove Inn

Located in the San Francisco Bay Area

Karen Brown Herbert (best known as author of the Karen Brown's guides) and her husband, Rick, have put 20 years of experience into reality and opened their own superb hideaway, Seal Cove Inn. Spectacularly set amongst wild flowers and bordered by towering cypress trees, Seal Cove Inn looks out to the distant ocean over acres of county park: an oasis where you can enjoy secluded beaches, explore tidepools, watch frolicking seals, and follow the tree-lined path that traces the windswept ocean bluffs. Country antiques, original watercolors, flower-laden cradles, rich fabrics, and the gentle ticking of grandfather clocks create the perfect ambiance for a foggy day in front of the crackling log fire. Each bedroom is its own haven with a cozy sitting area before a wood-burning fireplace and doors opening onto a private balcony or patio with views to the park and ocean. Moss Beach is a 35-minute drive south of San Francisco, 6 miles north of the picturesque town of Half Moon Bay, and a few minutes from Princeton harbor with its colorful fishing boats and restaurants. Seal Cove Inn makes a perfect base for whale-watching, salmon-fishing excursions, day trips to San Francisco, exploring the coast, or, best of all, just a romantic interlude by the sea, time to relax and be pampered. Karen and Rick look forward to the pleasure of welcoming you to their coastal hideaway.

Seal Cove Inn • 221 Cypress Avenue • Moss Beach • California • 94038 • USA
tel: (650) 728-4114, fax: (650) 728-4116, e-mail: sealcove@coastside.net, website: sealcoveinn.com

JUNE BROWN's love of travel was inspired by the *National Geographic* magazines she read as a girl in her dentist's office—so far she has visited over 40 countries. June hails from Sheffield, England and lived in Zambia and Canada before moving to northern California where she lives in San Mateo with her husband, Tony, and their children, Simon and Clare.

BARBARA TAPP, the talented artist who produces all of the hotel sketches and delightful illustrations in this guide, was raised in Australia where she studied in Sydney at the School of Interior Design. Although Barbara continues with freelance projects, she devotes much of her time to illustrating the Karen Brown guides. Barbara lives in Kensington, California, with her husband, Richard, their two sons, Jonothan and Alexander, and daughter, Georgia.

JANN POLLARD, the artist responsible for the beautiful painting on the cover of this guide, has studied art since childhood, and is well-known for her outstanding impressionistic-style watercolors which she has exhibited in numerous juried shows, winning many awards. Jann travels frequently to Europe (using Karen Brown's guides) where she loves to paint historic buildings. Jann lives in Burlingame, California, with her husband, Gene.

Travel Your Dreams • Order your Karen Brown Guides Today

Please ask in your local bookstore for Karen Brown's Guides. If the books you want are unavailable, you may order directly from the publisher. Books will be shipped immediately.

_____ *Austria: Charming Inns & Itineraries* $17.95

_____ *California: Charming Inns & Itineraries* $17.95

_____ *England: Charming Bed & Breakfasts* $16.95

_____ *England, Wales & Scotland: Charming Hotels & Itineraries* $17.95

_____ *France: Charming Bed & Breakfasts* $16.95

_____ *France: Charming Inns & Itineraries* $17.95

_____ *Germany: Charming Inns & Itineraries* $17.95

_____ *Ireland: Charming Inns & Itineraries* $17.95

_____ *Italy: Charming Bed & Breakfasts* $16.95

_____ *Italy: Charming Inns & Itineraries* $17.95

_____ *Portugal: Charming Inns & Itineraries* $17.95

_____ *Spain: Charming Inns & Itineraries* $17.95

_____ *Switzerland: Charming Inns & Itineraries* $17.95

Name _____ **Street** _____

Town _____ **State** _____ **Zip** _____ **Tel** _____ **email** _____

Credit Card (MasterCard or Visa) _____ **Expires:** _____

For orders in the USA, add $4 for the first book and $1 for each additional book for shipment. California residents add 8.25% sales tax. Overseas orders add $10 per book for airmail shipment. Indicate number of copies of each title; fax or mail form with check or credit card information to:

KAREN BROWN'S GUIDES
Post Office Box 70 • San Mateo • California • 94401 • USA
tel: (650) 342-9117, fax: (650) 342-9153, e-mail: karen@karenbrown.com

For additional information about Karen Brown's Guides, visit our website at www.karenbrown.com